UNDERSTANDING
REPRESENTATION

D0218123

About the authors

Roy Ashbury currently teaches at Queen Mary's College in Hampshire. A professional percussionist before taking a degree in Linguistics and Sociology, he discovered Film and Media Studies thanks to a course in Soviet montage cinema given by Peter Wollen. Roy has written about representing terrorism in news photography, African cinema and Murnau's classic *Nosferatu*, and is currently researching Japanese film history. He takes the view that Film and Media Studies are essential to a critical political practice.

Jo Cassey worked in formal education for thirteen years, as a teacher of GCSE and A Level Media Studies, as Education Manager at a Regional Film Theatre and as Director of a regional film education company. Jo has delivered many workshops and INSET for the BFI, as well as working as Regional Education Co-ordinator on the London Film Festival. Jo currently works for Skillset and is a Senior Examiner for AQA. Previous publications include: *Documentaries: A Teacher's Guide and Classroom Resources* (Auteur, 2000) and *The Tabloid Press: A Teacher's Guide and Classroom Resources* (Auteur, 2002).

Wendy Helsby has taught from primary to university level. Currently she is teaching Media Studies and Film Studies AS and A level at a sixth-form college and for the Open University. Wendy has been an examiner for Media and Film Studies and has led INSET courses for teachers and for GCSE students. She is on the BFI Secondary Teachers Advisory Panel. Her interest in media began with a Masters course in Communications and post-16 education and continued with her PhD research on the link between visual and verbal literacies. Publications include: *Language Puzzles* (Scholastic, 1993), *Teaching African Cinema* (BFI, 1998), *Teaching Television Advertising* (Auteur, 2004) and *Teaching Children's Comics* (Auteur, 2005).

Mark Ramey currently teaches Film Studies at AS and A2 Level. A Philosophy graduate and a Media and English school teacher, he developed his love of film when in 2000 he made the move from secondary to sixth-form teaching. He is now studying for an MA in Philosophy at Southampton University. Mark's interests are eclectic, ranging from postmodern theory and football to Nietzsche and the films of the Marx Brothers. This is his first published work.

Pauline Turner is Head of Media and Performing Arts at Portsmouth College. She has been teaching Media Studies for twenty years and Film Studies for the past ten. She edited the *Key Skills in Media* folder and worked on the specifications for Curriculum 2000.

UNDERSTANDING REPRESENTATION

Wendy Helsby
Roy Ashbury
Jo Cassey
Mark Ramey
Pauline Turner

Series editor: Dr Stacey Abbott

 Publishing

Series Editor's Note

The moving image is now an integral part of our daily lives, representing an increasing share of our cultural activity. New generations of students know the moving image more intimately and more intensely than their predecessors – but they are not always well served in relating this experience to the academic study of film and television.

Understanding the Moving Image is a new series of short orientation texts in the formal study of screen media, with each book offering an introduction to one important topic. All the books will be written at an accessible level, with no assumption of prior academic knowledge on the part of the reader, by authors with teaching experience and an interest/specialism in a particular area.

As befitting a British Film Institute project, the series will privilege the study of the moving image – notably cinema and television. Case materials will focus on texts familiar (and readily available) to the intended readership, without ducking the responsibility to raise awareness of longer traditions and broader horizons. All books will have a structure designed to facilitate learning for the individual reader, while remaining suitable for classroom use.

The books will be useful to the following:
- Post-16 students working for examinations in Media and Film Studies
- Course leaders and teachers from schools to first-year university and adult education
- The general reader with no prior background to the subject.

We are delighted to present the third book in the series, *Understanding Representation*, a fascinating exploration of the complex issues relating to representation in film and television.

Dr Stacey Abbott
for British Film Institute 2005
publishing@bfi.org.uk

First published in 2005 by the
British Film Institute
21 Stephen Street, London W1T 1LN
The British Film Institute's purpose is to champion moving image culture in all its richness and diversity across the UK, for the benefit of as wide an audience as possible, and to create and encourage debate.

Copyright © Introductions and editorial arrangement: Wendy Helsby 2005
Copyright © Individual chapters: named authors 2005

Designed, edited and set by Ampersand Publishing Services/Siobhán O'Connor, London
Cover design: Cube
Cover images: (front) *Billy Elliot* (Tiger Aspect, 2000); *Prime Suspect* (Granada Television); *One Flew over the Cuckoo's Nest* (Fantasy Film Productions, 1975); *Caméra d'Afrique* (Ministère Français de la Coopération, 1983); *Black Cat, White Cat* (Pandora Film Produktion, 1998); (back) *East Is East* (Film Four Limited, 1999). All images courtesy of bfi Stills
Printed in Great Britain by Cromwell Press, Trowbridge, Wiltshire

British Library Cataloguing-in-Publication data
A catalogue record for this book is available from the British Library
ISBN 1 84457 080 0

Preface

In all forms of media the political and the personal intersect, but perhaps nowhere more so than in the issue of representation. This book deals with the public forms of representation in film and television; however we must always remember that their effects are also very personal. During a career in education I have observed many examples of this, but two stand out in my memory. First, while working on a book on African cinema in the 1990s, I attended a conference at which obviously the majority of the delegates were black and male. As white and female I was very much 'the other', not only because of my appearance, but also because of the western ideologies that I represented. The other example comes from an earlier decade when I worked with gypsy families and travellers in mainstream schools and decided to use this experience to talk about representation with a group of GCSE media students. The vitriol that this topic revealed has also stayed with me as a clear example of how representation has both political and personal effects.

When first discussing this project with the BFI I decided to approach colleagues with whom I had worked over a number of years and whom I knew would be able to add expertise, excitement, knowledge and a variety of perspectives to the debate. As practising educators, working with students and professionals in the media, each has brought intellectual engagement to the issue of representation and applied it to areas in which they had a particular interest. There has been original research and analysis, as well as the synthesis of particular theoretical approaches in the work they have produced. As a result here is a book that has a range of approaches, styles, subjects and points of view to appeal to and to challenge different readers and readings. As with all products it has an exchange value: it provides the tools of analysis of ways of representing institutions, groups, places, ideas and people in the media, but at the same time it challenges those representations with philosophical and political interpretations. We hope that this will help the reader to interrogate one of the most important areas not only of media and film studies but also of the world in which we live.

Our thanks go to the team at BFI Publishing, including Wendy for her hard work in coordination, Stacey for her rigorous feedback, Caren for her helpful work on the stills and Siobhán for her careful reading of the script. In their own ways they all contributed to the clarity and focus of this book during its long gestation. My personal thanks go to my fellow authors for their understanding and patience, as well as their commitment to this project in already busy lives.

Finally, I would like to express my especial thanks to Richard O'Neill and Professor T. Acton (University of Greenwich) for their help in researching Chapter 7.

Wendy Helsby
August 2005

Contents

Authors' Note

Although separate chapters can be studied discretely, there are many points of cross-reference within the discussions. It is assumed that users of this book are likely to read the first chapter which gives a general and theoretical overview and will then choose to read the sections and chapters in which they are most interested. This means that there may be some repetition of points where this adds to the clarity of each discussion. The main texts discussed were currently available at the time of publication.

Part One
Messages and Messengers

1. Representation and Theories

WENDY HELSBY

How do we understand the concept of 'representation' in Media Studies? Do we look 'through a glass darkly' to see a version of the world constructed for us, or do we see a reflection of reality represented in the mirror of the media world? As the wicked queen in Snow White *discovered, sometimes mirrors do not reflect the reality we wish to believe. 'Mirror, mirror on the wall who is the fairest of them all …?'*

1.1 Reflection or construction?

The question of whether the media construct or reflect the beliefs, or ideologies, of society is addressed in this book through exploration of relevant contemporary issues. Most readers will be aware of both gender and racial stereotyping that have thrown up images such as the 'blonde bimbo' and the 'coon', which have rightly been challenged and criticised. Sometimes, however, it is not so easy to see and challenge our own more insidious beliefs and contemporary representations that are not often put under a critical microscope.

It is also true that those who challenge the status quo are often vilified as radical or 'loony' by their peers. It has taken many years and considerable pressure for society to accept and to legislate for gender and racial equality. Even legislation may not change deeply entrenched beliefs. The documentary *The Secret Policeman* (2004, BBC1) illustrated this point graphically. It was a piece of investigative journalism following police recruits in Manchester using hidden cameras, in which the views expressed by some of the trainees

Stephen Lawrence was killed on the street; the police were slow in responding and so failed to get a conviction against the accused racist attackers.

were extremely racist. This was in spite of all the messages to the contrary the recruits had been given in the official equal opportunities training initiated by the police following accusations of institutional racism after the Stephen Lawrence enquiry. There is a further discussion of this issue in chapter 4 on the police.

So how powerful are the media in constructing such opinions and beliefs? Or do they merely reflect the views of society? We begin by looking at some of the methodologies adopted in approaching this concept.

1.2 Theories

In any study of the media there is a theoretical underpinning, and here you will come upon the names of influential writers and theorists who have taken various positions when writing about how language and culture have been fundamental in the key concept of representation. The following is a summary of the ideas that inform the discussions in this book.

There are three basic theories of how language and culture connect with representation. First, there is the **reflective theory**. This states that language reflects the meaning that already exists or imitates (mimesis) the truth or reality that is inherent in the text. A critique of this theory would say that this does not allow for any alternative readings or different uses of codes. Secondly, there is the **intentional theory**, which states that the individual author of the text intends it to represent certain ideas. This means that each act of communication is unique in some way. A criticism of this theory is that, as we have to enter into the rules and conventions of a social system to be understood by others, the individual communication must inevitably lose some of its 'uniqueness' and must negotiate a shared meaning. Finally, there is the **constructionist theory**. Most media analysis work explores a constructionist approach, so this is the one on which we focus.

There are two major versions of the constructionist methodology. The first is semiotics, which was originally based upon a linguistic model. This used a scientific approach to analyse the structure of language. Roland Barthes and others developed this study into a wider field of texts to show how languages – visual, verbal and nonverbal – work in society. By extension this incorporated the idea of myth or ideology, and therefore context. Take the simple, often quoted example of the phrase 'a red rose'. Both the words and an image of them tell us about a certain type of flower and its colour. In the Western world if you gave someone a red rose, especially around 14 February, it would incorporate beliefs about romantic love. On the other hand, if you saw a red rose on the shirt of a rugby player it would indicate the English team and beliefs about patriotism would begin to emerge, while someone from Yorkshire would see it as a regional symbol. The red rose is therefore no longer neutral, but now has ideological meanings; it carries mythic significance depending upon the context.

The second constructionist theory is discursive and was suggested by Michel Foucault. This focuses more upon issues of power and knowledge. The emphasis here is upon cultural understanding and shared meanings. This emphasises the production of knowledge through a whole network of relationships (discourse) rather than just the meaning of a text. Thus it is much more rooted in an historical specificity than the linguistic or semiotic approach that tried to find trans-historical roots. Discourse tries to define and produce knowledge. It decides how we talk about a subject and it influences our ideas and practices. The important point is that in discourse there is also a power relationship. It deals with power because it also governs how we regulate others' behaviour and how we think and talk about objects and ideas. This power relationship will appear across a network of texts (intertextuality) and therefore consolidate this particular discourse. The production of discourses can be institutionalised and provide a common idea which Foucault called a 'discursive formation'.

The concept that texts (in the broadest sense) take on meaning and therefore knowledge relationships is the core of the constructionist idea of how representation works. Who produces the knowledge and therefore who controls the message are basic questions that a semiotic analysis would not ask.

Foucault did not, however, see this discourse/knowledge/power relationship in terms of a single classical Marxist idea of oppressive class power.

In the discursive approach the application and effectiveness of the power/knowledge link are important. If you possess a particular knowledge and you have the power to express this

Marxism was broadened from the class reductionist ideology, most notably by Antonio Gramsci with his definition of ideology as a hegemonic balance. Gramsci saw hegemony as a moving equilibrium and not reducible to class or economics. In this refined Marxist theory social groups negotiate to achieve a form of consent. For some groups the aim is to maintain or gain power in whatever form is most acceptable at the time and through means other than simply repression or revolution. There is in the hegemonic field a consensus or equilibrium constructed through the work of decision makers or opinion formers, including teachers, journalists and the media. The clever use of this hegemony will allow enough leeway to let the balance of power stay within the dominant groups and maintain the dominant ideology and status quo. Sometimes the leaders get this hegemonic balance wrong and a crisis of hegemony occurs, as was the case with Margaret Thatcher and the Poll Tax. You may also regard Tony Blair's entry into the second Gulf War as a point of disequilibrium and crisis.

knowledge, it can become the truth by which others will lead their lives. The knowledge might change over time, and hence the beliefs will change and we will behave differently according to the new ideologies. The person/institution who has the 'knowledge' will also have the power to represent the new truth or discourse. This circulation of discourses can be on the macro or the micro scale. Obviously the larger the body circulating the truth, the more influential it is. For instance, in the past Western countries have created a representation of the developing world as dependent because of mismanagement by its governments. This often failed to acknowledge the part that developed countries have played in this economic decline through their policies and institutions, such as the World Bank and the International Monetary Fund. But discourses can also be localised – for example, beliefs about subcultural groups within a small community such as a school or college.

As in semiotics there is a linguistic base to Foucault's theory. Discourse in its simplest form means verbal expression; however, our selection of language will reveal beliefs that are often subconscious and this is why Foucault suggested that discourse is a major factor in the exercise of power. Having evolved from its original speech-based meaning to become a concept that refers to much wider representations and beliefs, discourse has proved to be effective in deconstructing texts and understanding how these meanings and beliefs become dominant in societies.

These are important methodologies to consider when examining representation in a particular text or a range of texts. They raise questions to be asked both in the semiotic analyses and in the understanding of the discourses circulating around texts.

1.3 Image and representation

The media would claim that they have a function to entertain and are therefore not simply a window on the world or a reflection of the real world; however, the media do provide us with a paradigm of how to view the mediated world (McLuhan called it a 'global village', 1964). Media theorists would see the network of messages or discourses emerging from different sources, of which the media are one of the most powerful, creating a 'mental set'. Repetition of these messages reinforces the beliefs and makes them appear natural, 'just there', and so confirm the dominant world view, or the 'status quo', for their readers.

To take a simple example: at a superficial level we change our clothes from season to season as fashion editors and style leaders tell us what to wear in order to appear 'with it'. Flippant as this example is it can become dangerous if the message is more fundamental in changing attitudes and behaviour. This is exemplified in the attitude that to be fashionable you also have to be thin. People's self-image and self-worth can be seriously affected by the way they identify with those who are represented as style icons. Magazines aimed at preteen and adolescent girls have been criticised on more than one occasion for encouraging, through the images and advice they publish, anorexic and bulimic behaviour in teenage girls that has led in some cases to tragedy.

Marilyn Monroe, an iconic blonde, as she appeared in *The Seven Year Itch* (1955)

Representation is not only about viewing ourselves, but also about viewing others. It is a way of denying individuality by subsuming it into a particular stereotype. A classic example is that of the dumb blonde, who is frequently linked to the child-woman, or 'baby doll', icon. Here an element, blonde hair, is used as a fetish to represent a certain stereotype of femaleness. The Hollywood film star Marilyn Monroe became the icon representing this childlike blonde stereotype in the 1950s and 1960s, although there were many others moulded to play similar roles by the Hollywood system. Others have played upon this stereotype for comedic purposes such as seen in the Bubbles character in the television sitcom *Absolutely Fabulous* (BBC2 1992–2003) or Alice in *The Vicar of Dibley* (BBC1 1994–2000). Both Bubbles and Alice would not work as characters, however, unless we already knew about the discourses surrounding blonde women and child women.

With the child-woman example the argument goes that adult women are kept controllable and biddable by the excessive use of their forenames as well as being referred to as 'girls' by their employers, all of which serves to treat them as children. In *Coronation Street*, factory owner Mike Baldwin called all his female employees 'girls' and by their first names, while they called him 'Mr Baldwin'.

The distortion achieved by representing such groups through particular elements or discourse may be more obviously seen in the media, but as we have noted it also

The character of Bubbles from the television sitcom *Absolutely Fabulous*

What does the character Jeanne Dielman's dress and action reveal about her in this 1970s film? She in fact works as a prostitute while her son is at school

Who, or rather, what is Nelson Mandela? Is he a lawyer, a terrorist, a freedom fighter, a prisoner, the first political leader of the Rainbow Nation, a world statesman, the ex-husband of Winnie Mandela ...? He has been all of these things over his long life. Originally vilified, especially from within South Africa and by other segregationists such as in the United States, he is now lauded. This is because the power/knowledge base has changed and so the discourses and who is producing them have changed. The connection between the producer and the subject is fundamental to how representation works to maintain or change representations.

reflects upon the reality of people's lives. Just as thinness becomes desirable to such an extent it can lead to illness, so the image of the dumb blonde may well influence the way you perceive a woman with fair hair. It is this use of negative shorthand that is often criticised by media observers. In the above example the blonde hair objectifies the character or person as childlike and intellectually weak, rather than as an individual who is most likely not to have such characteristics.

There is never a single discourse, however, as all media texts can be read in a variety of ways and with many meanings that can only be constructed with our active consent as readers. A simple link between one element and an idea such as 'blonde hair equals blonde bimbo' can be read differently depending upon context and reader. Think of how many times the landlady in British television dramas is given brassy blonde hair. Here blondeness has other connotations such as being worldly wise. What is important is the objectification through characteristics such as hair, skin colour or ethnicity that can be used to categorise and even demonise groups. The Nazis were able to take this to the extreme and represent groups such as Jews, gypsies and the mentally ill through the iconicity of nose, skin colour and behaviour as subhuman. They were expert at using the power of the media through the repetition of its message to propagate this deceit, constructing a false view as apparently the truth or 'reality' to a highly educated population.

While we can unequivocally see the Holocaust as evil, sometimes it is difficult to see our own prejudices and beliefs as being questionable. Most of the readers of this book would believe that racial segregation or apartheid is wrong, but many people in various parts of the world have seen segregation or the euphemistic 'ethnic cleansing' as necessary. Just two of the better known more recent violent examples of this are provided by the Serb-Bosnian war and the events which took place in the Dafur area of the Sudan. In the period following World War II apartheid was seen as necessary by many of those ruling South Africa, but this institutionalised segregation came to be viewed very differently from the outside. If we look at the one individual who symbolises the changes in South Africa, Nelson Mandela, we can see how his image changed as political and social changes occurred and new beliefs or discourses dominated.

Stewart Granger's character Nino Barucci, in *Madonna of the Seven Moons*, is one image of a strong, sexually dangerous gypsy character

It is more difficult to see our own 'apartheids'. The word 'gypsy' has been mentioned with reference to the Holocaust. Did it bring to mind a particular image when you read it? If you were watching films in the 1940s the image of the male gypsy may have been the one of a strong and dangerous sexuality made famous by Stewart Granger in the melodrama *Madonna of the Seven Moons* (Arthur Crabtree, 1944). Exactly forty years later this image was still current and used in *The Company of Wolves* (Neil Jordan, 1984). Was this the image you had of the gypsy, or was it a different one? Maybe your image is more like Brad Pitt in *Snatch* (Guy Ritchie, 2000), that of an uneducated, feisty and wily 'pikey'. You may feel that films' representation of the male gypsy would not be influential in the real world because they are fictional and stylised, but entertainment value does not lessen their influence on our beliefs about such groups. This discussion centred on gypsies and other minority groups continues in Part 3.

Of course the media are only one influence; family and culture are among the others. But how do these groups acquire opinions and beliefs? As we argue in this book popular culture is one of the great conveyers of ideologies (Gramsci, 1971), and that is why it is important to study areas such as sports coverage and television soap operas in spite of what the tabloid press might claim. Does a soap opera such as

Protestors at Greenham Common: the feminist movement confronts 'Uncle Sam'

▶ Would the ideology regarding nuclear weapons have changed more quickly if *The War Game* (Peter Watkins, 1965), a powerful drama-documentary based on government leaflets about the effects of nuclear explosion on ordinary people in Britain, had been broadcast in the 1960s when it was made, rather than twenty years later in 1985? Would the media have drawn a different representation of the peace campaigners? Would we have seen a different discourse on the nuclear arms race? How would CND and the peace marches have been represented? ●

EastEnders that is watched regularly by millions of viewers reflect what is going on in society, or does it help to construct our belief about society? Does the voyeuristic pleasure of reality television in *Big Brother* or *I'm a Celebrity* also talk to us on another level about how we value such things as personal relationships and privacy, and fix in us attitudes about the group types which each contestant represents? On a macro scale Islamic fundamentalism and Western economic imperialism are currently in open conflict. How does each represent the other in the media 'global village'? Such representations penetrate and influence all of our lives – they are not just distant and theoretical murmurings.

As hinted earlier, attempts to change beliefs or ideologies, and thus the balance of power and knowledge, are often met with ridicule and hostility. Currently, major nuclear powers are trying to persuade new nuclear countries to give up or stop developing nuclear weapons. Attitudes to such weaponry have changed significantly since World War II and the dropping of atomic bombs on Hiroshima and Nagasaki by the United States. While the United States had technological supremacy at this point, the Soviet Union soon became a nuclear power, too, creating the fear of cataclysmic war. Small groups of protesters mounted campaigns and the umbrella organisation CND (Campaign for Nuclear Disarmament) was formed in 1958 with the slogan 'Ban the Bomb'. Regarded by the mainstream as being led by the 'loony left', including politicians such as Michael Foot, for several years CND organised mass marches at Easter from Aldermaston to Trafalgar Square in London. The press coverage in the main implied that they should really be doing what all right-minded people did at Easter – eating chocolate eggs! A similar treatment by the press was given to the women protesting against US cruise missiles at the Greenham Common Airbase in Berkshire in the 1980s. They were branded as feminists, with all the attendant connotations of being anti-authority and therefore anti-male. They were seen as examples of the stereotype of the hysterical female, much beloved by the Victorians. Stories were run about families left to fend for themselves while the mother was attacking the security of the country. Today it is generally agreed that to ban the bomb is the only sensible course of action, and cruise missiles have been removed from areas such as Greenham Common. The ideology has changed.

1.4 Representation and intertextuality

The interrelated nature of representation is reflected in many of the following studies. For example, mental health has links to race, as the headline on one page of the *Independent on Sunday* indicates: 'Blacks failed by our "racist" system of care for mentally ill' (Goodchild). The article claimed that mental health sufferers from ethnic minorities are more likely to be locked up than given proper treatment. In juxtaposition on the same page was a related account of a black man who was suffering from manic depression: 'Six police piled on top of me.' This echo of institutional racism links the chapter on mental health to that on the police. In the chapter on football the issue of gender, culture and race is raised by the film *Bend It Like Beckham* (Gurinder Chadha, 2002). Race, gender, the family and cultural identity are also explored in the film *East Is East* (Damien O'Donnell, 1999), which is discussed in the interview with Raji James at the end of the book. The way that servants have been economically tied into being sex workers links the chapters on beyond Britain to that on prostitution. It is these connections that illustrate the power of representation through the discourses of the media and through their repetition and their intertextuality.

To explore this idea we are going to consider some less obvious and perhaps more embedded contemporary representation and to show how each text feeds into the discourse of representation and is not a discrete item. The writers have chosen to look at familiar groups, but to approach them through different perspectives. For example, instead of looking at the representation of women as sex objects, one chapter looks at women as sex workers. Another minority group that is investigated is that of the diaspora of gypsies in Europe. In autumn 2004 the issue of gypsies buying land and building without planning permission became newsworthy and was renewed in March 2005 by papers such as *The Sun* with a tirade of anti-gypsy site articles. There were many interviews done with the local inhabitants, the local officials and government spokespersons, but few with those from the gypsy community. How often do we see gypsies and other powerless groups through their own eyes rather than those of the media? When such minority and scapegoat groups are in the news, how often do we see both sides reflected evenly?

Ninian Smart suggested seven dimensions to a religion. These were the practical and ritual; the experiential and emotional; the narrative or mythic; the doctrinal and philosophical; the ethical and legal; the social and institutional; and the material dimensions. Using these dimensions, it is possible to categorise football as a 'religion'.

Another chapter looks at football as representative of the nation. Football has traditionally been seen as a male preserve, but increasingly is being played and followed by women. It may seem to receive a disproportionate amount of media, news and gossip coverage. Does this indicate it is the new national heritage, a new religion? Does it fulfil Ninian Smart's (1989) seven dimensions of a religion?

In another chapter we look at how our world view might be altered if we lived outside of Britain and compared our views with others. One example of different viewpoints can be seen through representations of countries at war. Often British heroes are represented as the few against the many. The film *Zulu* (Cyril Endfield, 1964) used the representation of the small band of brave British heroes battling the savage hordes; however, a documentary gave a more balanced account and showed the failure of the army earlier in the day at the battle of Isandlwana against warriors armed with only spears and shields (*Timewatch*, 'Zulu – The True Story', 2004).

Another example of looking from a different viewpoint can be seen in *The Battle of Algiers* (Gillo Pontecorvo, 1966). In this film we are taken into the world of the Algerian freedom fighters whom the French regarded as terrorists. Similarly in the film *Camp de Thiaroye* (Ousmane Sembene, 1988) Sembene shows us the African soldiers' view of the French colonisers based on events after World War II. Both films provided alternative views to that shown within the Western media.

We should be able to look at many world events in this balanced way, but such opportunities are rare. Often balance comes from 'guerilla' production companies which challenge mainstream institutional working practices. Two such examples are Undercurrents videos that look at news items from different perspectives, and world cinemas that challenge Hollywood practices, sometimes referred to as Third Cinema (Pines and Willeman, 1989).

1.5 Representation and national stereotypes

One day when I was leaving Waterloo Station in London I saw a photo shoot. A man dressed in a beret and striped T-shirt, and holding a baguette, was being photographed. I do not know, but I guess it was something to do with advertising Le Shuttle, as its London terminal was in Waterloo Station. Why should I think this? It was obviously because of the stereotypical dress of the model. France, the nation, had been reduced to a few limited signifiers.

The concept of nation and nationality is an important part of our identity. How do Britons view themselves? In the imperial and colonial past it has been one of civilisation versus savagery. Comics frequently had pictures of white explorers being boiled alive by savage natives. Our views of other cultures and nations often are reduced to these simple oppositions.

Tourist guides and holiday programmes often reflect these simplified views. One word or image can conjure a whole raft of beliefs about a country or people as with my 'Frenchman' in Waterloo Station. We might challenge or conversely might wish to play up to our own national stereotype; however, when our image is metaphorically invaded and misrepresented or stereotyped by another culture we will be quite annoyed, as well as maybe amused, as with the upper-class, bowler-hatted Englishman stereotype beloved by other nations.

We are perhaps not so good at understanding our own misrepresentations of other cultures. Africa has often been portrayed as primitive, uncivilised and in a permanent state of crisis. Of course there are areas of deprivation and underdevelopment in this huge continent, but it is also the location of many well-developed civilisations with art and skills of high level and historically has given the world much in architecture, mathematics and literature (Ashbury, Helsby & O'Brien, 1998).

A good contemporary example of how national identity can change the perception of an event was the film *Saving Private Ryan* (Stephen Spielberg, 1998). This film focused upon the American forces during the D-Day landings. In the United States it was lauded for its 'realism'. On the other side of the Atlantic, however, it was its unreality compared to the French perception of D-Day that gave it a cool reception by the French critics. As one French critic stated, Hollywood is an 'industrial international image factory wanting to perfect globalisation in the domains of collective representations … [Spielberg] can do nothing but recycle traditional mythologies while covering up the vanity of the operation' (quoted in Hedetoft, 2000). A similar negative review talked about 'crude realism with romantic heroism' (ibid.). So what did a 'neutral' national voice say? In Denmark, where the film

▶ Look through a range of comics and graphic novels and note national stereotypes or representations of other races. Which nation is stereotypically the villain in British comics? ●

▶ What images or words signify other countries? For example, the Eiffel Tower; the Coliseum; palm trees; mountains covered in heather. What are the stereotypical images of the four nations that make up the British Isles? ●

was well received as a good (because of its nuanced portrayal of Allied soldiers) if not great film, it was commended for allowing the contribution of Americans to be celebrated and for reminding the younger generations of such sacrifices. The Danes had not been involved in the landings and so took the film at its face value. In other words, they were happy with its representations and the discourses to which it played.

The film was of course made for American audiences and the messages that the film gave to American viewers were ones that they would recognise. For Americans the beneficiary of the action was Private Ryan, who represented both America and Every(American)man. It was not Europe or democratic liberties that were at the centre of the action, which is what the French believed should have been the themes. Thus the complexity of any discussion about how nations and national events are represented is illustrated vividly in the debate over *Saving Private Ryan*. Unlike the mirror of the evil queen in *Snow White*, we are often told what we would like to hear rather than the other 'truth'. In a postmodern media world we may ask: whose truth is dominant? Our media mirror reflecting the world is fractured and its 'truth' always suspect. This idea is further discussed in Chapter 9.

1.6 Representation, ideology, realism

The issue of realism is intrinsically linked to that of representation. Most of us will have direct experience of the police in their official capacity on only rare occasions during our lives, if at all. Much of what we know about the police, such as the layout of a police station, comes from viewing police television programmes such as *The Bill*. We have to rely upon the programme makers for verisimilitude.

In areas where we have personal knowledge, however, we often feel that we can sift fact from fiction. For example, we have all been to school, so we perhaps think that we are justified in calling ourselves experts on the subject. We therefore feel that we can judge the reality of the representation of the school in programmes such as *Grange Hill* or *Teachers*. Our personal experience will influence how far we accept or reject what we see in terms of 'the school'. Does *Grange Hill* appear to be more real or 'hyper-real', especially to those whose experience of school may be a little distant? There is

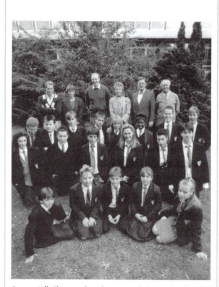

Grange Hill: Those with authority stand; the weaker kneel?

▶ If you have watched any of the programmes mentioned here, how far do you believe that they represent reality? ●

something else going on here beyond the surface reality of the wearing of uniforms or punishing the school bully. What you are seeing is a whole system of values or ideologies. These are implicit in the way that the programme makers have constructed the narrative and the way we read it. The values appear so obvious that we do not even notice them. If this is so, then we are accepting the programme makers' view of reality. Films also construct a view of education which is often nostalgic or gilded. If you are interested in this area go to Chapter 3 on teachers and schools.

Can discourses and 'reality' change? Sometimes it is easier to explore this idea if we take a text that was aimed at a different audience from a different period. If you had been at school during the middle of the twentieth century you might have learned to read using *Janet and John* early readers. They were used in hundreds if not thousands of schools. The middle-class family seen in the *Janet and John* books showed such pictures as Daddy in the garden with John building a bonfire and Mummy in the kitchen with Jane baking. Intrinsically there is nothing wrong with these images. Someone had to do the garden, and someone had to make the meal. But of course what happened was that these images became fixed as a truth not only about the types of words you learned to read, but also about the message values they conveyed. If you were a boy you could not go into the kitchen to cook because that was 'sissy-like' behaviour, and of course only 'tomboy' girls would enjoy building bonfires in the garden because that was a man's role.

There are also other forms of representation of reality as well as gender roles going on here. The *Janet and John* books provided an image of the average or 'normal' family: mother, father and two children. They suggested what a home should look like and the type of suburban environment in which it should be set. The image of 'place' was very middle-class. By implication they also suggested a particular attitude to education. If you came from an inner-city area, or from one of the new immigrant families arriving to help post-war Britain, or from a rural community, how much would you recognise yourself, your family or your environment in the books?

Films such as Ken Loach's *Kes* (1969) showed a very different reality of family life from that seen in *Janet and John*, or in *The Grove Family*, a lower middle-class family with two

▶ Has the stereotype of a chef really changed with the advent of Jamie Oliver's popularity? Is his 'domestic' side in play here? Chefs (as opposed to home cooks) have always been predominantly men. ●

Jamie's Dinners: Jamie Oliver's role as chef is signified by his dress, but what is suggested by his stance?

children and a dog (BBC TV 1950s soap opera), or *Mrs Dale's Diary*, in which the central character was a doctor's wife (BBC Radio 1950s soap opera), and to the ideology created by such programmes. The norm of two parents and two children living under the same roof was a strong belief for British society after World War II. Today this has changed. As you will read in Chapter 2 on the family, the ideology or the belief about what constitutes a family has been represented to us in many ways through soap operas and dramas. These are creating a new discursive formation (Foucault), particularly about the structure of the family unit.

Cultural differences relating to families and how they are represented are important signifiers to how we read texts from other countries and thus how we understand other people. Extended families and communal living are just two of many ways in which families exist.

But what happens before a family is created? In our society we would expect a young couple to 'fall in love'. We believe that romantic love is the way to meet the perfect partner. Whole industries are built upon this from producing red roses and Valentine Day cards, to Mills and Boons books and romantic genre films such as *Pretty Woman* (Garry Marshall, 1990). This view that people should be left to choose their own partners is, however, not always the norm. Other cultures may have different attitudes; Chapter 10 discusses this with reference to *East Is East*, while in *Black Cat White Cat* (Emir Kusturica, 1998), which is discussed in Chapter 7, the heads of two gangs try to arrange marriages in their families to fulfil traditional requirements.

In the past in Western Europe arranged marriages among royalty helped to gain or maintain the balance of power. Large landowners looked towards consolidating their holdings by buying into other families through marriage. Children, particularly girls, were seen as exchangeable commodities for this purpose. There are many examples of this in literature; Mr Rochester's first marriage in *Jane Eyre* was one of such convenience. If we come from a Western country where today arranged marriages are uncommon, it can seem strange to see marriages being arranged and we can stereotype the participants as being downtrodden or, worse, being abused by the power of the family patriarchy. Although this may happen, for many this is not the reality. We more often hear about those arranged marriages that go wrong than the many that are successful. In fact we know that the way of true love does not run very smoothly either. Today the statistics show that the institution of marriage is not as strong as it was. One-parent families and alternative partnerships are more in evidence. These issues are not normally the stuff of dreams and Hollywood's Dream Factory will not dwell upon them. It is film directors such as Mike Leigh who explore the darker side of families, as in *Secrets and Lies* (1995).

1.7 Representation and gender roles

The use of gender as a powerful delineator has been discussed many times, but it is still worth recalling it as an example of the way that beliefs or the 'discursive formation' can change. In the Victorian period women were given few opportunities to show their intellect. For many middle- and upper-class women their option was to run the household and to organise a social life. This could include charity work, which provided the only social security at the time. Those middle-class women who were working achieved this in spite of, rather than because of, their gender. Those who managed to take up a profession usually had to give up paid employment on marriage; others hid their identity behind a male persona, as did the Brontë sisters. Working-class women, on the other hand, have always worked to help the family income. The restored films of Mitchell and Kenyon (BFI, 2005) showed people leaving the cotton mills in the early part of the twentieth century; many of them were skilled women workers.

Adopted daughter finds her birth mother in Mike Leigh's *Secrets and Lies*

Various world wars and other events changed the general position of women. This still did not lead to a fundamental change in attitudes. For example, up to the middle of the twentieth century many women would give up work upon marriage and, if not then, certainly when they had children.

In fields such as science, as well as the arts, professions and business, women in the United Kingdom began to make inroads. By the 1960s the Women's Movement was challenging the role of women and their status in society. But the way that the press represented this major challenge to attitudes was to suggest that it was a few hysterical women burning their bras and challenging 'normal' language such as 'chairman'; they created a new stereotype of the aggressive feminist. By the 1990s, however, hegemonic challenges resulted in the appearance of

► How far do these statistics reveal such inequalities in the media workplace?

Research other work inequalities such as ethnicity, disability and race. Organisations such as Skillset (www.skillset.org.uk) are a good starting point for this type of research. ●

Gender of Workforce in Each Sector of the Media

	Men%	Women%	Total
Television (terrestrial)	50	50	24,900
Television (cable & satellite)	63	36	4,900
Independent production for television	58	42	13,300
Broadcast radio	52	48	20,700
Animation	62	38	1,500
Post-production	70	30	8,200
CD-ROM and other interactive media	73	27	23,100
Web design & development	62	37	15,200
Computer games	84	16	8,000
Commercials	53	47	7,200
Corporate production	64	36	3,200
Other	53	47	3,300
All workforce	61	39	133,500

Source: Census 2002 (from: www.skillset.org/uploads/pdf/asset_2775.pdf?1)

► Why were boys not trying to play netball? ●

The Vicar of Dibley: Popular television engages with the issue of patriarchy in the institutionalised Church

the new powerful, feisty woman. Helen Mirren was in charge of a murder investigation in *Prime Suspect* (ITV, 1991), and the Spice Girls and Madonna were setting new role models in popular music. Girls were even playing previously male games such as rugby and football, as in *Bend It Like Beckham*.

There were many areas from which women had previously been excluded and where they were now accepted, if reluctantly. For example, in the first episode of *The Vicar of Dibley*, the appearance of Geraldine (Dawn French) with 'boobs and a bob' as opposed to a male vicar with 'bad breath and a beard' was the key to this situation comedy, the central thesis of which was about the new role of women as priests.

Today we have legislation to enable women to be treated equally in the workplace and to have equal rights in regard to property and other areas. So who was correct? Was it the Victorian patriarch who believed that women should be the conveyers of family values and be free to conduct that role by staying at home and having few responsibilities and fewer rights? Or was it the feminists of the 1960s who regarded any form of patriarchy as anathema? How have the media reflected this changing discourse? What new issues on gender representation have arisen?

These are far-reaching questions. One way of trying to reach possible answers is to look at gender roles in advertising. Some commentators have seen changes from the 1950s housewife to the freer 'swinging' woman of the 1960s, who was able to take control of her own fertility (because of the contraceptive pill) and therefore became more predatory. But this also led to a more overt sexual woman who had been previously censored on television. This image was heavily criticised by feminists. The 'crisis in masculinity' in the 1980s and 1990s was fuelled by the image of the strong woman characterised by power dressing represented by the iconic shoulder pads. These women had tendencies to castrate metaphorically any male offender, by cutting his tie, for example. Advertising agencies followed this with the image of the 'new man' who helped with traditional female roles such as looking after children. There was then a backlash to this 'effeminacy' that became visible in the top-shelf magazine explosion of 'lad' magazines such as *FHM*, *Nuts* and *Zoo*, and the more overt exploitation of sex as a selling tool in advertising – 'men behaving badly'.

January 2004 saw the launch of Nuts and Zoo, while Cut appeared in August 2004, all male weekly magazines which illustrate the strength of this 'lads' market.

A link between these types of gender roles and the breakdown in moral values has been made by social critics and politicians. They believe such representations to be damaging the institution on which society's basic fabric is built – the family. Others, such as feminists, would see these representations as condoning a view of women as mere playthings rather than serious members of society and would see an 'old-fashioned' view of the family as a constraint upon freedom. Will women move back into the home? If you read articles in the press about powerful businesswomen giving up their work to become 'wives' and 'mothers' you might see this trend as a new ideology being used to create a domestic role for women as opposed to the 'superwoman' role of being mother, lover, partner and worker.

1.8 Representation and globalisation

If we take the focus off our immediate 'ethnocentric' world, how are we influenced by the way the media run particular stories about those outside our world? During the writing of this book there have been two dominant ongoing stories in the British press. The first is the threat of terrorism and the second is the issue of immigration and asylum seekers.

▶ What do you think about the issues of terrorism and immigration? Try brainstorming twenty words on each topic. Look at the words you have collected. If you grouped your words into subsets, can you see any larger ideas from the individual words? Where do you think most of your ideas originated? ●

It is impossible to be personally well informed on all the global or national events of the day, and we rely upon the media for information. We hear 'sound bites' from politicians and see confrontations on the television. We read stories in newspapers, magazines and on the Web. All of this material is filtered through many agencies, each with their own agenda. We call this 'mediation'. If we look at these ongoing stories of the past few years we can analyse how far the media have been instrumental in constructing meaning and of course how they have represented groups such as terrorists and immigrants. Researchers, such as the Glasgow Media Group, conduct detailed content analyses of how topics such as these are represented in the media. These are designed to show how the media is biased in its reporting and represents groups such as strikers differently to factory owners or politicians, and so provide us with meanings about control, power and the validity of each message.

Immigrants into a country are always an easily identifiable group. Sometimes they are encouraged in to help a country build up a population or fill skills gaps; at other times the welcome may not be so warm. The United States was a country where the immigrants moved across the continent and displaced the indigenous people. They then welcomed in new immigrants, mainly from Europe, who still had to go through a strict filtering process on Ellis Island. This is an historical example. Ask yourself, however, if groups such as Hispanics are still used as scapegoats for concerns about lowering standards and terrorism. In the film *Men in Black* (Barry Sonnenfeld, 1997) the opening sequence is of illegal immigrants being uncovered as alien terrorists, thus combining the two groups visually. In January 2004, however, President Bush decided to allow Hispanic illegal immigrants an amnesty in order to provide the US economy with necessary cheap labour.

Europe has similar concerns. The break-up of the Soviet Union and the consequent upheavals in the Balkans led to major movements of refugees in Eastern Europe – many fleeing war, but also people wanting to find work. Certainly in the British press Eastern European immigrants, many of whom come from already demonised groups, are referred to as problems and scroungers. To many people this appears the truth because of what they read or hear in the media that leads to negative stereotypes. The economic worth of this influx of potential workers to a country that is suffering a skills shortage as well as of people willing to work in vital low-paid work such as caring is ignored in the headlines. What will we think in fifty years once the dust and the media headlines have settled?

Inevitably the repetition of language and images associated with particular groups helps to create stereotypes. By themselves stereotypes are not negative. We all use stereotypes in our daily life to put individuals into particular groups. They are a shorthand route to everyday meaning such as 'student' and 'teacher'. It is when the stereotype conveys powerful negative constructs that media analysts challenge its construction. Negative stereotyping can lead to groups in society seeming to become the problem – Stanley Cohen (1972) called them 'folk devils' – and thus the excuse for the problem by becoming the problem.

It is in our nature as humans to create these scapegoats, whether it is the witch in Salem, the gypsy living on wasteland, the prostitute plying her trade, the immigrant family down the street, the football hooligan throwing bottles, or the strange behaviour of the mentally ill. Often the media will construct a moral panic over a particular issue by identifying a group who can be blamed for an ill in society and thus externalising the cause that is basically internal to society itself. They have hung their moral campaign around the scapegoat. In January 2003 a whole musical genre – rap – was blamed for gun crime as a result of the murder of two girls, and teenage antisocial behaviour is blamed on those who wear the 'hoodie'. Today in the United States the Arab, often seen as a Muslim fundamentalist and being viewed as anyone from the Middle East, is regarded as the folk devil. Chapter 9 focuses on this area.

This image of the Arab is one that has a long tradition in the West, probably ever since the Crusades. But interestingly in the United States the Arab stereotype can be seen to have had a more recent boost. In 1984, Jack G. Shaheen wrote that the only images that Americans see of Arabs on their television are as 'billionaires, bombers and belly dancers'. Why was the Arab the scapegoat? Shaheen suggests it is because the American media had run out of other folk devils such as the Italian American, as the latter's image was cleaned up and Italian Americans became more integrated into American

In August 2001 the Daily Express had this headline: 'Asylum: We're Being Invaded – Leaked Memo Shows We Are Losing the Battle on Immigrants'. The language is one of war and invasion. Almost a month later the World Trade Center in New York was destroyed. It would not be surprising if the people who read the Daily Express in August began in September to conflate the issues of immigration with terrorism. Language is a very powerful conveyor of ideology.

▶ Are there any current moral panics where a group is being represented as a 'folk devil'? ●

society. The energy crisis of 1973 allowed the oil producers, perceived to be all Arab, to be convenient scapegoats for the economic hardships that the United States was then experiencing. One can perhaps begin to see here why Iraq became a target for invasion three decades later.

It is through such discourses that we begin to define groups as 'not like us' and implying that they are not only different from us, but also in some way inferior to us. Richard Dyer (1985) suggests this is how stereotyping works ideologically. It becomes a non-neutral way of representing groups or types.

This way of defining others is often referred to as 'the other'. The idea of 'the other' appeared in the psychoanalytical work of Freud and was developed by Lacan and others. On a basic level it refers to the alien character of our unconscious from the point of view of our conscious self. It has, however, also been used in the media to convey the sense of an external something or someone representing the alien force as part of the binary opposition of the narrative – 'others' presented as opposite or different from the protagonists. The sense of us as civilised human beings constructs others in opposition and so they become uncivilised and dehumanised. Thus 'the other' is characterised by a sense of difference that cannot easily be bridged and appears to threaten the individual's existence and identity, and by extension the group with whom they identify. Thus we identify with certain groups by opposition to other groups. After September 11th 2001 the sense of the terrorist and the people they represented, often characterised as a Muslim fundamentalist, as being alien and not human was dominant in many media stories.

1.9 Have a go!

Each chapter in this book tries to give you a framework and typology that we hope you can use as a springboard for your own research into these and other areas which you might find easier to begin to study.

We have looked at a disability that is often shunned and hidden by society, that of mental health. Many media texts use mental illness. Once you begin to think about it, you will find many examples of mental illness as a narrative device that uses apparently unmotivated behaviour to generate reactions. Other discussions focus on institutions such as schools and the police, and the institution to which we all belong, the family. How essential is this in its present form?

One area that we have not looked at is how youth culture is represented. Popular music is often a focus of social concern and if you are a fan of a particular genre you could do research into how this has been represented in the media. Musical genres such as rock'n'roll and hip-hop often bemuse older generations and may appear as subverting and therefore dangerous influences. Dick Hebdige (1979) argued that the bricolage of each new style, such as 'punk' or 'garage' music, subverts the cultural norm and so creates a new representation of a group out of control. The music of Elvis Presley in the 1950s was regarded with deep suspicion as being 'black' music and not suitable for white audiences. His act was too raunchy to be shown on television except from the waist upwards. Half a century on, the music and the hip rolling now seem very innocuous and society has new musical scapegoats and folk devils. Popular culture breeds new stereotypes and new representations. No book can be as contemporary or as up to date as your own research – so, have a go!

When conducting research a basic structure or methodology helps to focus ideas. Questions that we used and which could provide a useful framework are:

- Who is in control of the representation?
- What codes and conventions are being used?
- Who is being represented in the text?
- Who is looking at or reading the text?
- In what particular position are the spectator and reader of the text being asked to look at this text? For example, are we supposed to bow down and worship or to look with powerful pleasures (voyeurism/scopophilia) at an image of a nude female in an allegorical or religious painting?
- Who has produced the text and for what reason? Is it to confirm the truth of a particular knowledge/power relationship or to challenge it?
- What messages and meanings are conveyed?
  (based on Richard Dyer's list, 1985)

Using these types of questions will help you to understand how representation works in the media today and you will also begin to see the way that representation works 'through a glass darkly'.

▶ Find a group, maybe one with which you identify or one whom you would categorise as pariahs, and study how they are represented in the media. Good examples can often be found in sports such as football and in popular music. ●

References

Ashbury, R., W. Helsby & M. O Brien, *Teaching African Cinema* (London: BFI, 1998).

Barthes, R., *The Elements of Semiology* (London: Cape, 1967).

Barthes, R., *Mythologies* (London: Cape, 1972).

Cartmell, D., I. Q. Hunter, H. Kaye & I. Whelehan (eds), *Alien Identities: Exploring Differences in Film and Fiction* (London: Pluto Press, 1991).

Cohen, S., *Folk Devils and Moral Panics: The Creation of the Mods and Rockers* (London: Routledge, 1972).

Dyer, R., 'Taking Popular Television Seriously', in David Lusted and Philip Drummond (eds), *TV and Schooling* (London: BFI, 1985), pp. 4–5.

Foucault, M., *Power/Knowledge* (Brighton: Harvester, 1980).

Froudon, J-M. 'Le Monde', *Cahiers du Cinéma*, no. 526, 1 October 1998.

Goodchild, S., 'Blacks Failed by Our "Racist" System of Care for Mentally Ill', *Independent on Sunday*, 28 September 2003.

Gramsci, A., *Selections from the Prison Notebooks*. Q. Hoare & G. Nowell Smith (eds) (London: Lawrence and Wishart, 1971).

Hall, S. (ed.), *Representation: Cultural Representations and Signifying Practices* (London: Sage, 1997).

Hebdige, R., *Subculture: The Meaning of Style* (London: Methuen, 1979).

Hedetoft, L., 'Contemporary Cinema between Globalisation and National Interpretation', in *Cinema and Nation*, Mette Hjort & Scott Mackenzie (eds) (London: Routledge, 2000).

Kuhn, A. (ed.), *Alien Zone II: The Space of Science Fiction Film* (Verso, 1999).

Lichenstein, D, 'The Appearance of the Other in the Attacks of September 11', February 2002 (www.divpsa.org/div39/section5/essay_lichenstein.htm).

McLuhan, M., *Understanding the Media* (UK: Routledge & Kegan Paul, 1964).

Mulvey, L., 'Visual Pleasure and Narrative Cinema', *Screen*, 1975.

Pines, J., & P. Willeman (eds), *Questions of Third Cinema* (London: BFI, 1989).

Shaheen, J., 'Arabs: TV's Villains of Choice', from *Channels*,
March/April 1984, quoted in Barry Duncan, *Mass Media
and Popular Culture* (Canada: HBJ, 1991), p. 95.

Smart, N., *The World Religions: Old Traditions and Modern
Transformations* (UK: Cambridge University Press, 1989).

Television and videos

The War Game (Peter Watkins, 1965, BBC television)
The Secret Policeman (BBC1, 21 October 2003)
'Zulu: The True Story', *Timewatch* (BBC1, 24 October 2003)
Undercurrents news videos
There's Only One Elvis (BBC1, 14 August 2002)

Part Two
Institutions

Introduction

'It's more than a game, it's an institution …'
TOM ON CRICKET IN *TOM BROWN'S SCHOOLDAYS*
BY THOMAS HUGHES (1857)

What is an institution? Education, religion even the British royal family can be called an institution. Institutions are some of the fundamental determinants of our lives – whether they are religion, school, police, family, social, the media, cultural or sport, they help to define our society. They are therefore more than the sum of their parts, and the relationship between the institution and us is much more complex than an economic or structural one.

Louis Althusser referred to ideological state apparatuses and repressive state apparatuses. The former would include the family, while the latter the police. In effect he was talking about institutions. Raymond Williams in his seminal book on language, *Keywords* (1976), shows how the word 'institution' is a noun of action or process. That is we can refer to the name given to the institution such as 'school', for example, but what we actually mean is the way that this group articulates a set of working practices, or rules, explicit or implicit, and how it is represented to us.

These rules are not only confined to the producers of texts. The consumers or spectators are also involved in these processes. As Christian Metz pointed out with reference to cinema, the institution of cinema involves technical, economic and regulatory factors, but also the experiences of the audience, the spectator and their reading of the text and its representations.

In the media the role and nature of texts lay claim to a representation of a truth and 'reality', but economic determinants suggest that the ownership or control of the means of production could indicate that there is a relative loss of identity in this postmodern world. Whose reality and whose truths are questioned? So in terms of institutions we need to ask:

- Who produces the text?
- What are their values and codes?
- What is the relationship to us as individuals?
- What are the dominant ideologies being promulgated through the institutional working practices?

The relationship between the state, the media and the industries that pay for them is crucial for an understanding of the institutions that run them. How are decisions made and who makes them? What pressures are they under? The BBC has had to respond to changes in political ideologies, technical determinants, the new regulatory authority and, like other institutions, a new world order in communications. It is having to ask itself how it can sustain itself as a public service broadcaster in an increasingly commercial media world.

Institutions gain their authority from wider sources than just themselves. They collect and disseminate information beyond individual texts. Consequently they help to construct a discursive formation (Foucault) that affirms a representation. So in the discourse around education, for example, films, television dramas, documentaries and news items are all helping to create the discourse.

As Williams's definition suggests, institutions are not inert structures. They respond and change to circumstances such as shifts in hegemonic power, ownership, political determinants, regulation, technological and economic pressures. In education there is a constant discussion on how the institutions of schools and colleges will work and be regulated. When viewing police programmes what do audiences understand about the law and what ideological tensions are there in the various roles the police are given and how have they changed over time? Similarly the institution of the family has changed in many ways over the past fifty years, particularly in its structure from the extended family to the nuclear family and now to the one-parent family. These changes have also been influenced by economic and regulatory factors, but are constructed by society and reflect its values. In a democracy we regard these as part of a negotiated consensus, and this inevitably means that institutions are often at the site of fractures of consensus. This section is going to look at how representations of the institutions of the family, of schools and education, and of the police reflect reality or construct it.

To recap:

- Institutions are enduring organisations and have a history of change. They are in the public memory.
- Institutions construct sets of rules and are regulated.
- Institutions are collectivist, they have common agendas.
- Institutions have shared values and shared working practices.

Having looked at some of the institutions that create society, the focus of this book then moves on to groups who are outside these institutions and are often in conflict with them.

References

Metz, C., *Film Language: A Semiotics of the Cinema* (New York: Oxford University Press, 1976).

Williams, R., *Keywords: A Vocabulary of Culture and Society* (Glasgow: William Collins, 1976).

2. Images of the Family

PAULINE TURNER

This chapter discusses images of the family and asks us to compare what we see on the screen with our own experiences of family life. How far are we expected to take what we see as real? How far do we distance ourselves from a text because we believe it to be outside our experience? Some texts might suggest that the characters would behave in a specific way because of where they come from or what kind of people they are. If this is the case, what readings are we expected to make of the text? This chapter will examine depictions of the family from a variety of genres: cartoon, soap opera, television sitcom and one film. How typical are they of the family groups they represent and who decided on that particular representation?

2.1 What is a family?

Most people will have a nursery book image of what a family might be. Usually, it's a mum and dad and two or three children, at least one of either gender. They live in a house together and the male parent works full-time, while the female parent works either full- or part-time, or stays at home to take care of the family. The children go to school and have outings with both parents at weekends and spend Christmas and holidays together. Often there's a pet, usually a dog. Sometimes reference is made to an older relative – a grandparent, for example. By this description I might be describing *The Simpsons* or *The Royle Family*. Both, we know, are constructions written for entertainment. Are we supposed to take them literally? Are the representations of their families

► What is your family like? How far do you think your family extends? If there is a remarriage in your family, what do you consider your relationships to be with those new members? ●

Baudrillard recognised that for a large percentage of people the world of television represents a reality that is 'more real' than their personal experience. Televisual representation has come to dominate our perception of the outside world. This theory was also posited by George Gerbner in the 1970s in his research into the effects of media exposure to what he termed 'heavy viewers'.

► Take a look at this website yourself. www.gov.statistics.co.uk ●

actually more real to us than, say, the world of *Billy Elliot* or the Fowler family in *EastEnders*? These questions will form part of the discussion in this chapter.

Government statistics suggest that what is actually occurring in society is not always being reflected on our screens – the representation is taken so far away from our own experiences or is so extreme that we cannot believe in it as a reality. We may not be particularly concerned about this, as one of the questions posed by this book asks us to consider whether we are bothered if what we see on our screens is real or not. We may not be consciously comparing our own experiences with those portrayed to us. Some critics such as the French writer Jean Baudrillard think that people are not concerned with whether what they see on the screen is 'real' or not – as for many people the media themselves are considered to be the 'real' world. This is known as the 'hyper-real'.

Current social trends give the lie to the so-called 'nuclear' or 'traditional' family and tell us that household composition has transformed in recent decades. In spring 2000 almost three in ten households in Great Britain comprised one person living alone, which was more than two and a half times the proportion in 1961. The proportion of households with two opposite gender adults and dependent children fell from two-fifths to less than a quarter, while the proportion of lone-parent households tripled. One in ten people in Great Britain lived in a lone-parent household in 2000. The most common household group was still those headed by a couple, but couple households with no children had increased from less than a fifth to a quarter (source: *Social Trends 31*).

So how does our experience as the viewer match what we see on television and the cinema? How far are we empathising with the programmes or distancing ourselves from them because they do not match our own understanding of the society around us? Baudrillard's point that audiences are not concerned with whether what they see on television is real or not might make the whole question pointless. In any case, does it matter?

Peter Tatchell, ex Labour MP and equal rights activist speaking on *The Media Show*, BBC2, February 1990, suggested that the whole idea of a family is a social construct, one engineered by the ruling classes for convenience. It offers protection for children, who in the human species require a

People in households in Great Britain — by type of household and family in which they live	1961 (%)	1971 (%)	1981 (%)	1991 (%)	2000 (%)
ONE-FAMILY HOUSEHOLDS					
Living alone	4	6	8	11	12
Couple					
No children	18	19	20	23	25
Dependent children	52	52	47	41	39
Non-dependent children only	12	10	10	11	9
Lone parent	3	4	6	10	10
OTHER HOUSEHOLDS	12	9	9	4	6
ALL PEOPLE IN PRIVATE HOUSEHOLDS (= 100%) (millions)	—	53.4	53.9	55.4	57.0
PEOPLE NOT IN PRIVATE HOUSEHOLDS (millions)	—	0.9	0.8	0.8	—
TOTAL POPULATION (millions)	51.4	54.4	54.8	56.2	

Source: Census — Labour Force Survey, Office for National Statistics

long period of nurturing (often around 18 years or longer), and therefore devolves specific responsibility to the biological parents rather than the collective responsibility of all adults towards all children – as in the Israeli kibbutz idea. He asserts that the whole construct of the family must be society's and be biologically determined, otherwise it would exist naturally within society and could not be destroyed. The family can be seen as a political unit. It serves a political purpose in that it controls and contains people, especially women. This is a very interesting idea to apply to a reading of soap operas, and we will be looking at this later in relation to *EastEnders*. The idea can also be seen as a version of determinism (Marxism). This suggests that the makers of media texts were, albeit unconsciously, constructing a view of society which most benefits the ruling classes and could even in some instances work against the best interests of the diverse ways in which families now need to be represented.

Determinism (Marxism) would suggest that subconsciously the writers and makers of a large part of the media construct representations that are in the best interests of maintaining the status quo – in favour of the ruling sectors of society (the governing system, the law, the Establishment etc.) and against anyone who might have an alternative way of doing things. Look at the way the media represent the annual worship of the Druids at Stonehenge every summer solstice. It is always reported from the point of view of the police and 'outraged' local residents, not from the point of view of the (minority) Druids.

Functionalism suggests that the media give people what they want to consume and is led by the tastes of its audiences. They reflect public attitudes and respond to change. For example, look at the way the representation of homosexuals has changed with public opinion over the years.

Graham Burton in *Talking Television* (Arnold, 2000) says, 'Representations endorse a so-called natural order of things. They support dominant ideological positions.' 'Commonsense' views of family life are sometimes constructed by such programmes as sitcoms and soap operas, and set up a false 'norm'. Thus, lone-parent families get a lot of undue attention in the press and by politicians. Similarly, couples of the same sex, whether male or female, who want to rear children are viewed with suspicion. Very little on our screens represents the statistic that a quarter of all households comprise a couple living alone with no dependent children. Functionalism would argue that we get what we want on our screens; that the films and television programmes reflect public attitudes and we are not interested in programmes about childless couples, or single people living alone, even though they comprise three out of every ten households.

So a key question remains when looking at our media texts: what does this film or television programme mean to me? Do my tastes shape content on television?

2.2 Families on television

Television programmes differ from films in being very much more culturally specific than films, which can cross more boundaries. This may affect our reception of, say, American sitcoms about families compared with British sitcoms. Our lack of personal experience of the way Americans behave at home might lead us to see all programmes as fictional or, conversely, totally representative and accurate. Television has also adopted and adapted the styles and formats from diverse sources, using radio, journalism, magazine, film, theatre etc. to produce an entirely new range of programmes. These are usually different generically from films. It could be argued that soap operas are not really a genre in their own right, but dramas – for years *Coronation Street* was claimed to be a drama, not a soap opera. The distinction is also blurred between whether programmes might be considered serials or series. Programmes such as *Friends*, for example, did have story strands running from episode to episode, but could also be seen out of sequence and make perfect sense to the viewer. Hybridity and overlap mean that genres are no longer quite so clear cut. This could also influence the way we receive and understand our television programmes. Television is also subjected more to market pressures from, say, advertising or the schedulers, than film, which is a further consideration in looking at how it constructs its representations.

2.3 Soap operas: *EastEnders*

The first television soap opera was centred on a family. *The Grove Family*, described as 'an average suburban family', ran on the BBC from April 1954 to June 1957. The most successful soap operas seem to be those concerned with families. Other soaps such as *Compact* (the magazine world), *United* (a football club) and *Triangle* (a shipping line) were all short lived and folded within two to three years of their inception. A quick look at all the currently running soap operas shows family concerns to be central issues, either as conflict within the family or the aspiration to achieve the perfect family, marrying happily and bringing up well-adjusted, stable children. The television series *Soapstars* ran a competition to find a new family for the soap opera *Emmerdale*, so bringing reality into fiction and thus conflating the ideologies.

EastEnders began its run with the Beale/Fowler family at the heart. This large family comprised a grandmother, mother and father, two teenage children and a new baby, and extended to the mother's twin brother, his wife and teenage son. With the shifting sands of plot lines and routine changes of character, the Beales/Fowler family some eighteen years later has only four of its original group, but other families have entered the arena and provided the soap opera with its rich and varied storylines.

One such family is the Slaters, who provide a less traditional presentation of a family, although in common with the Beales/Fowlers there is a grandmother, Mo, who lives with the family group. The rest of the family are Little Mo and Kat, her granddaughters, Zoe her great-granddaughter and Charlie her son. Originally Zoe was portrayed as a sister to Little Mo and Kat, but a later storyline revealed that Zoe was in fact not their sister but rather Kat's daughter, the product of an incestuous relationship with their Uncle Harry. Many families have skeletons within their closets and this eighteen-year-old secret might equate with what other young people might find out about their families at about this time in their lives. Mid teens is a typical time when young people unofficially enter adulthood and often start to be considered

▶ Scan a week's worth of television listings magazines. You can make a few general points from this about the different ways families are represented across a wide range of programmes. If you have time you could conduct a fuller content analysis. ●

EastEnders: the televisual community

▶ Watch a couple of episodes of *EastEnders* and count the number of times the word 'family' is used. In an omnibus edition in April 2003 it featured no fewer than 31 times! Why do you think the word 'family' is used so much? ●

old enough to know family secrets. A similar storyline was used in the BBC series *Playing the Field* (2001).

The word 'family' crops up frequently in *EastEnders*. Roy Evans and his son Barry run a car lot on the Square (2002). Roy advertises for a new member of staff, but Barry tries to put each applicant off, saying to his wife, Natalie, 'It's a family business and that's the way it's going to stay,' and to his father, 'It's Evans and Son – let's get our priorities right, Dad.' He is unsympathetic to his wife's wish to work in the business, however, as they have a new baby and Barry says that a baby needs its mother. This reinforces a patriarchal view of the world, but one that is increasingly anachronistic. How far do you think we are supposed to agree with Barry? He seems to be using his wife's pregnancy and the birth of their child to control and contain her, yet he is presented in the text of the programme to be very much a hands-on father. He does not extend these feelings to the return of a long-lost brother, Nathan, who appears to be the cause of some conflict in the past; after offering Nathan a job in the car sales business, it is Roy who says to Barry, 'Let's face it – we're all family. What better way to welcome him back to the family?'

In *EastEnders* in 2002 another new mother, Lisa, also had not yet returned to work and was relying on her partner Mark to support her. (Mark is one of the four remaining original Fowler family members, although played by a different actor.) Their situation is further complicated by the fact that HIV-positive Mark is not the father of the baby. In a conversation with his mother (the original mother, Pauline Fowler) he tells her that all he has ever wanted is his own wife and child, and that for a time he thought he was going to achieve this. As said before, the perfect family life with a partner and children seems to be the aspiration of most soap opera storylines. Certainly the baby's father takes the same view, and wants prolonged access and visiting rights to his child, having previously had only long-distance contact with his former wife and their son.

What are we to make of all these references to family and this portrayal of families in constant conflict? The preferred reading would seem to be that a happy family is the be-all and end-all, and that conflict within the family is to be avoided at all costs. Certainly there is much negotiation going on within the families – whether or not Natalie will be allowed to work;

whether Phil will be allowed to see his child on his terms. There is never a permanent balance of power, a clear hegemony, but the disagreements illustrate that power must be fought for and requires a lot of agreement between the parties concerned, and that agreement will only happen if the two sides share some basic values.

Richard Dyer suggests that that it does not matter whether or not we have typical representations on television, but rather what those representations are and what harm they might do to the well-being of the groups they represent (Dyer, 1985). Is the representation of family in *EastEnders* so far from the probable that we dismiss it; is it even damaging our view of what a family should be?

In *EastEnders* none of the families discussed portrays the configuration of two parents and two/three children, although an original cast member, Ian Beale, at one point had three children and lived with his third wife, Laura (their stepmother), in the Square. She also worked in the family business alongside her husband, but at that point in the storyline did not seem to have any power outside of the home.

But how representative of our own experiences are these groups, and do we identify with them or take the view that they are portrayed in this confrontational and melodramatic way as part of the entertainment? To put it another way: are the presentations of family in the programme damaging our understanding of what a family is? The opening comments relating to government statistics already illustrate the diversity of families, and, to return to the main theme, all of the characters seem to be in pursuit of happiness and harmony. Even if few rarely achieve it, this might be considered a positive attribute of the show.

2.4 Situation comedies: *The Royle Family*

Unlike soap operas situation comedy rarely shows a development of character or of situation. Part of the pleasure of the comedy for viewers is the anticipation of the outcome, the joke, and the repeated catchphrase. Circularity and repetition are fundamental to situation comedy's structure and popularity. Most of the characters are recognisable stereotypes, whether the snobbish Hyacinth Bouquet or the grumpy old man in *One Foot in the Grave*. But as in soap operas the family is again a tried and tested part of the

▶ Consider the representation of family within another British soap opera with which you are familiar. Who is the intended audience and how is that reflected in the representation of family? ●

The Royle Family: To the Royles, the shared experiences of television are a way of being a family

▶ Roughly calculate how much television you view in a week and how this differs for different members of the family. What attitudes do we have towards people who watch a lot of television, whether or not we watch a lot ourselves? Much of this attitude may be moulded by the language used by critics to describe heavy viewers – addicts, couch potatoes etc. – nearly all negative terms.

You might like to read more about audience effects. See I. Ang, *Watching Dallas: Soap Opera and the Melodramatic Imagination* (London: Methuen, 1985); M. Barker & J. Petley (eds), *Ill Effects: The Media/Violence Debate* (London: Routledge, 1997); and J. Fiske, *Television Culture* (London: Routledge, 1987). ●

formula. Even in a sitcom such as *Dad's Army* or where there is no apparent central family, there is still a pseudo family with the fussy father figure, the avuncular man, the potty grandparent and the naive youngster. Although formulaic, we can still laugh at older programmes because we recognise the institutions they represent. But even sitcoms change to represent a different view of society and its structures. *Absolutely Fabulous*, for example, and *The Royle Family* provided alternative situation comedies that built cult followings before becoming mainstream, using stylistically new ways to explore the changing institution of the family.

One element to remember about situation comedies is that, although they are rooted in reality (otherwise we would not be able to relate to them), they are unreal in the way that they do not develop a sense of a parallel realism as soap operas do. This means that representations can be overexaggerated, as in the two examples discussed below, without causing us to question their veracity. One thought to ponder about this genre is therefore whether this allows us to laugh at the stereotypes without transferring these ideas to our real lives.

The opening titles of *The Royle Family* position the audience as the ultimate voyeurs, our love of looking fully satisfied. We are inside the television set looking out into the Royles' sitting room; Jim Royle switching on the television activates each episode. We see life lived in front of the television set, with programmes serving as a constant background hum to the conversations and low-level activities of the family. The BBC News in February 2002 carried an item that stated that the average person watched around 21 hours of television per week; this would certainly seem the minimum to apply to the Royles, who seem to watch far more and whose watching is exaggerated for comedic purposes. Do we recognise our own viewing habits to be similar to these?

To the Royles, the shared experiences of the television programmes are a way of being a family. Discussing their individual preferences for daytime chat show hosts and singing the theme tunes to the shows are a change away from their ordinary day-to-day lives and illustrate the family's interpretations and uses of the shows. Do you recognise this as a family activity? There is of course an irony in the name, as the ultimate family in the United Kingdom is the royal family. Particularly since Victorian times, this family has been the most instrumental in forming our ideas, our beliefs, about 'the family'.

The Royles consist of mother, Barbara; father, Jim; married daughter, Denise; her husband, Dave; their son Baby David; and teenage son Anthony. This type of 'nuclear' family (heterosexual parents and two children) comprises about only two out of every ten households in this country, so we instantly ask ourselves how representative of modern families they might be. Although they do not live there, Denise, Dave and the baby are extremely frequent visitors. Other characters are Nana (who also does not live there, but would like to), Anthony's friend Darren, neighbours Joe and Mary, and their daughter Denise's friend Cheryl. Jim's friend Twiggy also makes several appearances. Each family member has his or her own character type and niche. One way of discerning their characters is through the iconography and symbolism of their appearance, or how the character is constructed visually. Patrick Phillips in his book *Understanding Film Texts* (2000), where he is discussing film characterisation, suggests using the following questions to help understand the impact of character. We might also usefully apply these to scripted television programmes, even though, as discussed earlier, film and television genres differ.

- How is the character constructed visually?
- How is the character constructed through dialogue?
- How is the character constructed through performance?
- What is the significance of the position we are put in as spectators for responding to character?
- To what extent is our response to character out of control of those who make the film?

These questions could be based upon Barthes' secondary codes.

If we consider Barbara Royle using some of these criteria, we can begin to understand her individual representation and her contribution to the family as a whole. Barbara Royle is middle-aged, harassed and worn down. She works in a shop and runs the home. She wears inexpensive, well-worn clothing: leggings or shortish skirts, and loose blouses. Her long hair is roughly piled on her head and has been dyed; the regrowth at the roots is clearly discernible. Through dialogue, she acts as a conduit for the rest of the family. She asks questions, then repeats the answers to the rest of the family, who might be sitting there or might just have entered the room, in order to elicit further responses. She remonstrates with Anthony when asked to do so by others in the family group – for example, if Anthony does anything to annoy Denise, she says, 'Mam, tell him!' which Barbara instantly does. She also takes Jim to task for using bad language or exhibiting antisocial behaviour. She never criticises Denise, even though Denise is portrayed as lazy and disorganised. Her own mother, Norma (Nana), she listens to patiently, but does sometimes laugh at after she has left the room. She has a synchronising motif by asking other people, 'Have you had your teas? What did you have?' and we wait for these questions and the other characters' responses and feel put out if one episode she does not ask them. This is part of the generic code of repetition.

Through her performance we see her as the centre of the family, without whom not much in the way of shopping, cooking or clearing up will be done. From our exceptionally privileged position as voyeurs of this family we keep our distance as regards understanding what really goes on in Barbara's head, as no one character is put above another when it comes to seeing their position more clearly than anyone else's. This, however, may occur in the audience's reception of the characters and storylines – the empathy we may individually feel, for example, with the harassed mother, or the teenage boy at the bottom end of a family group. To this extent, we may say that our response according to Phillips's criteria is outside the control of those who made the television programme and is asking us to consider, as Dyer suggests, what this representation means to us.

The discourses surrounding *The Royle Family* are many and varied. The storylines are unexceptional and mundane, instantly recognisable. Anthony wants to start a pop group. Barbara wants the sitting room decorated. The neighbour, Joe, has to go to casualty following an accident with a cheese grater. Denise's friend Cheryl is in constant pursuit of losing weight. Nana's neighbour dies. A review programme on the first series of *The Royle Family* had differing opinions as to its success. One of the contributors could not see the point of the programme at all and described it as the most boring thing

▶ Select another member of the Royle family to analyse using Phillips's criteria. Could you construct an additional Royle family member using these same criteria? If so, what would he or she be like? ●

she had ever seen. What, she wanted to know, was interesting about watching people watching television? This may be an example of what the writer Rick Altman called 'generic frustration' (1996), when a well-known format does not match the viewers' previous experiences. In this case, the Royle family is portrayed quite differently from families in other television sitcoms such as *2.4 Children* (BBC, 1991–1999) or *My Family* (BBC, 2000–2005), for example. The argument by the critics was hotly debated. The Royle Family satisfies many aspects of pleasure, the intense pleasure of watching others, voyeurism, and perhaps being able to feel vaguely superior to some of the characters. Also, the identification with parts of the personalities of the Royles and feeling that we might know someone like one of the characters with their quirky use of the television and individual interpretation of the point of some of the programmes. *The Antiques Roadshow*, we learn, is not about the beauty or intrinsic value of the articles, but a guessing game as to the final worth. If you watch the faces of the participants at the all-important valuation stage you may agree that the Royles have got it dead right. As far as the representation of the family goes the point is made above: many of the viewers will recognise aspects of personality in someone they know who's a bit like a Royle (which gives the programme some kind of realism) or entirely suitable for a situation comedy, and therefore possibly more real than their own experience (hyper-reality – Baudrillard). Perhaps they just take huge enjoyment from believing, rightly or wrongly, that they are not like this family. To take another of Dyer's points, he asks us to consider what harm the representations do to the well-being of the groups (in this case the family group) that they represent. The Royle family is written as basically a good-hearted group and even as possible negative representations of a working-class family. It is hard to see that any actual harm occurs unless we consider how they can be thought to be feckless and worthless by those who are in control of decisions about such groups. Will a politician, for example, want to vote out social security for the long-term unemployed having viewed Jim Royle?

A whole host of sitcoms over the years have also had the family at the centre. One of the most recent and successful is simply called *My Family*. The episodes centre on a middle-

My Family: Middle England's idealised nuclear family?

class family group of Ben, a dentist; his wife, Susan, a tour guide organiser; an elder son, Nick, who is unemployed, lazy and seemingly unintelligent; a daughter, Janey, who is intelligent but also very opinionated and full of her rights; and a younger son, Michael, who is a boffin and watches the antics of the rest of the family from an amused distance. They live in a large, suburban dwelling metaphorically a million miles away from *The Royle Family*. The title is interesting as it is not instantly clear who the 'my' of *My Family* is, and it is quite likely that the writers wanted different people to see different aspects of themselves and their families, and to identify with one or more of the characters. Not all mothers would identify instantly with the character of Susan simply because they are mothers themselves, but perhaps they would see aspects of people they know in, for example, the daughter, Janey, or Ben, the harassed father.

In 2002 the BBC piloted another sitcom, *All About Me*, which is a fusion of two families from different backgrounds and cultures. It features a boy of normal intelligence with cerebral palsy who watches the activities of his Indian mother and her white partner and his children, and comments occasionally via a voiceover. This family is so much at the far end of dysfunctional that it was interesting to see how the show developed and what the audience's acceptance was. For example, it has received criticism from Scope, the Cerebral Palsy society, for showing Raj as being unable to communicate verbally with his family via a voiced computer or similar, and presenting him as so totally isolated. However, it did address the issue of some people with disabilities being disempowered and frequently having able-bodied people speaking for them, as used in the title of the disabilities radio programme *Does He Take Sugar?* (BBC Radio 4). There is further discussion on the representation of mental disability in Part 3.

Raj might be speaking from a script, but then so are the rest of the cast, and positioning the reader from a minority viewpoint on occasion is a shift from the norm. It could also be said, however, that this device of the voiceover was very underused. The 'me' of the title was the character Raj, but there is probably less of his opinion than anyone else's. The following series to this show broadcast from autumn 2003 furnishes Raj with a voice computer partly in response to some of the criticisms. It has not been commissioned for a

▶ The actress playing Janey left the series and was replaced by a female cousin of the 'blonde bimbo' variety. This is a challenge writers often face – if you had to replace another family member from *My Family* (say, Michael goes off to university), how would you cope with this? What new family representation could you incorporate? ●

further series, however, as rather surprisingly the two families mixed together with considerable ease, given all of the cultural differences and ignoring sibling/stepbrother/stepsister rivalry. Perhaps *All About Me* was simply too unconvincing and saccharine sweet to make much of an impact.

2.5 Cartoons

Of all the cartoon families from *The Flintstones* (1960–1977 on television, plus several films) to *The Jetsons* (premiered 1962, Hanna Barbera's space-age answer to *The Flintstones*), the most famous and well loved of all must be *The Simpsons* (1987 to present). *The Simpsons* celebrates the underachiever and highlights many of the idiosyncrasies and pitfalls of human existence. It is the perfect text for understanding the concept of intertextuality; it draws on many other media forms and formats, including extensively from cinema, other television shows, magazines, cult figures and the whole notion of celebrity. It is massively imbued with references to popular culture. The former US president George Bush Sr, who said that we needed more families like *The Waltons* (1972–1981) and less like *The Simpsons*, could not have got it more wrong.

The Simpsons: the real American family?

The Waltons were a sugary sweet representation of a family during the Great Depression of 1930s America, who went through divorce, desertion, death, war and a whole gamut of extreme emotions. The Simpsons are a close-knit family unit and virtually every episode revolves around their experiences as a family and how they deal with day-to-day living. Homer may appear more like one of the children than an adult in some instances and Lisa too wise beyond her years, but they are rich material for examining what constitutes a family and what binds a family together.

In one episode, Marge wants to do something 'as a family', so they visit the Itchy and Scratchy theme park. Itchy and Scratchy are a pair of extremely violent cartoon characters who are an obvious reference to *Tom and Jerry* and other children's cartoons which exhibit cartoon violence while showing none of the consequences. This gives us a text rich in discourses on the point (and pointlessness) of theme parks and satirises the whole theme park 'experience'. It also puts the issue of the possible effects of violent media exposure on the individual and the group, and the true worth of a shared family experience such as a holiday.

The episode starts with Marge complaining that they do not do things as a family any more, and a visit to the theme park as a family outing is suggested. They arrive at the theme park and, after leaving their car in an enormous car park from which the car will be very difficult to retrieve, are instantly duped into spending more than they need to at the gate. Baby Maggie is deposited in a crèche where she is tossed into a cavernous ball pit and sinks to the bottom where several other babies are also floundering. The cartoon juxtaposes Marge's anxious face at the disappearance of her baby into the ball pit with Maggie sucking frenetically on her dummy. The viewer is left experiencing Marge's disquiet and the baby's bewilderment.

Outside the theme park is divided up into different areas along Disney lines, with 'Unnecessary Surgery Land', 'The Minefield' and 'Parents' Island' (sponsored by Laramie cigarettes), to name but a few. Homer, the adult child in all of us, loves all the attractions, but Marge voices her concerns at the suitability of some of the attractions and disapproves of the violent rides. She would seem to be the lone voice of adult reason. Lisa also wonders if overexposure to imagined violence which fails to show the consequences does desensitise you, but quickly joins with Bart in laughing at and seemingly ignoring the extreme acts to which they are exposed. Although Lisa is noted in the programme for her high intelligence, she exhibits a more childlike response in being 'sucked into' the theme park's values, as does her father, Homer.

In typical *Simpsons* fashion the holiday quickly goes wrong as the theme park's robots stage a revolt, leading Homer to declare, 'No one spoils my family vacation except me – and maybe my boy.' The situation becomes desperate, and the family are almost killed when the robots run amok and the electronics of the theme park break down completely, leading Marge to remark, 'Violence on TV may be funny, but it's not so funny when it's happening to one of us.'

As they leave the park and head home the final comment goes to Lisa, who says, 'It brought us together as a family – we got a lot of exercise out of doors and a whole lot of excitement.' As typically in a *Simpsons* episode, the cartoon ends happily; it does ignore some of the wider issues it shows (violence, machines as menace), but the central strand of experiencing things as a family is clearly highlighted.

There is an enormous body of research on the effects of media violence on the individual or group. A good starting point might be the English and Media Centre's website www.englishandmediacentre.co.uk, where there is a quiz on media and violence effects and a list of suggested reading.

The creator Matt Groening based *The Simpsons* on his own family; his construction of the Simpsons is intentional and deliberately represents the group through its members, their characters, verbal responses and their varying reactions to their lives, both individually and as a social unit. The episode's contents are designed to create certain ideas (such as how we experience theme parks) and suggest there is a preferred reading of the point of theme parks and their (to him) blatant fleecing of their customers. This means we must largely see things as Groening does. An acceptance of his view of the world that agrees with his intentional presentation of the rules and conventions of the social system as he sees it and our agreement that we think his presentation is feasible must be constantly negotiated with us, the audience.

The popularity of the show suggests that this may be happening at several levels. We could be in total agreement with the satire of the programmes and their presentations of the world around us, which concur with our own world view. We could read it as a cynical, exaggerated representation of people's experiences portrayed as anti-society and anti-family, as George Bush did. We may see it as nothing more than a piece of entertainment with amusing, totally unreal cartoon characters who are not meant to represent anything beyond a television programme and a range of children's toys.

The Simpsons seems to beg a discursive approach, with the emphasis on cultural understanding and shared meanings. The 'cartoon' style provides a means for how we talk about a subject; it discusses how we regulate others' behaviour and make sense of the world around us. It is able to push the boundaries by being in cartoon format and to explore ideas which would not be possible if real people were playing the characters. We also have the get-out clause at the end of the day that this is just a cartoon anyway. Whatever the subject content of each episode, Homer, Marge, Bart, Lisa and Maggie are always involved as a family. Even when one family member is highlighted it is in the context of how the whole family is affected by or how the members react to that person's experiences. Marge is a loving and thoughtful parent whose major reason for her existence is the well-being of her family and the continuance of her relationship with Homer. A patriarchal reading may suggest that Marge is powerless outside of the home, yet several episodes show Marge as

▶ Imagine a television sitcom such as *The Royle Family* being presented as a cartoon. How much further could we take the characters and situations? What would be lost of the acute realism of the family? Would the exercise work better with a sitcom such as *Gimme, Gimme, Gimme?* ●

contributing significantly to the Springfield community, trying out several paid jobs outside of the home and having her own needs met when it seems all the world puts upon her. Similarly, the superficially childish Homer can exhibit his own strong family values and suggest a parent with the best interests of his family at heart.

2.6 Films

Although the focus of this chapter is on families on television, the world of film has many examples of family life from the romantic to the realistic. One film which raises issues of what constitutes 'marriage' and 'family' is *Billy Elliott* (Stephen Daldrey, 2000). Billy and his family are represented as strong male characters with a strong sense of family, but there are other partnerships shown, such as Billy's friend at the end of the film and Mrs Wilkinson's relationship with Billy. In this one-parent family, the father is the head as his wife has died. He has a working son (at the pits, with him, although they are currently on strike); a schoolboy son, Billy, who is eleven; and a partly senile elderly mother living with him.

Billy is sent to boxing lessons, but migrates into the girls' dance class next door, where the dance teacher Mrs Wilkinson recognises he has real talent and ability, and wants him to audition for training at the Royal School of Ballet. There is no tradition of such a thing both in this part of the world and within Billy's working-class environment, and many taboos must be broken to allow Billy his chance. His older brother, Tony, is also a strong influence in the family, both in respect

In *Billy Elliot*, Mrs Wilkinson is the catalyst for Billy's ambition

to what is happening in the miners' strike and whether Billy may learn to dance. 'Nana' within the family appears to be senile and insists she could have been a professional dancer (who knows?). The point is that she has no power within the family because of her senility. It is to the dead mother that the final decision to allow Billy to audition for the Royal Ballet School is deferred: 'She would have let him,' 'She would have given him the chance.' This is what finally allows the brother, Tony, to support his father's decision. He is also spurred to this point after he sees what his father is prepared to do in order to get the money to take Billy to London for his audition. Billy's father, who is a staunch union man, is prepared to break the strike and return to work. This underlines for Tony the strength of his father's feelings. The decision to allow Billy to travel to London for the audition is clearly a family decision from which Mrs Wilkinson is excluded, except for her professional advice. Her screaming row with Tony and Billy's father after Billy's first missed audition did not change their minds at that point in the narrative to allow Billy his chance.

Finally, the emphasis is firmly on the family again when Billy's father and his brother go to watch the grown-up Billy dance in *Swan Lake* – one of the theatre ushers is asked 'to let Billy know his family's here'. The dance teacher is not with them, which would definitely have been too neat a conclusion – rather too much like the concluding moments in an episode of *This Is Your Life* (a television show recording the lives of minor celebrities).

What does Billy learn about how a family behaves in this film? He punches a boy offering him sympathy at his audition at the Royal Ballet School – but saw his father do the same to his brother when in disagreement. The films is set in the period of the Miners' Strike of the early 1980s, and Billy lives in an atmosphere of many conflicts 'resolved' by violence, with an oppressive police presence. His brother, Tony, has very fixed views about what is right and what is wrong, including his attitude to gays. He initially refuses to allow Billy to dance because of what other people might think: 'No brother of mine ...' However, when he sees that his staunchly union-supporting father is prepared to break the strike to work in order to earn the fares to London for Billy's audition, he persuades him not to go back to work, but will help his father find the fares some other way – this is the point at which the dead

▶ Watch *Billy Elliot*. Discuss whether Mrs Wilkinson is a substitute mother figure. Consider how her daughter describes her own family group. ●

Billy Elliot: Billy has to care for his grandmother in an extended working-class family

mother (presumably remembered quite clearly by the older Tony) is brought into the decision to allow Billy his chance.

▶ Examine the representations of family in other feature films dealing with young people, such as *Purely Belter* (Mark Herman, 2000) or *A Room for Romeo Brass* (Shane Meadows, 1999). Are they showing dysfunctional families or do they roughly accord with the Government Social Trends table referred to at the start of this chapter (see p. 35)? In what ways may depictions of the family define them as functional or dysfunctional? ●

What does this film's representation of a family mean to a modern reader? Billy's family is not set apart by divorce but by death, a different circumstance from most, according to statistics. Ballet is also something alien to many, perhaps typified most by Mrs Wilkinson's troupe of little dancing girls. Fewer people than ever have an elderly relative living at home with them. There is also a distancing from many people's lives by placing this story in the past representing industrial hardship in the North and Midlands of England. What is abundant in Billy Elliot's home is love, of all of the family members for each other – even though Tony refuses to consider that Billy might learn ballet initially, it is love for his father, for his dead mother and for Billy that finally persuades him.

References

Altman, Rick, 'Cinema and Genre', *The Oxford History of World Cinema* (London: Oxford University Press, 1996).

Ashby, J., & A. Higson (eds), *British Cinema, Past and Present* (London & New York: Routledge, 2000).

Barthes, R., *The Elements of Semiology* (London: Cape, 1967).

Barthes, R., *Mythologies* (London: Cape, 1972).

Burton, G., *Talking Television* (London: Arnold, 2000).

Creeber, G. (ed.), *The Television Genre Book* (London: BFI Publishing, 2001).

Dyer, R., 'Taking Popular Television Seriously', in David Lusted and Philip Drummond (eds), *TV and Schooling* (London: BFI, 1985), pp. 4–5.

Foucault, M., *Power/Knowledge* (Brighton: Harvester, 1980).

Hacker, J., & D. Price, *Take Ten: Contemporary British Film Directors* (London: Oxford University Press, 1992).

Hall, S. (ed.), *Representation: Cultural Representations and Signifying Practices* (London: Sage, 1997).

Martin, R., *TV for A Level Media Studies* (Oxford: Hodder & Stoughton, 2000).

Mulvey, L., 'Visual Pleasure and Narrative Cinema', *Screen*, 1975.

Murphy, R (ed.), *The British Cinema Book*, 2nd edn (London: BFI Publishing, 2001).

Phillips, P., *Understanding Film Texts: Meaning and Experience* (London: BFI Publishing, 2000).

3. Schools and Teachers

ROY ASHBURY

One can argue that film noir did not exist until film critics constructed it and posited a genealogy. Similarly, a case might be made that films about teachers articulate a hitherto unrecognised 'pedagogue genre', with characteristic tropes and themes, if not a consistent visual style. It is certainly true that a number of films, from Goodbye Mr Chips *(Sam Wood, 1939) to* Être et Avoir *(Nicholas Philibert, 2002), have portrayed teaching in ways which raise interesting issues of representation.*

3.1 Introduction

Before beginning, it might be worth saying what we are trying to achieve in studies of media representation like this. We are not engaged in a search for a 'holy grail' in the form of one 'true representation' of reality. Reality is complex, changeable and, especially in the case of cultural phenomena, often highly contested – no narrative can wholly transcend the 'mess' of conflicting social discourses and hold up a flawless mirror to human life. Representations are always political in that they intervene in social debates; positional and perspective-driven, they articulate specific agendas and commitments. In Media Studies we explore how media variously represent reality, the ways in which texts create narrative out of social life, the strategies employed and the reasons for particular images. We are interested in the contexts in which representations are created and the responses of audiences. This is not to say that we are indifferent to reality, and many of us resist the lure of a relativism in which all representations are regarded as

Here we have made only a modest start on what merits much more thorough research. I have, for one thing, concentrated on films which are easily available in the United Kingdom.

The great Russian linguist and semiotician of the 1920s Volosinov argued, in *Marxism and the Philosophy of Language* (1986, Harvard University Press), that all signs are subject to conflicting social meanings as part of the wider conflict between social classes and factions. Saussure had pointed out that the link between signifier and signified is arbitrary; Volosinov recognised that this makes the meaning of a sign something which can shift as the result of social struggles. Powerful groups attempt to fix the meaning of a sign in order to reinforce their supremacy over weaker groups.

A recent series of British TV advertisements extolling the pleasures of teaching has aroused the ire of many experienced teachers who feel that it will give new entrants to the profession unrealistic expectations. Representations can provoke passionate responses.

equally valid. Analysis of representations soon loses any purpose if not driven by a sense that they are inadequate to a reality existing outside of them, but we must equally avoid simplistic comparisons of 'reel worlds' to the 'real world'.

In the case of teachers and representations of education as a whole, even a cursory perusal of newspaper coverage or broadcast narratives, not to mention casual conversations in pub and bus queues, quickly reminds us that there is no simple consensus on the meaning of education, the quality of the teaching profession, the success of government policies, etc. And, of course, we all have our own, usually conflicted, memories of schooling to sustain different perspectives. Vividly contrasted images circulate – from chilling stories of playground stabbings to utopian teacher-training agency TV advertisements.

Nor has academic research identified an agreed reality against which all media representations might be measured. In social science debates, for example, there have long been sharply opposed analyses of the role of institutionalised education. No one denies the centrality of schooling in social reproduction, but this has been interpreted in dramatically different ways according to wider perspectives on the desirability of reproducing certain features of our social arrangements. What appears as functional in one optic is repressive in another. Throughout the history of compulsory schooling in the United Kingdom, apologists of the way in which schools produce 'good citizens' have faced criticism from those who have blamed the education system for reproducing inequalities of wealth, for perpetuating gender injustices, for racism and homophobia. Critiques of teachers – as tools of social control, as agents of an 'ideological state apparatus' producing submissive wage slaves and compliant consumers – have all challenged blandly functional notions of teachers as bearers of unproblematic 'social values'. Ever since the Education Acts of the nineteenth century introduced compulsory education as a way to counter the radicalism of the growing industrial workforce, nothing has been more political than education, and its development has always been part of wider social conflicts surrounding the distribution of wealth and power. Studies of representations of teachers and schools have to be premised on the recognition that they form part of a broader history of discourses and political clashes.

In addition, in any study of representations we must bear in mind that the producers and consumers of texts are not exclusively concerned, if at all, with questions of truth to reality. Media professionals work in many different contexts, within varied constraints, and their representational practices are shaped by numerous factors such as available technology, budgets, editorial control, corporate goals and censorship. Audiences for their part may vary in the needs they wish to satisfy by consuming media. What is being represented may be more a reflection of the 'reality' of an audience's hopes and fears than of what they take to be the real state of the world. Also, of course, audience readings of media representations should not be assumed to be passive and uncritical; audiences have their own experiences of social life to draw on, and media images are interpreted in light of a stored 'image bank'. In the case of media representations of teachers and of education, one has to consider, then, not simply how 'realistic' they are (although I do not dismiss this as a question), but also how they articulate the imperatives of producers and audiences. Or, to put it another way, the 'realism' of texts cannot ultimately be divorced from the context of transactions in which representations constitute a currency. Films about teachers have usually been made by commercial producers whose narratives enlist reality in an attempt to make entertaining, profitable releases within the constraints of censorship regimes reflecting wider configurations of power. This is a special kind of representational labour process in which all sorts of elisions, displacements and condensations take place in order to produce pleasure in audiences who will pay for the experience if it 'makes sense' to them and delivers emotional rewards. For both producers and audiences, 'representing reality' is embedded in a broader network of goals and desires.

3.2 Teacher as cultural hero

'All who treasure the memory of a beloved teacher will treasure Goodbye Mr Chips' DVD BOX DESCRIPTION

In the climactic scene of *Goodbye Mr Chips* (Sam Wood, 1939) the eponymous hero is dying. At his bedside are two younger colleagues who, lacking the narrative reach of the audience, talk sadly about what they perceive as his sterile life:

▶ What is the purpose of education? Is education the same as school? Are students encouraged to think for themselves? Does school prepare us effectively for life? Should we study things that do not have any obvious connection to a career? If you could redesign the education system, what changes would you make? ●

Goodbye Mr Chips: a nostalgic view of teaching as a conveyor of traditional standards

Robert Donat, who played Mr Chipping ('Chips'), was born in Manchester; Greer Garson, for whom Goodbye Mr Chips was her film debut and who played the role of Chips's wife, Katherine, was born in Northern Ireland and was working on the English stage when spotted by Louis B. Mayer.

'poor old chap … pity he never had any children,' they murmur. Overhearing this, the old man becomes indignant in a last blaze of consciousness; he bristles at their allegation that he was childless: 'I have thousands of them.' The camera tilts up to the wall behind the bed on which is superimposed an endless procession of schoolboys announcing their names; they are the pupils he has nurtured throughout the film, generations of young Englishmen whose characters have been moulded by his care. The audience 'knows' that he is right to feel a sense of immortality; the entire narrative is structured to deliver an unqualified legitimisation of teaching as a culturally pivotal profession. In any study of representations of teachers on screen, it is a good place to start.

Goodbye Mr Chips was one of a number of Hollywood films made in the 1930s by an industry which had learned how to appropriate profitably aspects of British culture, as well as talent, in a way that appealed to both American and UK audiences while still satisfying restrictive censorship regimes. As Aldgate and Richards (1999) explain, it was typical of inter-war films in its equation of British education with the public school and its portrayal of the latter as a benign defender of supposedly consensual values. They point out: 'although the interwar years were an era of virulent criticism of the public schools in literature, beginning with Alec Waugh's *The Loom of Youth* in 1917, none of this found its way to the screen.' Although using some location shots and staff and pupils from a real public school, the Brookfields School of *Goodbye Mr Chips* is a mythicised diegesis in which harsh realities of social exclusion are only faintly registered in order to 'resolve them'.

What gives *Goodbye Mr Chips* its distinctive force is that, while most subsequent films about teachers dramatise decisive events over a short period of time, it charts the hero's entire career. A frame narrative, the plot begins shortly before his demise, is reinforced by the film's title; we are immediately cued to read the story in an elegiac mode. A new term is beginning at Brookfields, an institution which the Head describes to a new member of staff as 'the heart of England'; a distant train whistle announces the return of the boys and we see them giving their names as they register, a recurring scene which signifies the cyclical nature of the school as an engine of seamless cultural continuity. At first assembly the

Head apologises to the boys that unusually Mr Chipping, or Chips, as he is affectionately known, is unable to attend due to a cold. We cut to the exterior, however, and through an imposing arch we see an elderly man in an academic gown; a closer shot reveals our hero with his wispy white hair; two tracking shots trace his hurried progress; colliding with a boy who is lost, he invites the lad to hold on to his gown as he proceeds to the Hall. The door is locked and the two polar characters, the new boy and the ancient schoolmaster, share a moment together; we see the old man's affection for children (in soft-focus close-ups), and the boy is soon at ease.

Even today, the mortar board and gown are emblematic of teaching, even though only a minority of people have ever encountered this costume personally. For decades British children's comics and TV series equated school with public school.

The sentimentality of the film is based on its redemption of time and the losses time brings. Chips is equally reassuring to the new teacher who is about to face his first class, telling him that he, too, once had to overcome his fear. Back in his digs, Chips dozes in front of a fire. A roll call of boys' names and a train whistle support a flashback dissolve to Chips as a young man about to board a train for his first day at Brookfields. In scenes on which one finds variations in many subsequent films featuring teachers, we see him fail lamentably in his initial efforts to win the trust of students. His first lesson is a disaster. While gangster films typically have a narrative structure of the rise and fall of the criminal protagonist, pedagogue films often have an inverse structure of failure before success. Despite warnings by older teachers, Chipping soon loses control of the classrom. He cannot find the right strategy; after experiencing anarchy, he attempts authoritarianism, but by doing so wins control at the expense of genuine respect.

A montage of sporting events now elides time and the narrative picks up Chip's career on the last day of an academic year some years later. He is older but unloved by the boys and is being passed over for promotion. At this narrative nadir, a deus ex machina materialises in the form of a German teacher who invites him on a walking tour of Austria. Here he meets Katherine. She restores his faith in himself and in teaching as a vocation. Married, they return to Brookfields, where her charm thaws the masculine climate; it is she who calls him 'Chips' and helps him to become a beloved teacher. Having helped Chipping become Chips, she dies in childbirth. The way is now clear for the boys to become his children.

It is interesting to compare the 1939 film of *Goodbye Mr Chips* to a recent British TV adaptation of the book in which Martin Clunes reprises Donat's Oscar-winning performance. Although closer to the original book in some respects – Chips meets Katherine in the Lake District – it portrays the school more negatively than either Hilton's original or MGM's version. It is clearly a place of social exclusivity, in which the few lower middle-class boys who attend it suffer from prejudice, and bullying is rampant and ugly. Also, the film is more positive about Katherine's feminist views; she argues with Chips about female suffrage and triumphs over the Head's conservatism by inviting girls to a school dance.

R. C. Sheriff, who wrote the great anti-war play Journey's End, *worked on the script for Wood's* Goodbye Mr Chips.

A montage of boys reporting at the start of subsequent autumn terms condenses the passing of time in a way which registers change, but which asserts an underlying continuity: as Katherine told Chips on the mountain top, a school is a 'world which is always young'. Chips grows older, but the boys do not; this is emphasised by casting the same young actor to play three generations of the Colley family. Chips has become a beloved figure in the school and, although it seems he will never achieve his ambition of becoming Head, he has found joy in teaching. He retires to lodgings next to the school.

The narrative's redemptive agenda has not, however, been concluded; World War I begins and, given the stress of manpower shortages, Chips is asked whether he would agree to return as Headmaster. Ironically, he now occupies the post he always longed for, but under tragic circumstances as staff and older boys leave for the front to die. In the greatest test of his role as guardian of cultural continuity, he demonstrates strength of character, imperturbability and liberalism. In an assembly in which he announces the death of a Colley boy of whom he was especially fond, he also mourns the death of Steffel, the German teacher who had invited him on the fateful walking tour of Austria and who has died fighting on the enemy side. Although muted, Chips deplores the waste of war and expresses no patriotic sentiments. He represents timeless values of decency; when the school suffers an enemy air raid he steadies the nerves of the boys by drawing parallels to classical history.

With the war over, we finally come out of the extended flashback to return to the frame: Chips asleep in front of the fire. A knock at the door wakes him; a new boy has been duped by older boys into thinking a master wants to see him. Chips thwarts the pranksters by asking the boy in for tea and cake. It transpires that the boy is yet another Colley. The cycle is beginning over again. Chips soon puts the boy at his ease, using for a final time the skills Katherine had first brought to the school. The boy looks forward to the future as Chips is reminded of the past. After the boy has gone, having said 'Goodbye, Mr Chips' in a shot framed by the door to the outside world, Chips dozes in his armchair and a sound montage of boys' names being read out, and of Katherine's voice, begins. The narrative can now let him die, his final moments invested with redemptive meaning.

What allows this mythic narrative to operate so smoothly, of course, is its deft treatment of anything that might create friction. As we see so little of British society outside Brookfields, criticisms of the public school as an engine of class and gender power are denied a grip. Only one scene allows class briefly to surface: Chips catches two boys fighting and learns that it was sparked off because they traded class-based insults of 'stuck-up snob' and 'town cheese'. This social fault line is, however, only grist to the narrative's ideological mill as the two die together, reconciled, as comrades in World War I. The gender exclusivity of the school is equally never treated as problematic. The boys display no interest in girls and, although they are startled on hearing that Chips is bringing his new wife to visit the staff room, the male masters quickly melt before her charm as she effortlessly takes on the role of serving their tea.

3.3 Blackboard jungles

In modern films it has proved impossible to represent schools in the way in which Brookfield is portrayed in *Goodbye Mr Chips*. Social and political changes during and after World War II rendered images of education as a benign arena of cultural reproduction increasingly problematic if not, as time went on, absurd. As narratives of cultural continuity became unserviceable, fictional schools were more convincing as sites of social tensions and even disorder.

In the immediate post-war years, British films registered a new conjuncture. With a Labour Government committed to a 'Welfare State', in which education was to provide greater opportunities for mobility in a more egalitarian society, the public-school system could no longer receive automatic acquiescence. The most interesting film of this period, *The Guinea Pig* (Boulting Brothers, 1947), articulated the shifts taking place. Responding to the Fleming Report (which had advocated a degree of access to public schools by state pupils), this film narrates the experiences of a lower middle-class boy, the son of an East End tobacconist, who is given the opportunity to attend a traditional public school. He initially suffers from prejudice and culture shock; however, while older teachers resist this experiment in class mobility, Mr Lorraine is a young housemaster who believes that some changes must take place if more disruptive change is to be

In *Saturday Night and Sunday Morning* (1960), Albert Finney plays the rebellious Arthur Seaton: 'Don't let the bastards grind you down … all I want is a good time … all the rest is propaganda.'

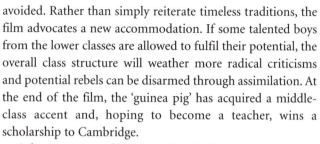

avoided. Rather than simply reiterate timeless traditions, the film advocates a new accommodation. If some talented boys from the lower classes are allowed to fulfil their potential, the overall class structure will weather more radical criticisms and potential rebels can be disarmed through assimilation. At the end of the film, the 'guinea pig' has acquired a middle-class accent and, hoping to become a teacher, wins a scholarship to Cambridge.

Other post-war films overtly challenged the utopian images of pre-war public-school films and were less sanguine about their ability to change. *The Browning Version* (Asquith, 1951) challenged the myth constructed by *Goodbye Mr Chips* with images of schools as bleak, 'joyless prisons' staffed by 'elderly failures' (Aldgate and Richards). The St Trinian's comedies (begun by *The Belles of St Trinian's*, Launder, 1954) mocked private education by portraying a girls' boarding school in which anarchy reigns and the teachers are social misfits, if not outright criminals.

For many post-war films, the narrative focus was youth; teachers, if featured, are marginal figures if not malign presences. In the 1950s classic *Rebel without a Cause* (Nicholas Ray, USA, 1955), for example, the high school is metonymically reduced to a school insignia, a set of lockers, and a trip to a planetarium in which an elderly teacher soon gives up trying to be heard ('Oh, what the heck!'). The new demographics of cinema and moral panics around youth made stories about timelessly 'good schools' unconvincing. For the 'teen film', school is a crucible for the formation of adolescent identities, rather than a place in which teachers test their vocation. In the 1960s, student protest and mordant critiques of education as a repressive arm of the state flourished and found perhaps their most powerful cinematic representation in Lindsay Anderson's angry masterpiece *If. ...* (Lindsay Anderson, 1968), a film in which a school very like that in *Goodbye Mr Chips* is transmogrified into a metaphor of an 'old Britain' of class prejudice, sexual repression and militarism.

The teachers in *If. ...* are inept or sinister figures (the school padre is perhaps a paedophile), while the Head is a pseudo-liberal whose attempts to understand the rebellion staged by Travis (Malcolm McDowell) and his friends are mocked as ineffective. Founder's Day, rather than reasserting

In *If. ...*, anger erupts into revolution

Four students were killed and nine injured when National Guardsmen opened fire on anti-war protestors during a demonstration at Kent State University, in Ohio

the timeless values of the nation, sees an apocalyptic showdown between the forces of tradition and 1960s counterculture in which staff, parents and old boys (not to forget a Crusader) are enthusiastically gunned down. The film was released as real world student protests rocked the world from Tokyo to Kent State, Ohio.

In a context in which schools are more likely to be represented as places of social control and repression, or as anarchic no-go areas, than as places of genuine learning, the films which focus on teachers as forces for good tend to distance their heroes and heroines from the institutions and represent them as individuals driven more by a personal desire to 'make a difference' than any concern with abstract notions of school tradition, and even having to fight the system on their students' behalf. In *To Sir, With Love* (Clavell, 1966), Sidney Poitier plays Caribbean Mr Thackeray, an unemployed engineer who finds a teaching post in a gloomy London school staffed by disillusioned teachers. Responding to contemporary social anxieties about 'juvenile delinquency', the focus of the narrative is his struggle to win the respect of the alienated students and to render them employable. As in Chips, his first lessons are naturally a disaster and he almost gives up in despair as they push him to the limit. Such scenes are common to films about teachers because they offer

In many films about teachers, the central role is played by a 'star'; as Richard Dyer has argued, stars can be seen as 'texts' who bring meanings, developed through previous performances and through publicity, to each new role. Sidney Poitier had achieved fame as the first black actor to achieve real stardom in Hollywood; his performances, in films such as *The Defiant Ones* (1958), had established his persona as including intelligence, sincerity, anger at injustice and control under pressure. Crucially, to white filmgoers, he was perceived not to be a 'hot head' espousing anti-white sentiments.

Lulu was a minor British pop artist of the 1960s who represented the 'acceptable face' of contemporary youth; her music was inoffensive, and audiences must have known she would prove amenable to persuasion in the film. With the rise of 'youth' in the 1950s and 1960s, enormous efforts were made to render them harmless consumers of fashion.

various pleasures: the classroom is a gladiatorial arena, in which the teacher is outnumbered and is being tested, but we are also encouraged to enjoy teaching as a form of theatre. Playing a teacher allows the actor to show off his or her dramatic skills.

When a star performer is involved, we can enjoy a new instance of the 'star text' safe in the knowledge that, ultimately, the students (trapped in the diegesis and blissfully unaware of the star persona) do not have a chance. In star vehicles especially, teaching is a practice of charisma and heart-felt rhetorical appeals rather than long-term and mundane activities. It is also little to do with teamwork. In *To Sir, With Love*, after an incident in which they set fire to tampons in class, Thackeray has a 'Eureka!' moment when he decides to treat the students as adults and focus on the social skills required for the world of employment and married life, rather than on abstract learning. He insists the boys address the girls with courtesy, and implores the girls to stop behaving like 'sluts' – his version of 'vocationalism'. Despite the scepticism of other teachers, and hints of racism in the wider community (though never expressed by the students for whom Thackeray's skin is not constructed as an issue), he wins respect and affection. One girl even develops a 'crush' on him, although the danger of this subplot is carefully curtailed. Claude Lévi-Strauss would have immediately recognised, in the film's magical resolution of numerous anxieties about delinquency, teenage sexuality and 'race', an example of a 'mythic' text. The students write a celebratory song for Thackeray (performed by Lulu, who plays one of the students and whose casting patently aimed to add 'teen appeal') and, although he finally gets an offer of an engineering job, he tears up the letter.

LouAnne Johnson, the teacher in *Dangerous Minds* (John N. Smith, 1995), follows in Thackeray's footsteps, but in the more ideologically charged diegesis of a 1990s America of 'hoods' and 'homeboys'. The film's ideological ambitions are immediately apparent as it opens with black-and-white 'documentary' images of urban decay edited to a rap soundtrack; this narrative's magical resolutions set out to address a social crisis with a 'racial' dimension. School buses collect young members of a black and Hispanic 'underclass' and transport them to the fictional Parkmont School

In *Dangerous Minds*, a Hollywood star (Michelle Pfeiffer) reasserts white authority

managed by a black principal who does not know what to do with them. So desperate is the school to find staff to teach 'challenging' (i.e. black) students, they offer LouAnne a full-time job despite her lack of proper teacher training.

While an ex-Marine and a divorcee, she is unprepared for the 'lion's den' of ethnic tensions, machismo, teenage pregnancies and gang rivalries into which she walks. Its claustrophobia is emphasised with telephoto shots which crush the classroom space. Derided and initially intimidated by the students, the film's heroine epitomises an America in which white authority is apparently losing control. With narrative predictability, the lesson is a baptism of fire and she leaves the class to tell her friend Hal, 'I can't teach them.' Played by Michele Pfeiffer, however, one does not imagine for a moment that she will really be giving up. The avuncular Hal tells her she must 'get their attention'; next day, dressed in jeans and a leather jacket, she begins the lesson by writing on the blackboard 'I am a Marine.'

This does the trick and she is soon teaching karate moves to two boys. Having made contact (a teacher who knows how to hurt people obviously impresses them), her pedagogy is a combination of 'do-gooder' sincerity and a grotesquely implausible use of the poetry of 'the two Dylans'. As Henry Giroux points out in his cogent critique of the film, the narrative exploits rap to signify social disorder and to give the film some credibility (as well as make money from a soundtrack

In all the films discussed here, teachers write very little on blackboards; however, when they do, the words usually seem to impress the students.

album), but denies black culture any role in the students' learning. Instead, Bob Dylan's song 'Mr Tambourine Man' and Dylan Thomas's poem 'Do Not Go Gentle into that Good Night' are represented as transcendent of social space and time, while LouAnne becomes (they tell her so) 'the light' to them. Her methods soon release the intellectual and literary potential of the students despite totally ignoring their cultural history. She visits their homes and a literary competition she organises has as first prize her taking one Hispanic student to a fancy restaurant. The narrative invests her personal triumph over the students' hostility with a wider significance; as Giroux remarks, the film reasserts 'whiteness as a model of authority, rationality and civilized behaviour'. The school is largely indifferent to her work, and she is only ever reprimanded by the straight-laced black principal for unauthorised trips and trivial infractions such as failing to knock on his door before entering. This takes on more serious consequences when he refuses to see a student who is subsequently killed. It is lucky this white woman has come along and it is only her belief in the students which is posited as effective. Disillusioned by the death of the student she had tried to help, she resigns; however, the class will not let her leave, as they need her now. Produced by Bruckheimer and Simpson, better known for 'high concept' blockbusters such as *Top Gun* (1986), this insidious film plays to anxieties about the 'underclass', but offers a complacent fairy tale in which, characteristically of Hollywood film, social systemic crises are 'solved' by well-intentioned and charismatic individuals played by movie stars whose own personae are the only real beneficiaries.

3.4 Teaching freedom

Perhaps the most seductive films about teachers are those in which the pedagogue is an individualist pitted against the school as a bastion of a generalised social conformity. In these films it is not the students who are rebelling against school and society – as they are privileged young people compared to the students in *Dangerous Minds* – but rather the teacher who is trying to help them escape the constraints of excessive conformity to which some of them subscribe, some even enthusiastically. The teacher is a subversive, an escape artist, a catalyser, and for some of the students a co-conspirator. Two major examples of this are *Dead Poets Society* (Peter Weir,

▶ What makes a charismatic teacher? Has a teacher had a major influence on your life? ●

▶ What elements make a good teacher? ●

USA, 1986) and *Mona Lisa Smile* (Mike Newell, USA, 2004). Both narratives centre on a teacher who rebels against the traditions of the school for whom they work and who encourages the students, at the crucial moment in their lives when they are on the brink of adulthood, to reject unquestioning authority.

In Peter Weir's *Dead Poets Society*, an exclusive boys' school is, despite its picturesque charm, nonetheless represented as a spiritually sterile place in which tradition stifles independence and creativity. The teachers are dull and in a brief opening montage place their emphasis on following rules, tests and grades. Consequently, the new English teacher Mr Keating (Robin Williams) startles the boys when for his first lesson he walks through the class whistling like a Pied Piper and invites them into a hall where cups and photographs of old boys are kept, largely unnoticed. In calm but passionate tones he makes an extraordinary existential appeal to them to 'seize the day' (*carpe diem*) and to 'make your lives extraordinary'. This is no neophyte teacher struggling to win respect, but a 'magus' who aims to liberate them spiritually through shock tactics. How could Robin Williams fail to inspire? In subsequent lessons he derides the introduction to a traditional poetry text book as 'excrement' and demands that the boys tear it out, leaving only the poems; he invites them to 'huddle up' round him conspiratorially as he tells them that poetry is essentially the highest form of human endeavour and other subjects only functional; he makes them stand on his desk to see the world from a new perspective.

Dead Poets Society: teacher as guru

His influence is especially powerful over those boys who are already feeling estranged from the school and their parents' plans for them. Neil Perry is a sensitive boy whose authoritarian father refuses to accept his son's artistic ambitions. Tod is a shy young man with genuine literary talent whom Keating helps, in a lesson that resembles an encounter therapy session, to come out of his shell. Reviving a tradition started by Keating when he was a student at the school, the boys meet in a cave and read poetry. It leads to tragedy, however, when Neil's father discovers his involvement in a production of *A Midsummer Night's Dream* and, despite his obvious acting abilities, takes him out of school with plans to enrol him into a military academy. Neil commits suicide. Keating is blamed and forced to resign in an

In the film *Mona Lisa Smile*, Katherine Watson (Julia Roberts) uses art to liberate conventional schoolgirls

ugly witch hunt in which the boys are forced to testify against him. In the final scene, however, Keating has to collect his things from his old classroom; the Head is now taking English. Keating walks through the class for the last time, but Tod Anderson can stand it no longer and he climbs onto his desk and cries, 'My Captain, Oh, my Captain', a phrase which Keating had made his own; despite the Head's rage, other boys follow suit. The rebel's efforts have not been wasted. He has planted a seed presumably no one can destroy.

In a similar vein, but with a female focus, is *Mona Lisa Smile*. Here the star is Julia Roberts playing art teacher Katherine Watson, a 'bohemian from California' who arrives in the autumn of 1953 at the prestigious all-girl Wellesley College to 'make a difference'. We learn this from a young narrator, the brilliant but archly conservative Betty who is the editor of the influential college magazine and who soon clashes with Katherine over art, but more fundamentally over the issue of a woman's social destiny. Betty and the majority of her peers are already socialised, as 1950s American middle-class girls, into seeing marriage and a housewife-mother role as their primary goals. Education is simply a way to acquire social skills while finding a 'good match'. Betty's marriage plans, encouraged by her ruthlessly ambitious mother, are almost complete. Only a few girls show signs of nonconformity. Gisele has had an affair with a stereotypically dark-haired, womanising Italian language teacher, while Joan harbours dreams of law school; Connie, a cellist, is looking for real love rather than a trophy marriage.

Katherine is apprehensive about her new job, clearly in an environment alien to her. Just as Robin Williams does 'quirky and charismatic' in his inimitable style, Julia Roberts does 'sensitive vulnerability' to perfection. Having received the generic warning that the students 'can smell fear' she arrives in an intimidating lecture theatre to find the girls primed to reject her with icy and unsisterly disdain. Using the lesson plans and slides of a previous teacher, she realises that, as dutiful students, they have learned everything down to the last dot and comma; what could she possibly teach them? Where poetry was the medium of transformation in *Dead Poets Society*, here it is art.

Luckily, there's a Proppian 'helper' – Chips had Steffel; Katherine is supported through her first crisis by Amanda, the school nurse whose female 'partner' has recently died and who is subsequently dismissed for supplying an unmarried Gisele with a diaphragm. Setting the film in the 1950s encourages the audience to sympathise with those not lucky enough to live today while enjoying the period detail and, more importantly, the pleasures that hindsight offers. (We all 'know' how repressive the 1950s were and the narrative can never be too troubling as we know that Katherine will be proved right.)

Propp (see glossary) defined seven basic rules for characters in classic narratives, such as hero, villain, dispatcher and helper. His theory is explained more fully in his book Morphology of the Folk Tale, *which was first published in 1928.*

Katherine's next lesson is the beginning of her fightback. She has torn up the syllabus and brought her own slides this time. She hits them with a reproduction of a painting of raw meat by Soutine – 'Is it art? Is it any good? Who decides?' Her voice now takes on authority. Like Mr Keating's standing on the desk, this is her version of the pedagogy of shock, of Shklovsky's 'Knight's Move' designed to challenge their preconceptions and to rattle their prejudices. The girls are startled, Betty is horrified, but some of them are open to new ideas; Gisele finds it 'aggressive … but erotic'. Later Katherine takes them to an empty warehouse to see a Jackson Pollock – 'stop talking and look'. Teaching consists of emblematic moments full of significance. We see little of the daily texture of teaching.

The American artist Jackson Pollock became famous in the 1940s and 1950s for his abstract expressionist paintings. Chaim Soutine, a Lithuanian Jew who studied and worked in France, was a major Expressionist painter of the first part of the twentieth century.

Viktor Shklovsky was a Russian Formalist critic who argued that the purpose of art is to make strange by 'defamiliarising' reality; he compared this to the way in which the knight in chess proceeds.

Art, however, is only a vehicle for Katherine's message of individualism and stand against conformity; specifically, she wants her students to reject gender stereotypes and a monocular focus on marriage as the key to a woman's happiness (although she never shows them any work by female artists such as Georgia O'Keefe, which one might have thought inspiring in this context?). Her lessons and her personal independence embody a challenge to the 'Stepford Wives' ideology which the school seems to endorse. Much of the film takes place outside of the classroom and enacts the way in which the four principal students (Joan, Betty, Connie and Gisele) negotiate in different ways the constraints and opportunities available to them in that historical moment. All are played by young successful Hollywood actresses, embodiments of female success. Betty subscribes passionately to convention and marries a 'suitable' young man, Spencer, with a promising business career. Still technically a student, Betty resents Katherine's demands that she turns up to classes and, as the editor of the college magazine, she writes a vindictive article alleging that Katherine is propagandising against marriage to her students. In a fury, Katherine brings a set of slides of advertisements into the lesson and does a Media Studies deconstruction of their underlying ideology; the images of women in the ads make a mockery, she argues, of notions that women have any brains. However, with poetic irony and inevitably, given the film's liberal feminist agenda and deployment of hindsight, Betty is cruelly and swiftly disillusioned as Spencer spends little time at home and is soon having an affair with another woman.

Gisele, on the other hand, has no home-making ambitions and her parents' divorce is cited to motivate her cynicism; however, she experiences the hurts of casual sex in an anticipation of what the audience knows will face 'liberated women' in decades to come. Is this film-making in a future anterior tense? Connie, whose cello playing seems to emblematise her emotional sincerity, wants true love, a 'companionate marriage', rather than the hollow marriage Betty has embraced. Joan is fiercely intelligent and could have a successful legal career if only she would accept Katherine's plea that woman can combine marriage and career. Joan sees them as opposed, as does her pleasant but insensitive boyfriend Tommy, and to Katherine's horror Joan suddenly gets married despite Betty's example. Joan tells Katherine in an anachronistic exchange (it resonates more with today's audience than it would have then) that by marrying she is exercising her right to choose and if she chooses a housewife role rather than a career other women such as Katherine (a pre-post-feminist) should not question it.

The conclusion of the film shares to a degree the bittersweet quality of *Dead Poets Society*, but 'with more feeling', as one might expect from a contemporary Hollywood film targeting a female demographic. Soutine and Pollock may be useful in the classroom as a way to pose questions about the nature of art, but this movie will not invite the audience to radically rethink the aesthetics of the moving image. Rather, Mike Newell concludes the film with 'classical' techniques; the college decides, after some discussion as her classes are popular, to renew Katherine's contract if she agrees to draconian restrictions on her freedom; she decides to leave. Meanwhile Betty is filing for divorce and she and Gisele are leaving for Greenwich Village, of all places, the iconic centre of 1950s bohemianism. All of Katherine's art class gives her individually painted versions of Van Gogh's famous flower paintings, presumably signifying their embrace of her gospel of nonconformity.

She finally leaves the college to the voice of Betty narrating her last 'flowery' editorial, heavily ironic as it was Betty who had been her most ardent enemy: 'she compelled us to see the world through new eyes … some say she is a wanderer, but not all who wander are aimless … especially not those who seek truth beyond tradition, beyond definition.' To a lush romantic score, we see Katherine in a taxi, laughing and crying as she sees all the girls following her on bicycles to wave goodbye. She has not changed the world, but, like Keating and Thackeray and Chips, she has 'made a difference' and corporate entertainment reassures its consumers that individuals still matter.

3.5 Being and having

One of the most interesting and critically acclaimed films about teachers in the past few years is *Être et Avoir* by French documentarist Nicolas Philibert. Part of a remarkable wave of successful documentaries to find cinema release in recent years, this film makes a fascinating contribution to the history of what have been mostly fictional feature film portraits of teaching, and one which raises all kinds of important issues about representation as a practice.

A more extensive study of teaching on film must obviously include documentary; Frederick Wiseman's *High School* (1968), for example, was one of several important cinéma-vérité films he made about American institutions. The reason I have not discussed it here is that it is currently unavailable on video or DVD; the film portrays the way in which the school's rituals and interactions inculcate conformity – the issues this representation raises are similar to those in *Être et Avoir*.

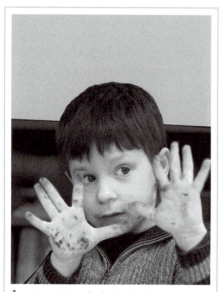

Être et Avoir. Jo Jo washes his hands and gains self-confidence

In all the films we have discussed, the day-to-day, unspectacular, mundane aspects of teaching go largely unrepresented; the demands of commercial entertainment produce narratives of teaching constructed around star performances and dramatic lows and highs deployed in narratively satisfying patterns. Philibert quite deliberately sets out to capture the texture of real world teaching – its slow work, its repetitions, the patience required; there are moments of discovery, but these are hard won and they are never definitive. Less theatre than a craft, teaching is represented as a slow-burning process rather than a firework display.

Philibert filmed for several months in a school in the small community of Saint-Etienne sur Usson in the French Auvergne, a mountainous agricultural region. The children are collected by minibus each day and the number of students is so small that one class contains children across a wide age range. They have a single teacher, Georges Lopez, whose quiet authority and obvious love for the children is powerfully conveyed. Much of the time is spent inside a single classroom where the children are learning the 'three Rs'. The camera observes the difficulty that children have in learning, and the need for a teacher who really engages with them, who is able to listen but also to gently push them forward. Philibert has said that his aim was to capture the essence of teaching as a combination of giving and demanding. Much of the time Lopez sits with the children and, with obvious experience, guides them through the maze of language. In one sequence, we see him teach them the difference between *ami* and *amie* – one boy finds it hard and insists on using the more colloquial *copain* and *copine*, but Lopez never grows impatient. In another moment, he is teaching a little girl which number comes after six; despite explaining it to her several times, and with other children telling her, she cannot seem to get it, but Lopez will obviously never give up until she does. One of the most memorable children in the class is little Jo Jo; he is lively, but not a natural academic, and Lopez is seen in several sequences carefully helping him to develop his skills. In an amusing encounter Jo Jo learns to wash his hands properly, while in another he begins to grasp the notion of infinity when Lopez quizzes him on the biggest number he can think of. We see him realise that thousands can come in two, threes and fours, that they can even come in hundreds.

There are days of fun and special events such as a happy session making pancakes, sledging in the snow and a summer picnic, but these are not the revelatory events we find in the fictional dramas and art is given no privileged status. The learning they involve is real, but it cannot be shaped into a sleek narrative machine.

The film also captures the 'pastoral' side of teaching, but again in 'slow motion'. One boy's father is seriously ill and in a very touching sequence we see Lopez talk to the boy and console him when he begins to cry. Another child, Natalie, is shy and finds it hard to communicate and Lopez discusses this with her mother. Later we see him talk to Natalie about her future and explain that he has talked to the teachers she will have in secondary school about her. But there are no miracles, and no conversion experiences. We sense that he is 'making a difference', but it will take time. As real teachers will recognise, he may never see that difference.

In fact, Lopez is retiring, which gives the film a degree of narrative closure. The film captures his last weeks and goodbyes at the school where he has taught for many years. In one moving sequence he talks to the startled children about his leaving, and their reactions clearly testify to the affection and respect in which he is held. At the end of the film, we see him wish them a happy holiday, knowing that it will be the last time he does this; a sustained shot records his effort not to break down in tears.

Clearly, *Être et Avoir* is a 'more realistic' film about teaching than super-charged narratives such as *Dead Poets Society*. As with all observational documentaries, the film sees you coming away with the feeling that one has glimpsed something of the unscripted reality of teaching. It is a real school with a real teacher and real children. The documentary reminds us of the materials from which the fiction films have selected, moulded, amplified. Philibert's skill is to make us feel the beautiful in the mundane; as he has remarked, 'Cinema isn't necessarily about spectacular events, but can be about simple things.' However, as any good Media Studies student knows, documentaries are not unmediated records of the real. *Être et Avoir* is, in its own way, highly constructed and, because of what happened subsequent to the release of the film, an excellent case study in issues of documentary realism and ethics.

▶ There has been an undercover investigative journalism documentary on secondary schools (*Classroom Chaos*, Channel Five, 27 April 2005). Do you think that this technique is legitimate in representing teachers, pupils and schools? Why? ●

▶ If you were going to document education in a British primary school, what would be your agenda? ●

With the development of lightweight camera and sound recording equipment, 1960s film-makers such as Robert Drew and Richard Leacock developed 'direct cinema', or 'cinéma vérité', a radical new style of documentary in which the aim was to capture life 'in the raw', as events unfolded, with minimum interference by the documentarist. They hoped their work would reveal reality more honestly than older approaches and eschewed voiceovers and interviews as artificial constructs. Sceptics pointed out that people are affected by the presence of cameras, and that editing inevitably introduces a film-maker's point of view. You cannot escape the fact that all representations are partial and provisional.

The DVD release of the film includes a revealing interview with Philibert in which he discusses its production. However 'observational' his style, he set out with a very specific agenda and spent five months looking for a school which would suit his purposes. He likes mountainous regions and combed the area for a small class with a quiet atmosphere and enough lighting to allow him to minimise the use of intrusive equipment. Most important, he wanted 'une belle rencontre' (a pleasant ambience) which could allow him to capture what he pre-defined as the essence of teaching; the intimate exchange in which a teacher gives of himself, but also makes demands on a student's skills. At one point Philibert says that whatever school he might have chosen, urban or rural, he would have made the same film in the sense that he was certain what he wanted the film to say. He was certainly not going to simply 'see what happened'. The very first shots of the film, we learn, were quite deliberately chosen to be metaphorical. The opening scene of cattle being herded in a snowstorm was, he comments, meant to suggest that education is a process of being directed onto the right path; the shots of tortoises crossing the floor of the empty classroom were expressly intended to signify the slowness of learning. Most interesting of all, the interview reveals that several of the scenes were prearranged rather than simply caught 'on the hoof' (as a die-hard observationalist would insist upon). Philibert himself proposed the idea that Lopez discusses his retirement with the children, and he also asked Lopez if he could talk to Jo Jo about infinity. The scenes in which we see the children doing their homework were also constructed, with Philibert making up some maths sums for one boy to do. The film was, to a degree, scripted so that Philibert could get the material he wanted.

Aware of the constructed nature of the documentary – and all documentaries involve similar practices – naive notions of 'recording reality' should quickly be dismissed. *Être et Avoir* is about a real school, but the film is not as distant from the constructed schools of the fiction films as we might first have thought. Philibert aimed to make a film celebrating the quiet heroism of teachers as part of his broader interest in how people learn to live together in society; he chooses not to critique the French school system. Choosing a small class with an experienced teacher provided him with the material he wanted, but he deliberately excluded the more stressful and negative dimensions of many teachers' experience.

Even accepting that his film is a portrait of one particular school, does Philibert capture it fully? Without seeing the footage he chose not to use, it is hard to say, but he admits himself that some children were less happy than others about being filmed and consequently figure only briefly. Jo Jo appears disproportionately and one cannot help but feel that his 'cheeky' looks were felt to be 'photogenic', as he is used in posters for the film. And is George Lopez represented truthfully? Does he never lose his temper? Outside of lessons in which he is in complete control, we see him only in a short scene working at night. He is interviewed only briefly about his motivation in becoming a teacher; it seems that he is single and is never seen socialising with friends, conveying the impression of a monkish man wholly dedicated to his vocation. How 'good' a teacher is he?

We are not really in any position to judge, of course, but even what we do see might be read 'oppositionally'. When the little boy insists on using the words 'copain' and 'copine', Lopez tells him that 'we haven't got to that yet', rather than taking the opportunity to build on what the boy does know and open up a little discussion of the appropriateness of 'ami' as opposed to 'copain' in different social situations. In one playground scene, if we watch carefully (I only noticed it on seeing the film for a second time), Jo Jo harasses another boy who not unsurprisingly retaliates and Jo Jo cries. Lopez, who has not seen the entire incident, arrives and immediately reprimands the other boy and demands he apologises to Jo Jo. Is his response to the boy whose father is having his larynx removed appropriate or clichéd when he tells him that 'sickness is a part of life'?

If this sounds critical for the sake of it, it is worth considering the aftermath of the film. After the film scored a success at the Cannes Film Festival (on the French DVD there is a fascinating short film of Lopez and the children attending the premiere), it was not long before both Lopez and some of the families took legal action against Philibert for exploiting their lives, suing him for a share of the money they feel he has made out of their 'performances'. It is a striking example of the way in which representations can have real-life consequences and, specifically, of a major difference

▶ Do any of the representations of teachers come close to the reality of teachers you have met? Discuss the most influential teachers in your school career. Can a teacher really change the lives of students? ●

Blackboards was the second feature film from this director. The first was The Apple *(1998), made when she was eighteen. She is the daughter of the Iranian director Mohsa Makhmalbaf, who produced the film.*

between fiction and documentary. Julia Roberts's performance in *Mona Lisa Smile* may be panned by a critic, but she will not be sued by the real Katherine Watson. As of writing, French courts have rejected the suits, but it certainly impacts on one's future readings of the film. When I watch it now, the 'saintly teacher' seems to have grown some claws. Perhaps Philibert could pacify him by making a film about the low salaries of rural schoolteachers in modern France?

3.6 *Takhté Siah* (*Blackboards*): teachers on a cruel road

In a narrative space distant both spatially and culturally from the films we have considered so far, we encounter in Samira Makhmalbaf's film *Blackboards* (Iran, 2000) itinerant teachers Said and Reeboir. They have no classrooms in which to practise their skills, but roam the bleak mountains on the border between Iran and Iraq in search of students. It is a cruel place and one which throws into a new perspective Western films which have represented the work of teaching.

In the opening shots we see them struggling along a dusty track with blackboards strapped to their backs. Like clumsy flightless birds, they are roaming a harsh landscape in the hope they might exchange lessons for food. With Iran and Iraq at war, it is a dangerous region of landmines and the threat of chemical-weapon attacks. Treeless, depopulated and sometimes obscured by fog, it seems impossible that anyone lives there. So hazardous is it that they smear their blackboards with red mud to camouflage them. The two men split up to try their luck in different directions.

Blackboards: on the Iran–Iraq border, education becomes a matter of life and death

Said eventually meets with a band of Kurdish refugees. These are almost all elderly men, who are attempting to return to their home in Iraq before they die. They agree to give him a bag of walnuts if he helps them to find their destination, but they have no time for his proffered pedagogy. His blackboard proves more useful as a stretcher and as a shield.

Reeboir, on the other hand, encounters a troop of young boys ('mules', as they refer to themselves) who are braving the hazardous mountain paths in order to carry loads of contraband goods across the border. For them, education is a luxury they cannot contemplate, and they rebuff Reeboir's offer of literacy lessons. It is only after enormous efforts that he persuades one boy, also called Reeboir, to practise the alphabet as they negotiate the trails. Soon, however, another boy is injured and Reeboir's blackboard serves as a splint for his leg. He learns later that they can all read, but had denied it because they had learned to fear strangers. Again, his skills seem irrelevant. Attempting to cross the border among a herd of goats, the boys are shot dead.

Said is no luckier. Amid the old Kurds is a sole woman, Halaleh, a widow with a young son. Her father is desperate that she remarry and, offering his blackboard as a dowry, Said marries her. The board then serves as a screen behind which he exercises his new conjugal rights. Expressionless and taciturn, Halaleh becomes his reluctant pupil. He clumsily tries to break through her unnerving silence by treating her like a student, writing 'I Love You' on his board as though in a spelling lesson and awarding her marks out of ten for her behaviour. When she does finally speak to him, however, it is to put him in his place: 'My heart is like a station; at every stop someone gets on or off … except my child.' When they reach the border, it is clear she intends to leave him behind. They divorce and we see her depart into the mist; the blackboard on her back has the now ironic sentence 'I Love You' still written on it.

Shot on location, with only one professional actor (Halaleh is played by Behnaz Jafari) and a cast including genuine 'mules', *Blackboards* is both realistic and allegorical. Makhmalbaf has said of the film: 'It has a lot of metaphors, but at the same time I'm talking about reality' (interview on the irandokht website). The peripatetic teachers with their blackboards on their backs are an imaginative construct.

Iran has produced a number of remarkable films which offer a startling contrast to news images of a country which most Westerners know little about and which the US Government seems intent on demonising as a 'terrorist state'.

I am aware that a major absence here is discussion of televisual representations of teachers; these include *Wacko*, *Please Sir* and *Grange Hill*; Channel 4's series *Teachers* is obviously an important text which deserves a study of its own. Its originality compared to the films discussed here consists in its portrayal of teachers as almost exclusively concerned with their personal relationships, sex lives, survival etc. than with any agenda of 'making a difference' to students. Consequently it was 'privileged' in being condemned by some sections of the teachers' unions, although more recent press coverage suggests it might actually have made teaching more fashionable!

Teachers: there are no positive role models in Channel 4's hit series set in a modern school

Poetic rather than documentary, the film is a moving evocation of social dislocation, misery and deprivation in the Middle East. To a Western film-goer such as myself, who also happens to be a teacher, *Blackboards* is a sobering experience, but also a politically energising one. Education is a human right, and too many of the world's children are denied it. This film makes me want to do something about it, while at the same time challenging me to question my assumptions about the usefulness of my knowledge. Here representations invite us to redefine our sense of reality, to learn more, to act. The narrative opens on to politics rather than offering a sense of completion or reassurance. It hardly needs saying that, since the film's release in 2000, events have given it greater resonance.

References

Aldgate, Anthony, & Jeffrey Richards, *The Best of British* (London: I. B. Tauris, 1999).

Giroux, Henry, 'Race, Pedagogy and Whiteness in Dangerous Minds', *Cinéaste*, vol. 22, no. 4.

Romney, Jonathan, 'Review of Blackboards', *Sight and Sound*, January 2001.

www.irandokht.com

Further reading

Tapper, Richard (ed.), *The New Iranian Cinema* (London: Tauris, 2002).

Filmography

Goodbye Mr Chips (Sam Wood, 1939)
The Belles of St Trinian's (Frank Launder, 1954)
To Sir, With Love (James Clavell, 1966)
If. … (Lindsay Anderson, 1968)
Dead Poets Society (Peter Weir, 1986)
Dangerous Minds (John N. Smith, 1995)
Blackboards (Samira Makhmalbaf, 2000)
Être et Avoir (Nicolas Philibert, 2002)
Mona Lisa Smile (Mike Newell, 2004)

4. Constables, Coppers, Rozzers, the Old Bill – the Police

WENDY HELSBY

How many words do you know that refer to the police? What do these words represent to you? What feelings do they create? Anger, respect, suspicion, admiration? James Halloran (quoted in Dennington & Tulloch) said, 'Television may provide models for identification, confer status on people and behaviour, spell out norms, define new situations, provide stereotypes, set frameworks of anticipation and indicate levels of acceptability, tolerance and approval ...' Television is thus a powerful mediator of messages, and it does this on a massive scale.

▶ Have you ever had contact with the police? How do you think this experience has influenced your view of the police when you watch them on television? List your personal rather than mediated experience of the police and what this unmediated view has told you about them. ●

4.1 Crime and television

It is more than probable that while you are reading this section that there will be a current news story of a brutal murder or other violent crime. It is also almost certain that in the evening television schedules there is at least one police drama or documentary. Programmers know that the crime genre is popular. 'Crime pays – at least in the world of TV drama.... There is a crime wave on television. Every channel has a new cop show. Even Channel 4, for the first time in its 22-year history, cannot resist its foray into the medium's most enduring genre and most reliable ratings puller' (Kinnes, 2004).

What is our fascination with law and order and, crucially, what issues about the representations of the police are raised? These two questions are interrelated and the answers may involve three basic points. First, crime and police series are said to gratify certain psychological needs in the audience

Does *The Thin Blue Line* represent the institution of the police accurately?

such as exploration of the fear of violence and so have a cathartic effect. Most of us will go through life without criminal violence as part of it, but in a police series there is more violence per episode than a person would witness in a lifetime. Secondly, police stories provide a hierarchy of deviance and allow us into different social worlds that we can explore vicariously. Finally, unlike other related genres containing violence, they focus on the political and legal institutions and explore how the authority invested in these institutions is executed. They show us the working practices of 'the law'. Television feeds off this audience interest. In so doing it has provided us with some influential and groundbreaking programmes. *Hill Street Blues*, a US police drama, for example, 'was hugely influential … changed the face of TV. It was the first epic, multistranded narrative that mixed reality and pathos' (John Yorke, Channel 4's head of drama, quoted in Kinnes, 2004).

4.2 Police and the law

Policing and the laws it administers on our behalf raise fundamental questions of how we believe our society should be regulated. What do you think? Do the laws put up the barricades and force the police to become confrontational? Or do the laws open up justice to all, with the police acting as social agents for everyone? Should the punishment fit the crime as retribution, or should it take account of social factors and rehabilitate the criminal? Police-related programmes articulate such philosophical questions within the 'realism' of the crime genre. The executive producer of *Murder Prevention* (first broadcast 30 October 2004 on Five), Stephen Heath, stated, 'The whole idea of whether you can prove intent to kill and stop someone before they have committed a crime poses interesting questions about how we police our society' (Kinnes, 2004). These are relevant questions in the context of such legislation as the Anti-Terrorism Act and issues revolving around Guantanamo Bay.

The police are society's agents of law and order, so that we come up against them when we have broken the rules; they also represent our personal and social security. As the upholders of law and public order they are one of the immediate responses you will get from a 999 call. The police put themselves on the line every Saturday night in most towns and cities in the United Kingdom in order to maintain public safety. They are the people who have to pick up the pieces when society's order breaks down. There are many incidents of police bravery, as well as tragic deaths. On the other hand, the police are often accused of abusing their powers, of being 'institutionally racist', of being sexist against female officers, of being corrupt and of brutality. There have been cases of wrongful imprisonment as a result of police evidence. These contrasting views mean that stories about the police are not only about law and order and catching the common criminal, but are also about how the individual 'copper' or detective becomes representative of our beliefs about the institution of the police.

4.3 Policing on television

'Crime and television are the two great cultural definers of our present era.' (Osborne, 1995)

Although the police will appear in crime sub-genres, such as in whodunits and the gangster genre, and in hybrid genres, they are often marginal characters. Here, however, we are concerned with them as the main focus of the narrative, as in *The Bill*, a police drama-cum-soap opera, and *The Cops* (BBC2, 1998–200), a police drama that was stylistically more like fly-on-the-wall documentary. As well as being found in entertainment, the police link with our real lives through narratives in factual news stories, current affairs programmes and in documentaries involving police activity. The media reflect a range of police-related activities such as forensic science, plainclothes detective work, courtroom dramas, criminal psychology, undercover police and the uniformed police 'on the beat'.

Both fictional and factual programmes help to explore and construct our beliefs about the police and help to create the consensus by which we judge what is acceptable and normal, and what we believe is beyond the pale in terms of policing in society.

As we have seen, one theory for the popularity of crime stories is that the audience can explore areas of transgression that few of us are likely to endure in real life. Police stories are particularly popular with women who perceive themselves to be more likely the victims of violent crime. There is also a

▶ What type of representation of the police do you favour? Do you prefer the police drama where the police are represented favourably as upholders of the rule of law; or do you prefer the type where they are fallible human beings and can be corrupt? What view would you take of the police if you had to make a television police drama? Create a synopsis of a new police series. ●

▶ Do a content analysis of a week's television by looking at the listings of terrestrial television. In how many programmes do the police have a central role? Try grouping the list into subgenres or groups. Are there any groups that stand out as popular? What does this say about the issue of policing in the media?

In one week (March 2003) on terrestrial television I counted twenty such programmes. What view of the police is revealed? Can you see a trend? Is it the anomic policeman – the one who gets results, but doesn't mind how? Is it the one who follows procedures meticulously and sticks by the rules? Is it the officer with a whole lot of personal baggage that they bring into the work place? ●

Agatha Christie with her eponymous characters Miss Marple and Hercule Poirot was sometimes referred to as the 'Queen of Crime Fiction'.

sense of voyeuristic pleasure in seeing the victims of crime. Plus there is the tension of suspense articulating around whether the criminal will be caught. The genre therefore provides a vicarious experience of transgressive behaviour, a fantasy of identification, a frisson of fear, and a catharsis. It allows the audience to have the pleasure of engaging with the unthinkable and to view the unwatchable, but while experiencing it in domestic safety. In the main we know that the narrative drive is towards social order, that the criminal will be punished, that law and order and the status quo will be reinstated. This will normally entail the criminal being captured, punished and contained. Emotionally there is therefore the thrill of the chase and intellectual challenge of solving the puzzle. The resolution is important to many of the pleasures gained from viewing crime dramas. Additionally there is the opportunity to play with philosophical issues of good and evil, right and wrong, and the morality of illegal actions in the pursuit of a conviction. Do the ends justify the means? Having achieved all of this, the crime and police story has to provide closure to the issues raised. The knowledge that justice has been done and been seen to be done are basic tenets of the classic crime story. But does this happen in real life?

The history of crime writing is an interesting area that reflects changes in society. Writers such as Chaucer in the fifteenth century through to Agatha Christie in the twentieth century have been fascinated by the themes discussed above. But it was not until police forces became established as an institution that the police/detective story developed. It is usually said that *The Murders in the Rue Morgue* (1841) by Edgar Allen Poe was the first detective story. From then on the police and their procedures became the focus for many crime stories, and as each new medium has appeared it has drawn upon our fascination with crime and our ambiguous relation with the police. For television the first play to be written was a whodunit, *The Underground Murder Mystery*, transmitted in 1937 and lasting 10 minutes.

In the early years of television after World War II many crime series were imports from the United States, such as *Dragnet* and *Perry Mason*. This pattern of import has continued with *NYPD Blue* (Channel 4), *CSI: Crime Scene Investigation* and *CSI: Miami* (Five). But there has also been a strong indigenous production commenting upon local concerns about law and order and the institution of the police. A TV series such as *Dixon of Dock Green* (BBC1, 1955–1976) popularised the 'village' bobby view of policing. It was a period of post-war consensus reflected in Dixon's cosy view of the world when he came out on to the steps of the police station under the blue light with an 'Evenin' all' to open the episode, then gave his homily at the end. The police here were represented as incorruptible authority. There was one episode about a bent policeman, but this was shown to be a complete aberration. Dixon was an idealised and romantic representation. He even had a 'village green' on which to work in spite of the fact that he was firmly located in London. His nostalgic appeal and the popularity of crime drama have seen the BBC resurrect Dixon on Radio 4 (June 2005) using the same type of stories as were used on television.

The 1960s introduced *Z Cars*, set in fictional Newtown, located near Liverpool. This series had a contrived naturalism resulting partly from new technology such as lightweight cameras. Police procedures were much more in evidence, and the police were seen to have a troubled relationship with keeping to the rules. The representation of a rough industrial north helped in providing this grittier view. Strong language was later emphasised in the TV series *The Sweeney* (1975), which gave an even more iconoclastic version of policing. The style was action packed, with space created for violence (Fiske & Hartley, 1978), and reflected a shift in the public's view of the institution of the police as stories of corruption, unsafe prosecutions and violence emerged in the press. Later there was another swing that brought in the introspective policeman such as Inspector Morse, ironically played by John Thaw who had starred as the violent Jack Regan in *The Sweeney*, and Inspector Jack Frost. Both of these men had unsatisfactory personal lives; their entire *raison d'être* was in providing security for society as their 'family'. With Morse and Frost in charge we could be safer in our beds. The 1990s introduced *Prime Suspect* (ITV, 1991), with a strong female lead played by Helen Mirren who took on the misogynist world of the police. *The Cops* (BBC2, 1998) showed us a more multifaceted and dirtier portrayal of the police, with a documentary style to reflect its content. *The Cops* was made by Tony Garnett's production company, which was also responsible for producing *Murder Prevention* for Five (first

Dixon of Dock Green: the paternal policeman

broadcast October 2004) and which shows us political and moral confusions within the police.

4.4 Police – the reality?

Given that there are so many different ways to represent the police and therefore many ways to interpret their roles, an understanding of these discourses can reveal much about our complex society. But in studying these representations it is important to keep in mind the basic questions:

- From where do the media get their information?
- Whose agenda is being set?
- What motives do they have in representing the police in particular ways?
- How far do political or social objectives influence the agenda?
- What influence do these representations have on our beliefs about the real institution of the police?

Remember these are fundamental questions to ask when considering representation.

Two of the key regular sources for journalists are the police and the law courts. It is inevitable therefore that there are crime-related stories in both local and national press and broadcast news. These are 'official' sources, so it is also inevitable that they are going to take a particular viewpoint that often entails seeing the criminal as being deviant. We know that in many cases criminal behaviour is the result of social deprivation, but the media rarely explore these issues when reporting crime. One programme that did explore this was a documentary on a group of men who as young boys had suffered at the hands of a paedophile and who became criminals (*Panorama*, BBC1, 6 February 2005). How deviant groups have been represented and why the law has criminalised certain types of behaviour are other aspects to consider. There is in society a consensus or discourse of what we believe is criminal. As Dennington states: 'Linking these interpenetrating worlds of "fact" and "fiction" which together constitute the one, dominant representation of social relations – the reality of fact and fiction and the fiction of reality that we hold to be the consensual view – is the shared image of the criminal. For the police, the public is that nonhierarchical but ordered structure of "law-abiding citizens". The criminal world, its deviant alter ego, can be read as an anarchic non-structure of law-breaking non-citizens, situated at the twilight perimeters of normal society' (Dennington & Tulloch, 1976, pp. 44–5).

These messages create discourses that coalesce around crime, the criminal, the deviant, the law-abiding citizens and the institution of the police. In order to show how such messages are given, the discussion will concentrate on certain seminal television texts that were regarded as innovative in their representation of the police when they were first broadcast. Further exploration of these ideas can be found in Chapter 6 on prostitution, Chapter 7 on gypsies and Chapter 9 on immigrants, which expand the focus.

4.5 Gender and police: *Prime Suspect 1* (ITV 1, 1991)

The police as individuals are members of society, but are also part of the institution of the 'state apparatus' (Althusser). Social issues are therefore integral to any representation of the institution and of attitudes to the police. For example, over recent years the presence of female police officers in charge of investigations has increased, but not without some antagonism from within the police force. This change reflects the way that equal rights and women's roles have developed in society as a whole. Television has reflected this change. In the 1990s Helen Mirren starred as a detective inspector in *Prime Suspect*. This was written by Lynda La Plante and was

Prime Suspect: Jane Tennison (Helen Mirren) asserts her authority as a senior police officer

▶ If you can view the first episode of *Prime Suspect*, ask yourself what the roles and representation of the two policewomen characters, Mirren and the uniformed WPC, are. Are they pliant or predatory? Are they professional or personal? ●

regarded as a breakthrough in having a woman senior officer as the main protagonist. In particular the first series reflected the feminist agenda and specifically the issue of the 'glass ceiling' for women in the police force with its macho culture. Having a female leading officer, as in *Prime Suspect*, reflected a change in the way the police have had to react after the case of Alison Halford, the senior policewoman who claimed her promotion was blocked because of her gender.

In the opening episode of *Prime Suspect* the Mirren character, Jane Tennison, has to win her spurs in a male chauvinist institution. We are shown Tennison as ambitious officer; Tennison as live-in lover; Tennison as comrade; Tennison as subordinate; Tennison as boss; Tennison as a woman. If you listen to the language being used in this episode you can hear how, as a woman, Tennison is referred to in comparison with the men. Another officer, who has been using prostitutes for his own 'purposes', is referred to as 'a bit of a lad' by his boss. This phrase has positive connotations condoning the behaviour as merely playful – 'sowing his wild oats'. On the other hand, Tennison, without any evidence of her sexual behaviour, is referred to several times as a 'tart'. Here the attitude of the policemen to women is seen as such that they can refer to their new chief in the same way as they talk about the prostitutes. She is also called a 'dyke' and referred to as a 'girl', the latter having negative connotations of belittling. The language used here can be seen to reveal the ideological beliefs of the police about gender and sexual behaviour.

The first series of *Prime Suspect* is about a serial killer whose victims are in the main prostitutes. It is Tennison, as a woman and without the male bias, who is able to talk to the colleagues of these women to find out vital information necessary in finding the murderer. The male officers see these women through their understanding of the stereotype 'prostitute' and not the people behind the stereotype. If you see this series, compare the way that the policemen interviewing the prostitutes in the station refer to them as 'a roomful of slags' and the way that Jane Tennison talks to the two women prostitutes in the pub, where one of them says, 'You don't mind drinking with us, then.'

La Plante also compares behaviour of male and female police outside of the job. In their spare time we see the men in the pub drinking with their 'mates'. In Tennison's spare time we see her in a domestic situation with her extended family. At one point there is crosscutting between a boxing benefit night with all the men from the unit and Jane rushing home to her family after her appearance on 'Crimenight'. At the end of the first series, however, Jane joins the men in the pub to celebrate arresting the murderer. Here she follows the working practices of the institution and its male culture, and in so doing her personal life has collapsed. There is a price to pay for being a top policewoman and it is not only the cost to family life is the message given.

▶ What does this say about her? Has she become an honorary man? What does it say about the institution? Has it accepted women as equal? ●

More recently *Merseybeat* (BBC1) started with a woman chief police officer, but she was removed after a series of plot lines which showed up her vulnerability as a woman; she even suffers rape. In both *Prime Suspect* and *Merseybeat* women were defined by their relationships with men and children outside of the police force. Compare this with the way policemen in similar roles are shown. There is often an attempt to give a social life to policemen, but it is usually within the context of the police station rather than separated from it, or there is an absence of a permanent partner. The way in which men and women have been represented in police stories and their position in the institution provide a rich area of research into how the institution itself is representative of society as a whole and the role of gender. There are many other examples in the media. You might in relation to this discussion, for example, like to view the Coen brothers film *Fargo* (1996), which has a pregnant police officer in charge of a murder investigation.

4.6 Society, nation and police

Another discourse in the crime genre is about the type of law-abiding nation we perceive ourselves to be. How does the national interest articulate with the ideology of law and order, and how is this represented in the police series? A three-year survey published in 1975 looking at the relationship between the Metropolitan Police and the London public showed 98 per cent respected the police and 90 per cent trusted the police. By 1980, however, the following comment was made: 'I believe that we are in the presence of a concerted campaign … to denigrate the police service. There have been attempts to depict the police as brutal beaters up and even

▶ What would you say would be the results of such a survey if it were conducted today? Do your own survey. Do people trust the police? If so, why? If not, what evidence do they have not to trust the police?

Ask if the violent portrayal of behaviour from both the criminal and the police is significant in their representation. What effect does this type of representation have on audiences? Do people believe society is more violent today? Do they believe the police should use violence? Should they carry guns? What image do they want of today's police? ●

In *The Bill*, the audience identifies with the police characters as the main protagonists of the narrative. What meanings does this image convey?

▶ How would you represent a criminal? Try these three criminal sketches:
● Draw a stereotype cartoon character of a criminal.
● Write a character profile for a criminal in a new police series.
● Compose a social services document on a 'real' person who has been imprisoned. ●

killers of persons in custody ... No organ of opinion in this country has done more to disseminate and endorse these mendacities than the BBC' (Eldon Griffithe in the House of Commons, reported in Clutterbuck, 1983, p. 66).

4.7 Narrative and the institution of the police

In crime genres the narrative has to be constructed both to retain the identification of the audience with the key protagonists and to maintain the suspense. Sometimes we are asked to identify with the anti-hero and to empathise with their situation, as in the gangster series *The Sopranos* (Channel 4, 1999, series 1), but in the police series we would usually believe that the 'hero' should be a representative of law and order. But what type of hero do we see represented? The types of protagonists in crime stories reflect how society understands policing. The kindly policeman who is interested in the old tramp or low-key shoplifter can be seen in a series such as *The Last Detective* (2003), an inheritor of the village bobby myth seen in *Dixon of Dock Green* and *Heartbeat*. The narratives and the characters are dependent upon the type of representation of the police each programme decides to give. With a limited serial or an ongoing series such as *The Cops* and *The Bill*, however, it becomes inevitable that the police as key protagonists are represented as fully rounded characters, while the criminals or rogues are stereotyped and marked by certain iconography. As they are usually not recurring characters the sketchiness of their portrayal can be seen to be a practical consideration, but the recurring iconography does beg the question of stereotyping. Indeed, one of the factors that made *Prime Suspect 1* so fascinating was that the culprit was presented as a charming and sympathetic character, one to whom Tennison in her vulnerable state could well have been attracted.

Villains or vulnerable suspects are often characterised as working class or, as in a classic Christie whodunit, inadequate members of society where the criminal is usually middle or upper class, the working classes being mere witnesses to the events. The demise of the villain often passes off perfunctorily. They are merely the device to show us the police as the representative of social and cultural authority and as hero, even if flawed. But when we are asked to identify with an anti-hero we are asked to become partisan to deviant behaviour. The anomic hero was one which Clint Eastwood developed in his Dirty Harry character, but it also appears in television police series such as *The Cops*.

4.8 Fact or fiction: *The Cops* (BBC2, 1998–2000)

In documentaries, and even more so in dramas, it is important for the director to provide dramatic conflict within the narrative; inevitably this will lead to distortion or manipulation of the basic 'truths'. The most difficult genre to assess on this scale of truthfulness, but one of the most powerful, is the drama that uses documentary realism, sometimes called the drama-documentary. Tony Garnett, producer of *The Cops*, has been heavily linked with drama-documentary over thirty years. He was involved with the *Cathy Come Home* (BBC1, 1965) and *Between the Lines* programmes. With reference to *The Cops*, Garnett has said that: 'No one is allowed to write for this show who hasn't spent at least two weeks out with the cops … I insist that the writers have to "bear witness" to the reality' (interview in *Vertigo*). The polemical effect of eliding the two forms of documentary and drama means we need to ask ourselves about the source of the representation and how balanced a picture of the reality of the institution a drama based on fact can be. The desire to challenge the Establishment may lead to manipulation and to negative representation in the same way as self-representation of that institution will emphasise its positive elements. The truth, as always, is somewhere in between. The media have tried to present this 'truth' in fly-on-the-wall documentaries such as the Roger Graef's *Police* series in 1982, where the Thames Valley Police was observed. This was one of the most notorious documentaries made about the police. Even documentaries are a form of constructed and mediated views, illustrated for example by choice of camera position and focus. In the case of fly-on-the-wall there is a suggestion of something as close to reality as possible. It is of course not unmediated, even though it promises objectivity. In the editorial stage hundreds of hours of film have to be cut to fit the schedules. These decisions among many others will have an impact upon representation.

In a famous sequence Graef showed the interview by police of a woman rape victim. The camera was positioned behind the woman and did not move, so the viewer was

The Cops: Did *The Cops* give a realistic view of the institution of the police?

▶ Look at several episodes from contemporary police series. List the similarities and differences in representing the police. Look at style as well as character. Compare the representation of the police and the criminal. How is the issue of gender raised in both the police and criminals? Are they heroic or are they in some way incomplete or inadequate? With what sort of crimes are women usually associated? How are other groups represented? For example, in the first episode of *The Cops*, a resident of a block of flats refers to the upstairs occupants by saying, 'They're no better than tinks.' ●

always positioned in the point of view of the victim. The unsympathetic police interview resulted in a public outcry at the handling of the female victim. This resulted in the police changing their procedures in interviewing rape victims. It was certainly a pivotal moment in the relationship of the audience to the way that the police were represented on screen. This effect was unintentional at the time, resulting from the limited space in the room and a desire not to intervene or interrupt the flow of the interview.

More recently there have been docu-soaps such as the one following Traffic Police in Yorkshire (BBC1) and *Crime Fighters* (ITV), which looked at the work of the special operation units. Each gives a very different view of the police.

Questions about style and form are relevant to how we view the police, particularly as a response to the stylistic changes in police series where a documentary feel has been used. In these programmes the camera and thus the viewer are part of the action, rather than observers. People walk in front of the camera obscuring the point of view. Ambient sound is foregrounded, and overlapping sound creates a reality effect through the confusion. Dialogue feels unscripted, with people speaking over each other or stumbling over words. This makes listening feel like eavesdropping. Action that is not necessarily relevant to the plot is included, so mimicking real life. These elements can be clearly seen in the 1990s stylistically innovative *The Cops*. Tony Garnett, the producer, referred to this style as 'distilled naturalism' (BFI Media Conference, 2000).

Not only was *The Cops* challenging stylistically, but it also pushed the boundaries of the representation of the police that Garnett referred to as 'Trojan Horse drama' (ibid.). By this he meant that *The Cops* was sold as a member of the popular police genre, but that inside it were messages about the authority and accountability of institutions in society. In *The Cops* the police were seen as the reflections of their criminal counterparts – taking drugs; accepting bribes; lying. The first episode opens with a young woman in a club taking drugs. We follow her as she leaves at daybreak to go to work, and it is only then we find out she is a policewoman. Garnett said, 'One of the things we tried to do with *The Cops* was to introduce "stock" characters whom the audience could immediately recognise; we reinforced their prejudices to begin with, but then totally turned them around by making the "stock" characters behave in a way that the audience wasn't expecting. In rethinking their judgement of the character, the hope was that the audiences would have to rethink its own prejudices' (*Vertigo*).

The first episode of *The Cops* also shows us how a policeman, Roy, targets unofficially someone whom he believes is responsible for a colleague's heart attack. It shows us the problems of an Asian policeman in being accepted by the Asian community, while the young policewoman we met in the opening sequence is also seen having to assert her authority on a sceptical public: 'You're only a slip of a tart.'

A more traditional representation is taken by the police drama-cum-soap operas *The Bill* and *Merseybeat*. These focus on the relationships of police characters rather than on the crimes committed. They provide a different representation of the police. *The Bill* was originally launched in 1984, mimicking the fly-on-the-wall style of documentary, and the ring of authenticity is given through the Metropolitan Police's cooperation. This type of cooperation has been encouraged by senior police officers to create a positive image of the police. It was suggested that the police could spread a particular message to their officers – for example, about new initiatives – far more effectively in episodes of *The Bill* than through an official circular to police stations. This shows how popular the programme was and still is with members of the police force, as well as with ordinary viewers.

In contrast, when *The Cops* was finishing a BBC spokesman dismissed the suggestion that the lack of police cooperation led to the demise of the series: 'We didn't have a great deal of cooperation after the first series, but it was never a factor. There were plenty of people who'd left the police force who were willing to tell how it really is' (www.mediaguardian.co.uk/broadcast/story).

The ambiguous relationship with institutions in society is clearly seen in the way that the police are represented in the different television shows discussed above. But it was even more clearly revealed in the programming in the 1990s when *Heartbeat*, which reflected the nostalgic view of policing and a reversal to the status quo, was broadcast alongside *Between the Lines*, which centred on police corruption and used a realist aesthetic to interrogate the institution.

► Consider the Tony Martin shooting of Fred Barras case in Norfolk that obtained notoriety regarding the policing of rural communities. How do you think the police are viewed by groups with whom they are frequently in conflict, such as gypsies and prostitutes? This episode also raises issues about ethnic minorities in the police force. Similarly, in *Prime Suspect 2* the issue of race is raised with one of the colleagues of Tennison. In *The Thin Blue Line*, however, a situation comedy, although the characters were multiracial they did not play to their ethnic stereotypes. Find other contemporary examples of these issues. ●

DCI Tom Barnaby and Seargent Dan Scott are the archetypal veteran and novice in *Midsomer Murders*

4.9 Realism and the police

The question of realism is fundamental to the concept of representation. If the representation of the institution of the police is considered unbelievable, then there is a resistance to its reading. The audience will take on a negotiated or oppositional position unless they feel that this is generic verisimilitude and suspend their disbelief. This is what happens in a whodunit such as *Midsomer Murders* (ITV). Midsomer is a small rural community where the body count in one episode must match that of a reasonable-sized town. What helps the gap between fiction and reality is the emphasis on iconography such as uniform, vehicles and now more frequently guns.

The police series also lays emphasis on the police procedures, the routine and the hierarchies of police structures. In *Prime Suspect* we see Helen Mirren in the incident room piecing together the evidence. In the mise en scène are photos of the crime scene, telephones, computers, people in police uniform and so on. The sound design is complex with overlapping dialogue. The technical style and the detail help to lay claim to a degree of realism that aligns with the documentary claims to reality and reflect the procedures that underline the apparent impartiality of the police and its representation as a professional force. In *Prime Suspect 1* Tennison appears in a crime investigation series in the style of *Crimewatch UK* (BBC1) – a TV programme within a TV programme. This then becomes a multilayered viewing experience for the audience that helps to construct generic verisimilitude by articulating with and referencing our other media experience, so blurring the division between fact and fiction.

But more fundamentally the police series also has to conform to society's view of the police – that is, a cultural verisimilitude. As with any institution this is often contradictory. The police themselves would obviously wish to have a particular representation, and this is probably best seen in the series such as *Crimewatch UK*, where real police are helped to investigate crime by the audience and is a programme that comes close to representing the reality of police work. Although introduced by two professional presenters, one of whom also presents the news, the ultimate truth, the work of the police, is foregrounded. We see in the mise en scène police answering telephone calls from the public as though they were in their police stations. A policewoman or man gives updates on current cases, and we have identity 'mug shots'. In addition part of the 'narrative' of the programme focuses on the procedures of collecting evidence from witnesses and appealing for help. This links with police news conferences when a particularly heinous crime has been committed, such as the murder of two young girls at Soham. Here the police appeal to the public is mediated through its reporting on television and elsewhere.

Fictional programme makers must build upon these images of reality seen on our screens. To do this they adopt a range of styles from the naturalistic view of urban decay given by *The Cops* to the nostalgic rural view of *Midsomer Murders*. Neither of them is 'real', but which is closest to reality? How do we judge their relationship to reality? A representation that allows for the audience to decide upon the truth and motivation of the key protagonists and so injects ambiguity can be very unsettling. In the main audiences wish to be reassured and believe the dominant view that good will overcome evil and that the police personify this battle and are the heroes in such a fight. Where the audiences' view of the police is left ambiguous we can see that this may lead to a breakdown in trust in society. This was why *The Cops* created such a furore when it showed police taking drugs and breaking the law.

In the past the dominant view of the police in the media has been accused of being 'politically reactionary' (Clarke, 1987, p. 45) and of reinforcing the police's view of themselves (Clarke, 1981). Does this still exist in police series? *The Cops* was a show that challenged the reactionary view. Are there similar programmes on television at the moment? Currently new crime and police series are being developed: Channel 4 has *The Ghost Squad* about rooting out police corruption; ITV has *Lie with Me*; BBC3 has *Conviction* about an old-fashioned cop cracking under the pressure of contemporary police methods; Five has *Murder Prevention*; and ITV is reviving Inspector Morse and Agatha Christie's Miss Marple. The crime and police series are certainly not moribund. Do any of these series provide us with an alternative view of policing? Does the political agenda set by Garnett in *Murder Prevention* and the documentary style used provide us with a 'real' or truthful view of the police, or is it merely another slick drama?

▶ These were referred to as 'state apparatuses' by Louis Althusser. Some he categorised as ideological; others as oppressive. How far do you think the police are represented as agents of the state creating views of the way the state is organised, and how far do they impose or repress other views? ●

4.10 State apparatus

Like other institutions such as education (*Teachers*; *Grange Hill*) and health (*Holby City*; *Casualty*; *Hospital*), the police are part of the state structures.

A political activist who wished to challenge structures of society and the political institutions would certainly want to emphasise and represent the view that the police are often the agents of official repression. This view could also believe that they are sexist, racist and class-ridden. On the other hand, the police and those who support their role would want to present a view of being impartial in their reflection of society's consensus and the need of the police to protect our civil freedoms. It is only occasionally when there is a crisis in this consensus, a crisis in hegemony, that policing is seen by these latter groups not to provide an impartial view. The interview with the rape victim and the Stephen Lawrence death were two such notorious events. A series such as *The Cops* provides us with the alternative and perhaps more uncomfortable view. But which represents reality? Which is a true representation of the police? Tony Garnett would certainly claim that *The Cops* reflects his view of the 'relationship between the police and the community' (*Vertigo*), even if fictionalised. But Garnett would also claim to have a left-wing view of society and has a keen and acerbic view on politics. So again we have to ask those questions: who is representing and who is being represented?

Discourses centred on the police reveal the ambiguous nature of their representation often depending upon the emphasis given. Is the discourse focused upon the issues of crime, legality, justice, community and family or of national pride in an institution? Are we articulating the ideas of the decent law-abiding citizens who are threatened by the disruptive and deviant criminal, or is there an alternative discourse? Television goes beyond our viewing in the home. It is part of the complex interaction of society. The police series does not reflect a neutral view of policing, but rather it actively constructs a representation of a social reality. In so doing it also articulates the contradictions and tensions around policing practices and the police as an institution, messages about crime, professionalism, individualism, authority, the role of minorities, comradeship, bureaucracy, gender, the family and moral panics. This is perhaps the answer to the question posed at the beginning of the chapter about the popularity of the crime series. It provides a site for ideological struggles over the way that society functions. It can also provide a site for consensus on how society is controlled. Its representation on television tells us much about society.

References

Althusser, L. (trans. by Ben Brewster), *For Marx* (London: Verso, 1996; originally published 1969).

Barthes, R. (trans. by Stephen Heath), *Image Music Text* (London: Fontana, 1977).

Clarke, A., U203 *Popular Culture* Unit 22 and TV11 (Milton Keynes: Open University, 1981).

Clarke, M., *Teaching Popular Television* (London: Heinemann, 1987).

Clutterbuck, R., *The Media and Political Violence*, 2nd edn (London: Macmillan Press, 1983).

Creeber, G. (ed.), *Television Genre* (London: BFI Publishing, 2001).

Dennington & Tulloch, 'Cops, Consensus and Ideology', *Screen Education*, Issue 20, Autumn 1976, pp. 37–47.

Fiske, J., & J. Hartley, *Reading Television* (London: Methuen, 1978).

Kinnes, S., 'Cop a Load of That', *Sunday Times*, 24 October 2004.

MacMurraugh-Kavanagh, M. K. (ed.), transcript from Q & A seminar at University of Reading reported in 'Bearing Witness … Tony Garnett on "cops, the community and the TV audience"', *Vertigo*, pp. 21–2.

Osborne, R., 'Crime, media, violence', in *Campaign for Press and Broadcasting Freedom*, March/April 1995.

Stewart, C., M. Lavelle & A. Kowaltzke, *Media and Meaning* (London: BFI Publishing, 2000).

Selected television series

Dixon of Dock Green, BBC1, 1955–1976

Z Cars, BBC1, 1962–1978

The Sweeney, ITV, 1975–1978

The Bill, ITV, 1984–

Crimewatch UK, BBC, 1984–

Inspector Morse, ITV, 1987–2000

Prime Suspect 1, ITV 1 – written by Lynda La Plante, 1991,
   Granada Television Ltd
Heartbeat, ITV, 1992–
The Cops, BBC2, 1998–2000 – World Productions, executive
   producer Tony Garnett
Merseybeat, BBC1, 2001–2004
Murder Prevention, Five, 2004 – World Productions

Part Three
Minorities

Introduction

In this section we look at groups who have in their various ways been targets for opprobrium in society. Unlike institutions they are not powerful, influential or identifiable as part of the structures of society, either in ideological or repressive 'state apparatuses', as Althusser called them. These groups have been marginalised, often outside institutions, and are feared and certainly branded as different from the rest of society. They are regulated, but because they are on the edges of society they may not agree or conform to the regulations set up to control them. They may have their own set of values that do not fit with society's values or working practices. They become the outsiders and the scapegoats for problems in society and frequently moral panics occur around such minorities.

We have chosen three groups from this category to study: the mentally ill, prostitutes and gypsies.

We have many words in our language to talk about people whose behaviour suggests that they are not within the paradigm of 'normal'. Mental illness can take a variety of forms from mild depression to the criminally insane. Between these extremes we can cover illnesses that are short term and curable to the longer term and incurable, from self-harm to senile dementia, from phobias to schizophrenia. For others mental dysfunction has a genetic cause, such as in Down's syndrome which can usually be identified visually. But often we can be unaware of illnesses in people who are apparently healthy and without any physical signs of mental illness.

Whatever the cause, when we see 'unusual' behaviour we can become extremely alarmed or we may react by laughing at it to cover our embarrassment. Why should this be so? The behaviour may be unusual, but mostly it is harmless and we could see equally unusual and bizarre behaviour in people who claim no disability. Even so people will often protest if they think a home for people with mental illness is being located near to them. 'Nimbyism' (an acronym that stands for 'not in my back yard') takes hold. Is it because of the way the media have represented and reported mental illness? There have been a few sad cases of people suffering from an illness, such as schizophrenia, who have been the cause of the death of an innocent person. But there have also been cases of sane people setting light to and inflicting harm on defenceless mentally troubled victims. Who is more 'mentally disturbed'? Do we suggest that every would-be perpetrator of such crimes be locked up?

The media have often used mental institutions as metaphors for society. From *The Cabinet of Dr Caligari* (R. Wiene, 1919) to *One Flew over the Cuckoo's Nest* (Milos Forman, 1981) the message is that an analogy can be made between society and the institution. Often the question is posed, as in *Caligari* – who is mad: the inmates or those in control? Are we not 'all a little mad'? (Marion Crane in *Psycho*, Alfred Hitchcock, 1960).

Another group that has an ambivalent relationship with the media is prostitutes. Prostitution is a powerful economic reality in many women's lives. Sex is a commodity that they can sell or that others can sell on their behalf. Who has control, how prostitution is regulated and the subsequent consequences are important issues that help to construct the representation of gender. Mostly female, although there is a cohort of young men involved, the world of the prostitute is often used in the press to both titillate audiences and to criticise its sexual licentiousness. The *Sun*, with its Page Three girls, and the top-shelf magazines use images of women for voyeuristic pleasure. But selling sex on the streets is a prohibited occupation. It becomes a woman's problem rather than one of how people in society wish to spend their leisure time.

This hypocritical position is explored in the chapter on prostitution by looking at mainstream texts such as *Pretty Woman* (Garry Marshall, 1990), where Julia Roberts plays a hooker, as well as at texts that explore the reality of the lives of prostitutes.

Finally, another group that is often stigmatised is discussed. The gypsy nation is resident in many areas of the world. As it has spread, so have the issues surrounding a group of people who appear to have a different set of rules and different cultures. In modern societies we generally regard itinerants as dubious people. Even the travelling salesperson has a reputation built upon the fact that they cannot be pinned down. Similarly the sailor with a girl in every port is often represented as a picaresque or Tom Jones type character. But these are individuals and give no threat to the generally ordered view of society and its rules. Gypsies, on the other hand, as an identifiable group are seen as a threat. They appear to bring chaos, to not fit into the regulations that permanent settlers have adopted and to not play by the rules.

This section explores how the media have reported on stories where gypsies or travellers have been involved and how language has helped to construct as well as reflect a view of these groups. Additionally the views of gypsies and how they see themselves are offered. The section also explores how gypsies are represented in films from both Hollywood and other world cinemas. Such discussions on diasporas also open up how we see ourselves as a nation and how we view other nations. This leads therefore into the final section on representing nations.

5. Mental Illness

JO CASSEY

'Is mental illness contagious?'
HATHOR IN *STARGATE SG-1*, EPISODE 14, 1997

When reading this chapter it is important to note that in the context of this discussion I have taken 'mental illness' to mean conditions such as depression, psychosis, suicidal tendencies and schizophrenia. In addition I am assuming the stance that the construction of an audience's understanding of the term is bound up with issues of femininity and masculinity, normality and deviance, sexuality and the culture of violence.

Understandings of mental illness are constructed, represented and proliferated throughout mass culture. It is extremely rare that an audience can applaud the realistic portrayal of mental illness within a television or film text, so it is little wonder that there is a lot of stigma attached to this area. When a character is suffering from a mental disorder such as depression, schizophrenia or suicidal tendencies, they tend to fall into one of two opposite extremes: the violent sociopath or the quaint and down-at-heel. The reasons behind the illness and the characters themselves tend to be negatively stereotyped. In addition men tend to fare better in a narrative that depicts mental illness; they are represented as either suffering less from mental health problems or are seen to cope better with them.

I am interested in analysing the extent to which mental health is represented accurately or positively. I want to examine whether representation challenges an audience's

The Madness of Prince Charming (produced by Planet Wild and aired on 17 July 2003 on Channel 4) was clearly a play on the film title *The Madness of King George*. This documentary focused on the troubled life of 1980s pop icon Adam Ant, whose music made him millions before mental illness took its toll in the form of manic depression. 'Depression is like having a fist smashed in your skull.' (Adam Ant)

Statistics on mental health in the United Kingdom

How many people in the United Kingdom have a mental health problem?
▶ 1 in 4 people will experience a mental health problem in the course of any one year

What are the main types of mental health problems?
▶ 1 in 6 people will have depression at some point in their life.
▶ Depression is most common in people aged 25–44 years.
▶ 1 in 10 people is likely to have a 'disabling anxiety disorder' at some stage in his or her life. For manic depression and schizophrenia this figure is 1 in 100.

Who develops mental health problems?
▶ 20 per cent of women and 14 per cent of men in England have some form of mental illness.
▶ 18 per cent of women have a 'neurotic disorder' such as anxiety, depression, phobias and panic attacks, compared with 11 per cent of men.
▶ Men are three times more likely than women to have alcohol dependence and twice as likely to be dependent on drugs.

What about mental health problems among children and young people?
▶ 15 per cent of preschool children will have mild mental health problems and 7 per cent will have severe mental health problems.
▶ 6 per cent of boys and 16 per cent of girls aged 16–19 are thought to have some form of mental health problem.

What is the prevalence of mental health problems in older people?
▶ 15 per cent of people over 65 suffer from depression.
▶ Up to 670,000 people in the United Kingdom have some form of dementia.
▶ 5 per cent of people over 65 yeaars of age and 10–20 per cent of people over 80 yeaas have dementia.

What about suicide and self-harm?
▶ 75 per cent of all suicides are by men.
▶ 20 per cent of all deaths by young people are by suicide.
▶ 17 per cent of all suicides are by people aged 65 or over.
▶ Approximately 142,000 hospital admissions each year in England and Wales are the result of deliberate self-harm. About 19,000 of these are young people.
▶ Self-harm is more common in women than in men.

What is the relationship between mental health problems and offending?
▶ 10–20 per cent of young people involved in criminal activity are thought to have a 'psychiatric disorder'.
▶ In England and Wales an estimated 66 per cent of the remand population had mental health problems compared with 39 per cent of the sentenced population.

What are the costs of mental health problems?
▶ The total cost of mental health problems in England has been estimated at £32 billion. More than a third of this cost (almost £12 billion) is attributed to lost employment and productivity related to schizophrenia, depression, stress and anxiety.
▶ More than 91 million working days are lost to mental ill health every year. Half of the days lost are due to anxiety and stress conditions.

Source: Statistics on Mental Health factsheet 2003, Mental Health Foundation

perception of mental health issues and whether the representation invites empathy, distaste or anger. How do we glean meaning from this representation? When considering questions such as these I think it is important to remember that an audience will respond to a media text largely according to their 'norm references' (i.e. what they have been socialised from birth to perceive as 'normal' or 'typical').

Significantly in the research of National Mental Health charity MIND it was found that 'the media has tremendous power in creating and perpetuating discriminatory attitudes towards people with mental health problems' (Dunn, 1999). In MIND's report *Not Just Sticks and Stones* (Read & Baker, 1996) 60 per cent of the mental health service users who took part blamed the media for the discrimination they faced.

In the majority of cases where representation of mental illness is concerned, the mental illness depicts a violent angle. The media has '… a preoccupation with violence, particularly when it is random and seemingly inexplicable' (Professor Anthony Clare, article in *NHS magazine*, autumn 1996). When considering film, this argument is supported by a consideration of the horror genre and particularly of the 'slasher' sub-genre. Most of these texts contain a protagonist who is deemed a psychopathic character (*Psycho*, Alfred Hitchcock, 1960; *Halloween*, John Carpenter, 1975), or the film resolves itself using a character who is mentally ill (*Scream 2*, Wes Craven, 1997). This makes for an easy plot device in that the audience does not really need to dwell too deeply on the character's motivation – the mental illness is explanation enough. This also means that the character can behave in an unpredictable manner, serving to heighten the tension within the narrative.

The Madness of King George (Hytner, 1994) is a tragi-comedy that focuses on King George III (Nigel Hawthorne), who is slowly sliding into insanity, and the resultant political and royal backstabbing. The king is not on the best of terms with his son and heir, the Prince of Wales (Rupert Everett), and his subjects have no respect for him. Witnesses consider the king's behaviour to be increasingly strange and unbefitting of a royal, resulting in a loss of faith in his ability to rule England. The king must prove his sanity to his wife, Queen Charlotte (Helen Mirren), and his doctors.

Like the Alan Bennett play it is based upon, this feature film explores the compatibility between madness and power. The

▶ Brainstorm as many words as you can think of which are used in everyday life to describe someone who is perceived not to be mentally 'normal' or has acted stupidly (e.g. 'mad', 'loony', 'dumb', 'idiot', 'spastic', 'schizo' 'nutter' etc.). When you have completed your list consider the extent to which these terms are discriminatory. You could also research the derivations of these words and phrases. ●

Reel Madness, held on 19–22 June 2003 at the ICA in London, was the first national film festival dedicated to film portrayals of madness and mental distress. Organised by the Documentary Filmmakers group, Mental Health Media and Rethink, one of the key aims of the festival was to counter negative stereotypes. As a precursor to the festival a poll of 215 films that depicted mental illness was conducted whereby the public could vote for their favourite. The top ten films to receive the most votes were: *Analyze This, Awakenings, As Good As It Gets, Betty Blue, Breaking the Waves, Fight Club, Girl, Interrupted, One Flew over the Cuckoo's Nest* and *Shine,* but top of the poll with 22 per cent of the votes was *A Beautiful Mind.*

'His majesty was all-powerful and all-knowing, but he wasn't quite all there' Marketing tagline for *The Madness of King George*

king is a proud ruler reduced to a helpless patient; he is manic and deluded, but because he is the monarch no one can tell him to be quiet. Here the mentally ill person is presented to us as a confused, kind old man – he calls his wife 'Mrs King' – as opposed to an obsessed, evil monarch. The audience is positioned to feel an enormous sympathy with the incapacitated protagonist, as we see him soil himself, ride the back of his aides, slide down banisters and be dragged away nearly naked and screaming against his will. The manifestations of the king's illness are humiliating for him, and we share that humiliation. The remedies administered by the king's physicians include purgatives, bloodletting and keeping the monarch in isolation.

At the other end of the spectrum are films that, whether successful or not, consciously explore issues of mental disability such as *Spider* (David Cronenberg, 2002), *Girl, Interrupted* (James Mangold, 1999), *Twelve Monkeys* (Terry Gilliam, 1995) and *K-PAX* (Iain Softley, 2001).

5.1 *One Flew over the Cuckoo's Nest*

'*Madness has always had the power to frighten and fascinate*' (Headlines *leaflet*, Mental Health media)

One Flew over the Cuckoo's Nest (Milos Forman, 1975) is an independently produced $4.4 million film directed by Czech

'For both *Spider* and *Red Dragon* I met people in high-security hospitals and the thing that struck me is that these people are human beings … when you meet them, you can see all the fragility and vulnerability and confusion in their faces. I think that when we see someone across the street who seems odd to us, they can be more normal than we imagine. They go against convention, maybe in the way they dress or walk or speak. We judge them too quickly. Underneath it all, they need to be understood.'

'Split Personality' – profile on Ralph Fiennes, *Screen International*, 22 November 2002, p. 13

director Milos Forman and co-produced by Michael Douglas and Saul Zaentz (Kirk Douglas had owned the film's rights for some time, following his role as McMurphy on Broadway, before the film was greenlit). The film is an adaptation of Ken Kesey's eponymous 1962 bestselling novel, which was a product of the author's own experiences as a worker in a Californian psychiatric ward, as well as of the specific counterculture in which it was written. (Kesey was a persistent user of LSD at the time, which prompted him to have hallucinations while working as an orderly.)

A grim satire, the film is set among a group of patients and workers in an Oregon state hospital, an authentic mental institution. The film is narrated by an inmate, 'Chief' Bromden (Will Sampson), who tells the story of an energetic con man, Randall Patrick McMurphy (Jack Nicholson). McMurphy seeks out institutionalisation as a means of escaping the rigours of prison farm work, his punishment for dating a 15-year-old girl, and ultimately tries and fails to take on the system.

The film itself can be read as an allegory, with the hospital depicted as a place of rebellion led by an energetic, flamboyant, wise guy and anti-hero (McMurphy) who kicks against the Establishment, institutional authority and attitudes. The latter are personified largely by the matriarchal Nurse Mildred Ratched (Louise Fletcher), the patients' supervisory nurse. McMurphy is the antithesis of all that Ratched represents; he is exuberant, vital and vulgar, and everything in his personality suggests a lack of control. Ratched represents a bureaucratic and corporate mindset. She appears almost detached and lacking in emotion, and fosters a sense of discord among the patients by pitting them against one another in group therapy sessions so that they remain submissive to her and totally emasculated. McMurphy represents anarchy and disobedience; she represents rules and order.

The group of inpatients is a bizarre social mix. Chief Bromden (a.k.a. Broom), a dignified towering Native American, is an elective mute; Billy Bibbit is a stuttering, impressionable paranoid who is fiercely afraid of his mother; Dale Harding is an ineffectual intellectual who is relatively sane, but unable to overcome the shock of his wife's infidelity; Charlie Cheswick is an insecure neurotic who lacks self-confidence; Martini is profoundly immature; and Taber, a cynical, trouble-making sadist.

Jack Nicholson stars in *One Flew over the Cuckoo's Nest*

Jack Nicholson was ideally placed as the anti-hero here, a figure that rebels against oppressive bureaucracy, insists upon his or her rights and adheres to an ethos of live free or die (he is ultimately killed by Chief in a mercy killing). Previous films such as *Easy Rider* (Dennis Hopper, 1969) and *Five Easy Pieces* (Bob Rafelson, 1970) saw Nicholson revelling in the role of a rebel misbehaving amid the 1960s baby boomers counterculture, moving away from the bohemian beatnik movement of the 1950s.

▶ Sometimes the line between fact and fiction is somewhat blurred. For example, following the release of *Girl, Interrupted*, actress Winona Ryder, who played the lead as the suicidal Susanna, was caught shoplifting in Hollywood. The press responded throughout her court appearances by referring to her role in the film, as if there were some connection and one headline screamed 'Winona Ryder: Shoplifter Interrupted'.

Similarly, Angelina Jolie, who in the film plays Lisa, a charismatic sociopath, is often depicted as a somewhat kooky woman who in real life claimed to wear a vial of her former husband's blood around her neck and has a knife fetish.

Consider the way in which actors who star in films which depict mental illness are represented in the media at the time of a film's release. To what extent are facts manipulated to suit the needs of the film promotion? ●

Question: What do the following lead actors have in common?

Joanne Woodward (*The Three Faces of Eve*, Nunally Johnson, 1957); Cliff Robertson (*Charly*, Ralph Nelson, 1968); John Mills (*Ryan's Daughter*, David Lean, 1970); Dustin Hoffman (*Rain Man*, Barry Levinson, 1988); Daniel Day-Lewis (*My Left Foot*, Jim Sheridan, 1989); Geoffrey Rush (*Shine*, Scott Hicks, 1996); and Angelina Jolie (*Girl, Interrupted*, James Mangold, 1999)

Answer: They have all received an Oscar since World War II for their portrayal of a person with a mental disability.

One Flew over the Cuckoo's Nest: Nurse Ratched (Louise Fletcher) tries to control the rebellious McMurphy (Jack Nicholson)

One Flew over the Cuckoo's Nest *was the first film to sweep the Oscars since* It Happened One Night *(Frank Capra, 1934); it was nominated for nine awards and beat off stiff competition from* Jaws *(Steven Spielberg,1975) and* Nashville *(Robert Altman, 1975) to win all of the major categories: Best Picture; Best Screenplay; Best Actor; and Best Actress. Ultimately, the film grossed $300 million worldwide, making it the seventh-highest grossing film ever at the time.*

With his logical mind, McMurphy bucks against what he considers bureaucratic illogic and attempts to alleviate the dull monotony of life on the ward with fractious games, pranks and 'illegal' excursions. He soon senses who his main opponent is when he encounters stiff opposition from Ratched, whose system of vice-like control via pills and electric shock treatment enables her persistently to maintain the upper hand. McMurphy becomes antagonised by Ratched's domineering attitude in chaotic group therapy sessions; one of her key strengths is her ability to remain cool, unwilling to yield her power, as she subtly contrives to make McMurphy appear the misfit patient. When he questions the rules she calmly replies, 'Don't get upset, Mr McMurphy,' with her ever-permanent self-satisfied smile.

Ratched cunningly agrees to 'let majority rule', safe in the knowledge that her authority and power will always win over the malleable, drugged-out patients. In controlling the patients Ratched is serving her own sexually repressed ego rather than the therapeutic needs of her patients.

In one of the film's funniest sequences, McMurphy hijacks the field trip bus and takes the men on a fishing trip, accompanied by Candy, a prostitute friend whom he picks up on the way. McMurphy convinces the harbour manager that they are a group of doctors from the state mental institution, and the group venture out on what proves to be a highly enjoyable, liberating fishing trip. Ironically the trip has been more therapeutic than any group session at the hospital, but ultimately the men are caught and McMurphy is labelled 'dangerous', with Ratched now adamant that he be kept in the hospital indefinitely.

One of McMurphy's biggest lessons (and a crucial part of the film) comes when he realises that not only is he to remain incarcerated after his 68-day sentence has ended, but also that very few of the men are actual inmates. They are volunteers, opting to hide in a locked ward from the law, their families and, ultimately, the despair of their lives in the outside world, so voluntarily submitting to Ratched's desire for power. The inmates are no more insane than the employees of the institution, and McMurphy is one of the few that have actually been sectioned (i.e. detained against their will and given treatment, as they are considered a threat to themselves and others as a result of mental illness).

So we see an explicit connection being made between the institution and other societal organisations, with the mental institution seen as a way of repairing the damage done by Church, school and family to the inmates. The institution is a microcosm for the rest of society, where life seems inhabited by social misfits.

The final irony is played out towards the end of the film when McMurphy bribes the night watchman with alcohol and smuggles two prostitutes into the ward. A wild party ensues where the men are temporarily liberated and the ward is destroyed. McMurphy has the opportunity to leave through the open window, but agrees to stay when Billy reveals how disappointed he would be. Instead, McMurphy arranges for Billy to lose his virginity with one of the prostitutes. The next morning Ratched discovers the debauchery and immediately humiliates Billy by threatening to tell his mother; the repressive nurse knows exactly how to exploit his weaknesses. Symbolically Billy reverts to his stammering self and, wracked with guilt, he commits suicide by slitting his throat. Upon learning of his death, McMurphy goes berserk and attempts to strangle Ratched (the third use of the throat image in this scene), as he blames her for his death. But he is restrained by the orderlies and later returned during the night, a lobotomised glassy-eyed obedient captive. Lobotomy is seen

Lobotomy – a psychosurgical procedure involving selective destruction of nerve fibres or tissue that connect the frontal lobes to the thalamus. It is performed on the frontal lobe of the brain and its purpose is to alleviate mental illness and chronic pain symptoms. The bilateral cingulotomy, a modern psychosurgical technique which has replaced the lobotomy, is performed to alleviate mental disorders such as major depression and obsessive–compulsive disorder which have not responded to psychotherapy, behavioural therapy, electroshock etc. (Source: http://www.chclibrary.org)
A government working party, as recently as 1996, recommended that mentally ill patients in Scotland who are incapable of giving consent should still undergo neurosurgery for mental disorder. About twenty-five operations are performed annually in Britain. Interestingly, the working party considered that attitudes to neurosurgery continued to be affected by people's responses to films such as *One Flew over the Cuckoo's Nest*: 'modern techniques of neurosurgery bear little relation to operations of the early period, yet it is images of the film which underlie much of the debate.' (source: www.bmj.com)

Lobotomised characters have recently featured in *Quills* (Philip Kaufman, 2000) and *From Hell* (Albert Hughes & Allen Hughes, 2001), to create dramatic impact.

here as psychiatric vengeance. The final scene sees Chief denying Ratched her overall victory; he sets McMurphy free in an act of mercy killing. Then, as an homage to McMurphy's liberating example, he escapes the hospital, fleeing the cuckoo's nest for good. For him at least there is some hope of survival.

One Flew over the Cuckoo's Nest can be read as an anti-psychiatry text and was, ironically, made in the aftermath of the decarceration movement when surgical and electroshock therapies were already in decline. But one can argue that it reflects society's disillusionment with the psychiatric methodologies that had previously enjoyed so much acclaim.

5.2 Television genres: soap operas

'And it is easy to slip into a parallel universe. There are so many of them: worlds of the insane, the criminal, the crippled, the dying, perhaps of the dead as well. These worlds exist alongside this world and resemble it, but are not in it.'

(Susanna Kaysen, Girl, Interrupted, *1995, p. 5)*

Let us now consider the genre of soap opera – one of the most popular fictional genres on television. All terrestrial channels have their soap brand champion (BBC1 – *EastEnders*; ITV – *Coronation Street*; Channel 4 – *Hollyoaks*; Five – *Night & Day*). As a genre they have been hailed as '…firmly rooted in the tradition of British social realism …' (Martin, 2000, p. 101) and are often accused of being too depressing by the popular press because they focus on gritty issues such as rape, murder and infidelity. How, then, has mental illness faired in this popular arena? And to what extent can the genre's representation of mental illness be argued to be the highlighting of just another social issue?

A key example is the storyline from *EastEnders* involving Joe Wicks. Joe was a seventeen-year-old character, introduced to the series in March 1996 as David Wicks's long-lost son. David had left his family behind when Joe was only eight years old, so was surprised to see Joe when he turned up looking for him in Albert Square. Joe had run away from his home in Bolton following a car crash in which his sister was killed; he blamed himself as they had swapped car seats. Unprepared to accept Joe back in his life, David contacted Joe's mother, Lorraine, to come to fetch him. The father–son relationship became increasingly strained, however, when Joe started behaving somewhat strangely. David found a dead cat under Joe's bed and from there on Joe's degeneration was rapid; he became obsessed with aliens and paranoid about being poisoned, and wrapped his television in foil. His bedroom wall became a collage of newspaper clippings and he was convinced that Grant Mitchell was the devil. Initially Joe was treated for depression via prescription drugs, but his condition was exacerbated when he stopped taking the pills prescribed to him and he tried to commit suicide. It was when he took his mother, Lorraine, prisoner that he was sectioned and finally diagnosed as schizophrenic as a result of post-traumatic stress.

As the storyline was continuous (the plot line lasted eighteen months), the programme was able to consider the emotional effect that schizophrenia can have on a family and its impact on individual relationships. The scriptwriters did attempt a reasonably positive outcome – upon release from hospital Joe fell in love with Sarah Hills and got engaged.

So the BBC did actively explore the area of schizophrenia and interestingly did it through the show's biggest teen heart throb (Paul Nichols), presumably to have a greater impact, particularly on a young audience. The programme attempted to raise awareness about the issue through its portrayal of schizophrenia and garnered the annual Mental Health Media Award in October 1997. Unlike the national press, who when dealing with the issue tend to portray sufferers as violent and/or social misfits, the programme's scriptwriters worked closely with the National Schizophrenia Fellowship (NSF) to make Joe's illness as realistic as possible. Interestingly the NSF was flooded with calls from sufferers and their families after 22 million viewers watched Joe Wicks's departure from the series. Research published by MIND (1997) indicated that many secondary school teachers felt that *EastEnders* had raised the profile of mental health and increased students' awareness: 'The guy in *EastEnders* was a real heart throb so they all fell in love with him and there was a sympathy element whereas if he had been an old fella it would have been different' (MIND 1997).

But the decision was made by the BBC to avoid dwelling overmuch on the issue; the character had served its purpose and was written out after eighteen months, a brave move as

▶ Many contemporary television soap operas have depicted mental illness within major storylines (e.g. Jimmy Corkhill's nervous breakdown and suicide attempt in Channel 4's *Brookside*, Joe Wicks's schizophrenia and attempted suicide in BBC1's *EastEnders* and Lisa Hunter's self-harming in Channel 4's *Hollyoaks*). To what extent can these programmes be argued to be socially responsible in bringing issues such as these to light? Do they promote greater knowledge and understanding? Are the programmes arguably on a moral crusade?

Can representations such as these be considered as an enjoyable 'reality'? ●

Paul Nicholls attracted a large young female audience to the show. Nevertheless, it would seem that the programme had managed to attract unprecedented attention to the topic and had made inroads at breaking down the stigma attached to mental illness.

One reason for *EastEnders'* success where so many others had failed is the level of modality operating within the text. The audience was positioned to respond positively to the way in which mental illness was represented because the plot line was believable and arguably 'realistic', in other words it had 'high modality'. An audience is positioned to feel comfortable with the messages and values of an issue when the representation rests easily within their expectations of that particular issue.

By contrast, when Channel 4's *Brookside* portrayed Jimmy Corkhill as taking a class of secondary school students hostage while suffering from clinical depression, it could be argued that an audience would invest less in this representation because the situation was less believable (i.e. it had 'low modality'). Jimmy was posing as a teacher; he was not even qualified to teach, yet had 'blagged' his way into the job. This situation was far less convincing and almost comical, based on the character's previous behaviour, where his main role was as the programme's 'loveable scally', and the circumstances were less believable.

> *'For better or worse, movies and television contribute significantly to shaping the public's perception of the mentally ill and those who treat them.' (Steven E. Hyler)*
> Wedding, Boyd & Niemiec, 1998, p, 1.

5.3 Other texts

'Madness has always had the power to frighten and fascinate.' (Headlines leaflet, Mental Health Media)

A marked historical example of the power of film to persuade or 'educate' according to its representation is the Nazi film *Victims of the Past (Opfer der Vergangenheit)* (1937) which was made during the Holocaust, under the direct orders of Hitler, as a propaganda film about the mentally ill. It was screened by law in all 5300 cinemas in Germany and used by the Nazis as justification for the extermination of people who were labelled as mentally ill. The film's fundamental argument was that keeping these people alive was against the basic principles of nature, and its motivation was to gain support for the notion that the destruction of 'lives not worth living' was valid. As many as 30,000 German citizens, regardless of their religion, were killed as a result.

Unlike propaganda, a text whose primary function is to entertain will not set priorities on the way in which it represents the truth. This is linked to a second consideration: the extent to which a text subscribes to a commercial imperative. If the motivation behind a text is to make money (e.g. box-office gross), then the way in which the issue is represented may well be manipulated to gloss over the reality. The marketing strategy behind the film will be devised to ensure that the film will be of optimal appeal to a mass market. Consider the marketing taglines of the following mainstream films:

'From mental to gentle' – Me, Myself and Irene
'Sometimes the only way to stay sane is to go a little crazy' – Girl, Interrupted
'Young and depressed in America'– Prozac Nation

Films which involve some form of mental illness will often dumb down the depiction of 'reality' in the pursuit of commercial appeal.

Similarly, if the subject matter is not deemed appealing to a mass audience, the storyline is adapted accordingly. A good example of this is *A Beautiful Mind* (Ron Howard, 2001). Made for $60 million and shot between March and July 2001, the film was marketed as a biopic based on the life of Nobel Prize–winning mathematician John Nash (Russell Crowe). It ran with the 'smaltzy' taglines 'He saw the world in a way no one could have imagined' and 'I need to believe that something extra ordinary is possible'. Controversy arose, however, around the extent to which the storyline was manipulated to suit the needs of the cinema-going public. The life of a man who suffered delusional traumas and was a certified paranoid schizophrenic was suddenly turned into an uplifting tale of love conquering adversity – a classic example of mediation to enforce the commercial imperative of the Hollywood Machine. Interestingly, the film raises the issue of

▶ *Schizo* (Pete Walker, 1976) was marketed via the tagline 'When the left hand doesn't know who the right hand is killing you're dealing with a schizo'. Consider the way in which taglines are used to promote a film.

Research a number of films that depict mental illness in some way. What are their taglines? What do you think the film's USP (unique selling point) is? How does the tagline address the target audience? Would you say that this was a positive or negative representation of mental illness? ●

► Hollywood tends to represent a person who has a mental illness as one of two extremes: either as a violent (e.g. *Psycho*) or as a quaint character (e.g. *K-PAX*). Watch some of the film texts that have been recommended in the filmography at the end of this chapter and consider the way in which the characters' mental illness has been depicted. Is it a positive portrayal that encourages the audience to feel empathy? Or is it a more negative representation, through which disdain and repulsion are expressed? ●

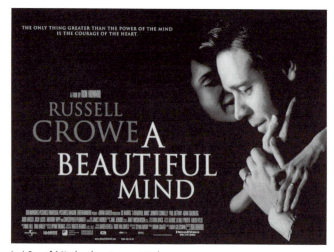

In *A Beautiful Mind* madness is romanticised

the extent to which genius verges on insanity and involves the audience in Nash's delusions, for he is constantly haunted by figments of his troubled mind. '... [T]he movie plays on our willing suspension of disbelief ... [it] is pulling us into the mind of a paranoid schizophrenic' (Philip French, 'And Every Second Counts', *Observer*, 24 February 2002).

However, the truth is easily manipulated for the sake of the mainstream. The film ignores Nash's alleged homosexuality and the fact that his wife, Alicia (Jennifer Connelly), divorced and later remarried him. Further, the narrative is rendered much more palatable with the conventional tearjerker ending (aided and abetted by an end title accompanied by Charlotte Church singing 'All Love Can Be') to encourage audience satisfaction, a key element to guarantee a film's success and good word-of-mouth. Triumph of the human spirit is director Ron Howard's stock in trade (*Apollo 13*, 1995; *The Grinch*, 2000; *Cocoon*, 1985; *Far and Away*, 1992 et al.). Here we are witness to a dramatic portrait of a man who is the victim of his peculiar gifts, but who somehow manages to survive his illness with true grit and the love of a good woman. Misery and madness give way to personal triumph.

By contrast, newspapers are guilty of perpetuating negative stereotypes which are orientated around mental health issues. Emotive words such as 'psycho', 'nutter' and 'lunatic' are frequently used by journalists in their reporting as an easy way of grabbing their readers' attention, and their

► Many film texts which depict mental illness are based on real-life stories (e.g. *Awakenings; Girl, Interrupted; A Beautiful Mind; One Flew over the Cuckoo's Nest*). To what extent have historical events been manipulated in these biopic texts? How important do you think audience appeal and box-office gross are when considering the way in which people and issues are adapted for the purposes of a film narrative? ●

usage is rarely questioned; language has the ability to demonise. Consider this headline and quotation from the *Sun* on 11 March 2005: 'Bananas in Pyjamas – Michael Jackson lived up to his wacko image ...' When the media uses provocative labels in such a throwaway manner it encourages people to do likewise, and so these words become embedded in our culture – they become part of everyday parlance. This practice feeds the public's ignorance and fear of people who have mental health problems rather than encouraging sympathy and understanding. A study by the Glasgow University Media Group (1996) based on audience research confirmed the belief that people who saw a strong link between mental health and violence largely derived their beliefs from the media. This is corroborated by the Health Education Authority's analysis of media coverage in 1996 which concluded that 46 per cent of all press coverage of mental illness was about crime and that stories emphasising that link were given greater prominence. The study also found that 40 per cent of tabloid newspapers and 45 per cent of Sunday tabloids employed stigmatising, pejorative vocabulary such as 'nutter' and 'loony'. Pieces giving advice or guidance on mental health issues accounted for less than 8 per cent of all coverage.

Is it any wonder then that a recent report published by the Department of Health concluded that the public's attitudes towards people with mental health problems have shown a marked deterioration since 2000? Rather, people are becoming increasingly intolerant and fearful of those suffering from a mental health problem. In society 'nutters' are portrayed as either a drain on our society's resources or as a threat to the public; they are relegated to the bottom of the pile and hegemony is maintained

> 'The thing about madness is it is shorthand more often than not for behaviour which is inexplicable or horrifying. As a consequence, the mad become, in the public consciousness, capable of horrifying things.'
> (Dave Harper, Senior Lecturer in Clinical Psychology, University of East London, quoted in the Guardian, 15 July 2003)

With facts such as these it is understandable that the public perceptions about mental health are negative; other forms of

The *News of the World* described Aaron Barschak, the 'comedy terrorist' who breached security at Windsor Castle to give Prince William a kiss at his twenty-first birthday party, as a 'nutter', 'madman' and 'lunatic' in its coverage of the event in June 2003. Former world heavyweight boxing champion, Frank Bruno MBE, was presented as mad by the tabloid press when he suffered a mental breakdown in September 2003: 'Bonkers Bruno Locked Up' (*Sun*, 23 September 2003). The paper went on to run a sympathy campaign for the popular celebrity and encouraged readers to send it letters of support for it to pass on to Bruno.

Lifting the Lid! disability film festival
An annual film festival that is both unique and inspiring in that it screens films which have been made by the disabled. The festival has been in existence for five years and runs at the National Film Theatre in London (it was originally screened at the now defunct Lux, London). The festival was heralded for being 'the first move towards an annual film festival ... where the work of disabled film-makers, directors, scriptwriters and producers is given a platform'. Interestingly, among the short films to be screened in 2003 was *An Artist's Guide to Schizophrenia*, a documentary about artist Aiden Shingler. (Source: *Sight and Sound*, vol. 13, issue 8, August 2003)

media are not encouraged to buck that trend. Far be it for a film or television text to take the moral high ground when the all-too-precious audience figures and box-office gross are at stake.

Media texts tend to conform to neat categories (or genres) so that audiences feel orientated. Different genres will treat 'mental illness' differently (e.g. musical comedy will have a light-hearted portrayal, whereas a thriller will have a more intense portrayal). When considering the way in which mental illness is represented within the moving image, a key consideration is the motivation behind the medium. If the fundamental aim of a media text is to entertain, then we will 'read' that representation differently to that found in a text which aims to educate (i.e. an audience is being positioned to respond differently).

Clearly it must be remembered that in any representation of mental illness, the depiction is likely to be distorted and, as any representation has an element of intervention, it is unlikely to be authentic – that is to say, the work of some one who is mentally ill themselves. The mentally ill have little or no opportunity for self-representation, so any portrayal is likely to be deeply fictitious, subjective and manipulated to suit the needs of the text and ultimately the producers of that text.

'… when life itself seems lunatic, who knows where madness lies? Too much sanity may be madness! To surrender dreams – this may be madness; to seek treasure where there is only trash! And maddest of all – to see life as it is and not as it should be!'

Miguel de Cervantes in Man of La Mancha (Hiller, 1972)

References

Darke, Paul, White *Sticks, Wheels and Crutches: Disability and the Moving Image Catalogue* (London: BFI, 2003).

Dunn, S., *Creating Accepting Communities: Report of the MIND Inquiry into Social Exclusion* (MIND, 1999).

Gabbard, Glen & Krin, *Psychiatry and the Cinema* (American Psychiatric Publishing Inc., 1999).

Kesey, Ken, *One Flew over the Cuckoo's Nest* (London: Penguin, 1962).

Laing, R. D., *The Divided Self* (London: Penguin, 1960).

Martin, R., *TV for A Level Media Studies* (London: Hodder & Stoughton, 2000).

Perkins, Charlotte Gilmore, *The Yellow Wallpaper* (London: Virago Press, 1987).

Philo, Greg (ed.), *Media and Mental Distress* (London: Longman, 1996).

Philo, Greg (ed.), *Message Received* (London: Longman, 1999).

Plath, Sylvia, *The Bell Jar* (London: Faber & Faber, 1971).

Rabkin, Leslie Y., *The Celluloid Couch: Annotated International Filmography of the Mental Health Professional in Movies and Television from the Beginning to 1990* (Lanham, MD, & London: Scarecrow Press, 1998).

Read, J., & S. Baker, *Not Just Sticks and Stones* (London: MIND, 1996).

Showalter, Elaine, *The Female Malady: Women, Madness and English Culture 830–1980* (London: Virago Press, 1987).

Wedding, D., M. A. Boyd & R. M. Niemiec, *Movies and Mental Illness: Using Films to Understand Pscyhopathology* (Boston: McGraw-Hill, 1998).

Wolfe, Tom, *The Electric Kool-Aid Acid Test* (London: Black Swan, 1969).

Zimmerman, Jacqueline Noll, *People Like Ourselves: Portrayals of Mental Illness in the Movies* (Lanham, MD: Scarecrow Press, 2003).

Filmography

Now, Voyager (Irving Rapper, 1942)

Spellbound (Alfred Hitchcock, 1945)

The Snake Pit (Anatole Litvak, 1948)

The Three Faces of Eve (Nunally Johnson, 1957)

Psycho (Alfred Hitchcock, 1960)

Shock Corridor (Samuel Fuller, 1963)

Titicut Follies (Frederick Wiseman, 1967)

Schizo (Pete Walker, 1976)

Sybil (Daniel Petrie, 1976)

Rain Man (Barry Levinson, 1988)

Awakenings (Penny Marshall, 1990)

Benny and Joon (Jeremiah S. Chechik, 1993)

Forrest Gump (Robert Zemeckis, 1994)

Twelve Monkeys (Terry Gilliam, 1995)

Shine (Scott Hicks, 1996)

Sling Blade (Billy Bob Thornton, 1996)

The Idiots (Lars Von Trier, 1998)

Girl, Interrupted (James Mangold, 1999)

The Other Sister (Garry Marshall, 1999)

Memento (Christopher Nolan, 2000)

Nurse Betty (Neil LaBute, 2000)

Quills (Philip Kaufman, 2000)

Requiem for a Dream (Darren Aronofsky, 2000)

A Beautiful Mind (Ron Howard, 2001)

I Am Sam (Jessie Nelson, 2001)

Me, Myself & Irene (Bobby & Peter Farrelly, 2001)

About a Boy (Chris & Paul Weitz, 2002)

K-PAX (Iain Softley, 2002)

Red Dragon (Brett Ratner, 2002)

Spider (David Cronenberg, 2002)

Prozac Nation (Erik Skoldbjærg, 2003)

Useful websites

www.disabilityfilms.co.uk – comprehensive
    filmography/resource

www.mind.org.uk – MIND mental health charity

www.bbc.co.uk/health – BBC on-line

www.channel4.com/health – Channel 4 on-line

www.sane.org.uk – SANE mental health charity

www.mentalhealth.org.uk – Mental Health Foundation

www.rcpsych.ac.uk – Royal College of Psychiatrists

www.doh.gov.uk/mentalhealth – Department of Health

www.rethink.org – Rethink mental health resource

www.ctono.freeserve.co.uk/id23.htm – Mad Pride

www.rethink.org/at-ease – @-ease mental health resource
    for young people

6. Prostitution

ROY ASHBURY

Social groups vary enormously in power, in wealth, in political influence, in access to communication technologies. Some have little ability to control the ways in which they are represented. This chapter deals with how one relatively powerless group of women has been portrayed in the cinema.

A well-worn cliché describes prostitution as the 'oldest profession'. Like all 'sound bites' this conceals as much it reveals, highlighting continuity rather than diversity. Prostitution takes many different forms and the meanings attributed to it and the responses it provokes are complex and contradictory. Even within a single community perspectives clash as to how it should be regulated and what explanations might be given for its existence; different societies have divergent legal frameworks within which it operates; across history, it has been tolerated, celebrated, stigmatised – often all at the same time. In media representations prostitutes have been by turns sacred and profane, and for every story of 'crack whores' there has been one of 'happy hookers'.

Historically, prostitution was never universally condemned. Herodotus described the existence of 'sacred prostitutes' in ancient Near Eastern societies – women who represented deities and would have sex with temple worshippers. Excavations at Pompeii revealed that brothels were accepted features of Roman life. Some English and French courtesans of the eighteenth century achieved great wealth, celebrity and even political influence. Today, some

Representations are infused with power relations. 'People think "prostitute" – and that's it, you can't be anything else. But I don't act like a "prostitute" when I'm a prostitute – the stereotype chewing gum, looking brassy, overdoing the make-up – suspenders, black stockings … It's what the media have made out a prostitute to be.'
Yasmin (from Roberts, *The Front Line*, 1986)

▶ Where does prostitution begin and end? To what extent do you think that people use sex as a way to achieve status, advance careers, secure material gains? Is this not a form of prostitution? Discuss. ●

Courtesans have featured in many novels (e.g. Nana by Emile Zola) and have been the subject of several historical studies, as well as important paintings by artists such as Toulouse-Lautrec, Degas and Manet.

In early modern Europe women were drowned and burned for prostitution. Prostitutes were forced by the Nazis to wear black triangles as symbols of shame. In the aftermath of World War II, French prostitutes had their heads shaved as punishment for having serviced German troops – scapegoats for national humiliation. In the United Kingdom today, the largest group of unsolved murders is that of street prostitutes, and yet popular British newspapers show little compassion for 'vice girls'.

▶ Newspaper research project – Select at least two contrasting newspapers and monitor them for a month. When they report prostitution, in what ways and using what language do they portray it? ●

A closely related issue, which has also led to fierce feminist debates, is that of pornography. What is it? Is it harmful? Should it be banned? Is it acceptable in some forms, but not others? Is it a manifesto for rape and violence against women? Or can it be, when produced and consumed consensually, a valid and even life-affirming form of visual expression? Are the women involved in the porn industry inevitably 'sex slaves', or can it empower them?

countries have legalised prostitution (including Holland, Germany and Australia), and recent decades have seen the growth of articulate prostitute rights campaigns.

More commonly, however, prostitution incurs stigma. Various attempts have been made to declare the 'truth' of prostitution. Religious responses have deployed ideas of 'sin'. Medical discourses have often blamed prostitutes for epidemics of sexually transmitted diseases. Seventeenth-century theories imagined sexual diseases were 'brewed' in the wombs of prostitutes. In nineteenth-century England, concern about syphilis led to the infamous Contagious Diseases Acts, provoking an important repeal campaign led by Josephine Butler. Since the 1980s, some responses to AIDS blame prostitutes while expressing little concern about the risks they face from clients.

Psychological theories have attempted to identify experiences in the course of childhood that might explain why a woman becomes a prostitute. Does a lack of fatherly love or abuse by a male relative produce low self-esteem, masochism and/or a desire to revenge oneself on men? Sociologists are suspicious of purely psychological accounts on the grounds that human behaviour is shaped by family and community structures, economic forces and cultural values. Research by social scientists such as Eileen MacLeod emphasises the impact of gendered socio-economic inequalities which put some women under such duress that prostitution becomes a meaningful, albeit hazardous, career.

Feminists have been sharply divided over prostitution. For many, it is a form of rape, a fundamental violation of a woman's human rights, and the quintessence of male domination. No woman can meaningfully consent to it. Prostitution must be abolished as part of a wider battle to defeat predatory male sexuality, a lynchpin of patriarchy. Other feminists argue that accepting nothing less than its total abolition is unrealistic and even harmful – not only to women engaged in prostitution, but also to the feminist project itself. Coercive prostitution is an unquestionable evil, but many prostitutes are women for whom it is, however regrettably, the least worst option facing them in societies in which many women suffer low pay, few occupational opportunities, pitiful welfare benefits for single mothers, and domestic violence. Under such circumstances prostitution is a survival strategy for women despite its dangers. The risks are only magnified by laws and social stigma that undermine prostitutes' ability to work safely. They do not 'sell their bodies', but negotiate payment for sexual services that they are prepared to provide; hostile social reactions make that negotiation more hazardous than it needs to be. 'Sex radical feminists' claim that 'sex workers' subvert patriarchy precisely because they demand that men pay; prostitutes challenge restrictive ideologies of female sexuality; feminists should support their 'sex-worker sisters'. The growing sex-workers' rights movement asserts that prostitution is analogous to other work, but currently resembles the unregulated industries of Victorian England before health and safety laws and trade unions eliminated their most exploitative features. Men control the sex industry, but this is all the more reason to support sex workers when they organise to win some control. They suffer enough stigmatisation without other women adding a 'feminist' version in which prostitutes are denied volition. Dividing women and reproducing the 'good girl'/'bad girl' ideology only reinforces patriarchy.

Legal regimes are equally diverse. In some countries prostitution is a criminal offence, while other nations have legalised it, varying in the extent to which they attempt to actively regulate it (licensed brothels, etc.). The framework of UK law on prostitution was laid down for decades by the Sexual Offences Act 1956 and the Street Offences Act 1959. Prostitution is not in itself illegal, but anything that would make it a viable career is illegal, with more than 35 offences. The 1959 Act made it a crime for a 'common prostitute' to loiter and solicit in a public place for the purpose of prostitution. A woman becomes a 'common prostitute' after two police cautions for soliciting; on the third occasion she can be arrested; in court the charge will state that the woman, a 'common prostitute', was soliciting. Until 1982, the punishment could include imprisonment. The Sexual Offences Act 1956 criminalises persons who aid and abet prostitution, by renting rooms, running a brothel or living off 'immoral earnings'.

'Kerb crawling' became illegal in the 1985 Street Offences Act. The Crime and Disorder Act of 1999 introduced Anti-Social Behaviour Orders, which are being used to exclude prostitutes, on pain of imprisonment, from specified areas.

▶ List the words you associate with people who are very sexually active. Are there any differences between the quality of words used for men and those which are used for women? ●

Research by Sue Lees (Losing Out, Hutchinson, 1986) showed that young women feel policed by labels such as 'slag' and 'slut' if they display any sexual independence.

In all areas of representation, language is incredibly important. What words do you use to talk about a social group? Contrary to the playground chant that 'sticks and stones may break my bones, but words will never hurt me', words are powerful labels that can shape our perceptions and actions. A language is a framework of judgement and decision-making. Words can hurt and offend; they can incite hatreds and reinforce prejudices; they can obfuscate; they can also heal, illuminate and aid in understanding.

In the discussion of sexual behaviour, words such as 'slut' and 'whore' are heavy with negative connotations and judgmental moralism; 'sex worker' and 'working girls' are terms preferred by those who wish to break down rigid distinctions between 'normal' and 'deviant'. Many experts in the field reject 'prostitution' as a noun describing a group of women, preferring to talk about 'women who are involved in prostitution'; they hope by doing this to separate the activity from the person involved in it, rather than using words which suggest that there is such a thing as a certain type of 'prostitute person'.

To add to the complexity, some women who are sex workers embrace the term 'whore' in a defiant gesture of rebellious re-appropriation of language against patriarchal semantics.

With cheaper travel and glaring economic inequalities across the globe, prostitution in all its forms has become increasingly internationalised. The Internet has revolutionised the communication of sexual imagery, information, contacts etc.

The 2003 Sexual Offences Act has attempted to regulate much more closely every aspect of sexual behaviour and created many new offences. Most controversially, it is now illegal for two young people under sixteen to engage in any form of sexual behaviour even if consensually – even to kiss – although the Home Office says that it is unlikely the police would ever prosecute.

The Criminal Justice and Police Act 2001 made kerb crawling an arrestable offence and criminalised advertising the services of a prostitute by way of cards in telephone boxes. The Sexual Offences Act 2003 increased the penalty for keeping a brothel, and created for the first time a specific set of offences dealing with the sexual exploitation of children – severe penalties have been introduced for 'paying for the sexual services of a child' (both sexes up to the age of eighteen) and 'causing or inciting child prostitution'. The 2003 Act treats young people involved in prostitution as victims rather than as offenders.

UK law has long treated prostitution predominantly as a 'public nuisance'. Only in recent years, with concern about the abuse of children and international sex trafficking, has the focus broadened. In the 1950s politicians were anxious to get women back into the home; street prostitutes could not be allowed to 'corrupt' other women and undermine the nuclear family. This is why the 1959 Act does not require the police to produce any evidence that a citizen feels they have been inconvenienced and an actual nuisance caused. In recent years, 'nuisance' has been couched more in terms of the way prostitution allegedly attracts crime to an area, lowers property values and leads to 'normal women' being harassed. Several towns and cities have seen residents' campaigns with support from the local press leading to punitive treatment of kerb crawlers and vigilante assaults on street prostitutes.

The 1956 Act was intended to protect prostitutes from exploitation, but the legislation often proved to be a blunt instrument, as it does not distinguish between coercion and the consensual arrangements into which a woman might enter to minimise the risk of violence against her. It was, in effect, paternalistic legislation, which treats women as requiring the law to rescue them even when they do not want to be rescued. Why on earth, you can hear the male legislators say, would you take a prostitute's views seriously?

The 1959 Act is, in addition, highly stigmatising, labelling a woman a 'common prostitute' when charges are read out in court which contradicts the basic legal principle that a person should be presumed innocent until proved guilty. It prejudices a woman's right to a fair trial, as well as making it easy for the police to abuse their powers – a woman so labelled may be arrested simply for walking down the street; her reputation condemns her.

Whatever their rationale, Britain's prostitution laws have been ineffective. Street prostitution has not been stamped out and the laws have encouraged a growth in off-street prostitution. These laws are also sexually discriminatory. Even with new kerb-crawling laws, it is still women who bear the brunt of the law, not their male punters. They are also in effect class laws, as the majority of street prostitutes are working-class women who, lacking the resources of middle-class women, are the most vulnerable to arrest.

Arguments for de-criminalisation suggest that Britain's laws make prostitutes more vulnerable to violence and exploitation than they might otherwise be. If two or three women work in a flat, which provides some security, they can be arrested for running a brothel. If they work from home, their partner can be arrested for living off immoral earnings. Anyone caught putting a prostitute's ads in a phone box, so that she does not have to solicit in the street, is a criminal. Well-lit streets with people in the vicinity offer some safety, but soliciting and kerb-crawling laws drive women into remote and deserted urban corners where a woman is at greater risk from a 'dodgy punter'. Although soliciting is not an imprisonable offence, fine default is and if a woman goes to prison she faces losing her children to 'care', which undermines attempts to build a normal life.

The stigma surrounding prostitution, which is only encouraged by the law, makes some men feel that the women are 'legitimate targets' of rape and violence because, after all, who cares what happens to a 'whore'? And if the law will not protect them, who will? The pimp, if anything more stigmatised than the prostitute, often with stereotypically racist overtones, may sometimes seem to 'working girls' to be the only man prepared to offer some support when other men (police, punters, 'respectable men') will not. As for the prevalence of drug abuse among prostitutes, might it not be reduced if 'the game' were less dangerous and proper health care accessible?

In July 2004, the Home Office announced a radical overhaul of what then Home Secretary David Blunkett called Britain's 'outdated, confusing and ineffective' prostitution laws. The consultation paper, *Paying the Price*, announced that all options, including legalised brothels and 'tolerance zones', will be considered.

For decades, feminist critiques of the British legal system argued that the law and its implementation have been rife with gender discrimination and 'double standards'. There are many examples of police officers, lawyers and judges expressing the view, implicitly if not explicitly, that women often have only themselves to blame when subject to male violence. Men find it hard, traditional ideology asserts, to 'control themselves' when faced by 'provocative' clothes and sexually active women.

Prostitutes have long faced judicial indifference and even contempt as especially 'loose women'; when the Yorkshire Ripper was tried for his serial violence against women in the north of England, one legal opinion was that the really tragic thing about the case was that he murdered 'ordinary women'. If he had confined himself to prostitutes, presumably the tragedy would have been much less?

Irma la Douce (1963): Jack Lemmon and Shirley Maclaine star in Billy Wilder's risqué comedy about the relationship between policeman and prostitute

When Western film-goers discovered the riches of Japanese cinema in the 1950s, Kenji Mizoguchi was one of three great auteurs who attracted attention; the other two were Akira Kurosawa and Yasujiro Ozu. Mizoguchi made several major films featuring female prostitution, the narratives of which indicted the oppression of women. He had a personal reason for this interest – his elder sister had been sold to a geisha house and had supported him through his education with her earnings.

When examining media representations of prostitution, one needs to be aware of the discursive struggles that swirl around it at every level of society.

6.1 The fiction film

'In the UK more money is now spent on prostitution than on cinema going. In financial terms that's £770m on prostitution as opposed to £400m on taking in a movie.'
(Herald, *Glasgow, 4 February 2003*)

As 'sexual outlaws', prostitutes often appear in contemporary film as signifiers of 'low life', adding a frisson of excitement for audiences vicariously enjoying forays into forbidden social worlds, much as tabloid newspapers salivate over 'kinky' misbehaviour involving 'vice girls'. Frequently, their narrative role is confined to that of egregiously abused corpses demanding a police procedural; however, because prostitution embodies issues of sex, money and power, many film-makers have seen its dramatic potential as a 'lightning conductor' for important social anxieties and debates. The following are just a few memorable films from different national cinemas in which female prostitution has been central to the narrative force: *Belle de Jour* (Luis Buñuel, 1964, France), *Nights of Cabiria* (Federico Fellini, 1957, Italy), *Leaving Las Vegas* (Mike Figgis, 1995, USA), *The Life of O'Haru* (Kenji Mizoguchi, 1956, Japan), *Pandora's Box* (Georg Wilhelm Pabst, 1929, Germany), *Pakeezah* (Kamal Amrohi, 1971, India) and *Pixote* (Hector Babenco, 1981, Brazil).

There have been important fictional prostitutes in every popular film genre: in the Western (*Stagecoach*, John Ford, 1939; *Unforgiven*, Clint Eastwood, 1992; *Painted Angels*, Jon Sanders, 1998), in comedy (*Irma La Douce*, Billy Wilder, 1963; *Milk Money*, Richard Benjamin, 1994), in crime drama and film noir (*Klute*, Alan J. Pakula, 1971; *Scarlet Street*, Fritz Lang, 1945), in horror (*Peeping Tom*, Michael Powell, 1960), in science fiction (Pris in Ridley Scott's *Blade Runner*, 1981, is a 'pleasure model replicant'), in melodrama (*Walk on the Wild Side*, Edward Dmytryk, 1962) and in social-issue films (*Lilya 4-Ever*, Lukas Moodysson, 2002). Further, for some auteurs, prostitution has been a recurring theme throughout their careers. Mizoguchi is perhaps the most well known example of this.

6.2 Early cinema

'Some things should not have pictorial representation in public places.' (US Supreme Court Justice Mckenna, 1915)

To those whose stereotype of silent film is speeded-up chases with amusing stop-motion tricks, it is surprising to learn that films featuring prostitution were common well before synchronised sound. Two important sub-genres of film melodrama in the first decades of film were so-called 'fallen woman films' such as *The Downward Path* (1902) and films about the 'white slave trade'. Narratives of women seduced and abandoned, kidnapped or otherwise driven into prostitution were highly successful. *Traffic in Souls*, a 1913 film about a woman rescuing her sister from coercive prostitution, was so profitable that its producer Carl Laemmle felt confident enough to build Universal City, one of the homes of the Hollywood system.

Film developed into a major medium amid dramatic changes in human experience. It grew at a time of rapid urbanisation, intensifying industrialisation and technological innovation. In the United States, large-scale immigration was creating a 'melting pot' of ethnic identities and tensions. In Europe, the leading powers were 'sizing up' for a major confrontation over power and colonial possessions. One of the most significant areas of social change was in gender relations. An older ideology of woman's proper destiny (to be pious, pure, submissive, domestic) was being undermined by growing numbers of women entering the workplace, and by women campaigning for legal and political rights. The role of marriage, the place of sex in human relationships, birth control and the basis of divorce were all 'hot' topics of public discourse and would continue to be so throughout the twentieth century.

Many women were avid movie-goers. The cinema offered a space for them to enjoy entertainment that was not weighed down with traditional etiquette. Women went alone or with friends, and their tastes were an important consideration for film producers. 'Movie-struck girls' helped to lay the foundations of cinema, creating many 'stars' and genres, as well as promoting the growth of fan magazines. But was the cinema a 'good influence' or, on the contrary, a new form of moral corruption? What were audiences watching in the dark

Kevin Brownlow's Behind the Mask of Innocence (London: Jonathan Cape, 1990) is a brilliant study of social issues represented in silent cinema.

Hollywood fan magazines in the 1920s and 1930s even urged female readers to stay in their home towns so that Hollywood dreams did not become nightmares.

Not her real name, Theda Bara – an anagram of Arab Death – became an icon of predatory female sexuality.

The Payne Fund was a conservative foundation that sponsored research into media effects; although much of the research revealed a complex situation with no simple cause-and-effect links between media and behaviour, the highly publicised book-length summary Our Movie-Made Children *(Henry Foreman, New York: Macmillan, 1935) was a simple hypodermic model.*

spaces of 'nickelodeons' and storefront cinemas? In addition to what was happening on the screen, was not there a 'promiscuous' mingling of unmarried men and women in the stalls in front of it?

Debate intensified as cinema's popularity broadened, as films became longer and visually more powerful, and as some film-makers seemed 'hellbent' on peopling the screen with seductive 'vamps' such as Theda Bara in *A Fool There Was* (Frank Powell, 1915) and girls 'on the make' as personified by Barbara Stanwyck's film roles in *Ladies They Talk About* (Howard Bretherton & William Keighley, 1933) and, especially, *Baby Face* (Alfred E. Green, 1933). In the United States, Hollywood became synonymous with excessive lifestyles and lurid sex scandals – a 'modern Babylon'. 'Movie-struck girls' were pouring into Hollywood in search of stardom, and some of those who failed swelled the ranks of Los Angeles's prostitutes. What most troubled society's moral guardians were narratives in which 'gold diggers' or 'party girls' (*Party Girl*, Victor Halperin, 1930) shamelessly exploited their sexual charisma and 'traded' sexual favours for social mobility (furs were a recurring signifier of 'glamour' and 'success' in films such as *Easy Living*, Mitchell Leisen, 1937), in effect 'prostituting' themselves. What could the effect be on impressionable young women, portrayed as 'dopes' unable to resist film's hypodermic effects? These fears seemed to receive 'scientific' justification when Payne Fund researchers such as Blumer claimed, in the 1930s, that 'movies taught delinquent girls to barter their sex for money' (Rosen, 1973).

What conservatives demanded were films in which 'fallen women' suffered terrible fates; they were only satisfied if adulteresses, never mind prostitutes, shared the fate of Anna in MGM's 1935 adaptation of Tolstoy's novel *Anna Karenina*, where she committed suicide, because sin must never be enjoyed. Liberals, on the other hand, were more compassionate if a woman was redeemable. If she had been sold into prostitution, or seduced and abandoned by a cruel man, or had taken to the streets as the result of fundamentally noble motives, she was eligible to be rescued by the love of a good man. (In Josef von Sternberg's *Blonde Venus* of 1932, Helen raises money for medical treatment to save her husband's life and to support her child.) In any event, the subject had to be represented as 'tastefully' as possible with no explicit representations of sexual exchanges. Society as a whole, however, should not be indicted for prostitution.

In the United States, local censorship pressures became so troublesome to the film industry that Hollywood set up a self-regulation body to try to nip the problems in the bud. When the Catholic League of Decency urged boycotts of films, and municipal bodies banned films, Hollywood lost money; it was better to try to appease the critics. By 1933, Hollywood films were under the close supervision of the Production Code. It stipulated there must be no sympathy for 'evil' and that 'no picture shall be produced which will lower the moral standards of those who see it'; 'the sympathy of the audience shall never be thrown to the side of crime, wrong doing, evil or sin'. A range of social issues became unacceptable for the screen, and this included prostitution. The very words 'prostitute' and 'whore' became taboo. Scripts were submitted before production began so that much of the censorship was unseen by the public. Joseph Breen, administrator of the Production Code for more than twenty years, made it clear that film-makers would not satisfy him with a few cuts or with 'moral endings' tacked on to otherwise 'unhealthy' plots. A film's narrative had to defuse any appeal of 'sin' throughout with 'compensatory moral values', 'voices of morality' and the punishment and repentance of 'wrongdoers'.

Joseph Breen was, as his correspondence revealed, virulently anti-Semitic; he saw Hollywood Jewish movie 'moguls' as institutionalised 'pimps' corrupting white Anglo-Saxon morals.

In Britain, the British Board of Film Censors ruled many subjects 'unsuitable', even banning films that got past the American Production Code (such as Jack Conway's *Red-headed Woman* in 1932). It imposed such restrictions on producers that there was, as Tom Mathews comments, 'an almost total lack of physicality on the British screen'. It was a rare British film that even hinted at prostitution, which is why a novel such as Arthur Greenwood's *Love on the Dole* (1933), in which a desperate Sally Hardcastle exchanges sex for survival, took so long to reach the screen. It is also why, when it did, the prostitution was only implied, rather than honestly confronted.

Greenwood's novel Love on the Dole *also worried the censors because it portrayed the police as brutal tools of the state.*

Film producers resented censorship on an artistic basis, but also because it prevented them from tackling subjects with popular appeal and commercial potential. The appeal of many 'stars' was their sexual charisma; it is pretty certain that many members of the audience enjoyed the very things that their 'betters' wished them not to see.

In John Ford's *Stagecoach*, Dallas is thrown out of town a fallen woman, but proves herself a capable nurse and midwife on the journey to Lordsburg for the upper class wife of an officer, impressing the hero Ringo, whom she eventually marries. Despite censorship restrictions, Ford's portrayal of the prostitute Dallas is a sympathetic one; of all the women in the film, she is represented as the most authentically American.

Serious treatment of contemporary prostitution was ruled out in Anglo-American cinema. Fritz Lang, for example, complained that: 'the Hays Office warned us that we couldn't show the heroine as a prostitute. We had to put a sewing machine in her apartment, so that she was not a whore but a seamstress' (talking about his 1941 film *Man Hunt*; quoted in Pascall and Jeavons, 1975).

Even setting films in the past, a popular strategy by film-makers to reduce a censor's ire, was only partially successful. David Selznick had a number of run-ins with the Production Code, most notably the original script of *Gone with the Wind* (1939) which featured a sympathetic prostitute, Belle Watling, nursing wounded soldiers during the siege of Atlanta. Breen rejected the scene as making her 'too sympathetic'. In the final film, she makes only a fleeting appearance as a signifier of Rhett Butler's raffish masculinity.

Given the censorship restrictions on Hollywood, films in the 1930s and 1940s could feature a prostitute in a sympathetic way only if her past were veiled and the narrative redemptive (as, for example, John Ford's classic Western *Stagecoach*, 1939).

6.3 Film and the post-war 'Sexual Revolution'

The parameters shaping the representation of prostitution began to change during the seismic shifts in culture after World War II. Economic growth, new technologies and a more youthful population all laid the basis for shifts in sexual behaviour to which film-makers responded and which some actively wanted to celebrate.

Television reduced cinemagoing as families adopted suburban and home-centred lifestyles; popular music grew with affordable radios and recordings, catering to a major youth market; films had to offer something 'special' if they were to compete. Sexual mores changed as women gradually increased their earning power, enjoyed more educational opportunities and contraception became more accessible. Colour, widescreen and younger stars were all successful responses to competition from television, but the censorship restrictions of the past were now a straitjacket preventing films from reflecting new social attitudes and tolerances.

The impact of European 'art film' is also relevant. The post-war years saw a creative resurgence of film-making in

Europe. A wave of directors achieved international fame for their aesthetic inventiveness and daring subject matter. Many of these films were successful in the US market, adding to a sense that Hollywood was not delivering 'adult' entertainment. Many of these European films treated sex in a more explicit way. Nudity, premarital sex, adultery, rape and prostitution were among the subjects brought to the screen by Italian neo-realism, the French New Wave and Sweden's Ingmar Bergman. Even British films, such as *Room at the Top* (Jack Clayton, 1959) and *Saturday Night and Sunday Morning* (Karel Reisz, 1960), began to portray sexuality more openly, if drawing a line at an exploration of prostitution. (In Michael Powell's *Peeping Tom*, 1960, a prostitute does make a memorable appearance in the famous opening scene, but only as a victim of the serial killer whose troubled soul is the real focus of the narrative.)

A number of European films signified prostitution in radical new ways. Italian director Federico Fellini's bittersweet *Nights of Cabiria* (1957), for example, narrates the life of a poor prostitute whose touching optimism despite all her knock-backs invites the audience to share her pain when the man she loves betrays her. She is almost saintly and emblematic of the 'crucifixion' of the dispossessed. If anything is 'fallen' it is the world around Cabiria. In Jean-Luc Godard's *Vivre sa vie* (1964) and *Two or Three Things I Know about Her* (1967), prostitution is a metaphor for a capitalist society in which everyone is compelled to exchange use of their bodies and minds for survival, even film-makers. More explicit sexually was Luis Buñuel's *Belle de Jour* (1964) in which the beautiful and outwardly respectable wife of a wealthy man chooses to work in a high-class brothel in order to exorcise her sexual fears. The film suggests that bourgeois respectability only vainly represses the 'perversity' of human sexuality.

Set in the sleazy world of 1950s Soho, *Peeping Tom* was unusual in drawing back the curtain on British sexual mores and hypocrisies; in one scene, we see 'respectable men' surreptitiously buy pornography from 'under the counter' of a newsagent's.

6.4 New censorship regimes

Under the stress of social change and growing competition, censorship regimes retreated. In Britain the BBFC, under John Trevelyan, took a more liberal approach to 'adult' films if Trevelyan accepted that they had artistic intent. In the United States, the Production Code was relaxed and film-makers pushed at the boundaries. In 1952 the film medium finally got First Amendment protection. In 1956, prostitution

Billy Wilder was one of many German film-makers who went to Hollywood to escape Nazism. His most famous film is Some Like It Hot *(1959), a cross-dressing comedy starring Marilyn Monroe.*

was permitted as a subject if 'treated within the careful limits of good taste'. The Code was further amended in 1961 so that 'sex aberrations' could be represented on screen with 'care, discretion and restraint'. In 1966 a major Code revision shifted the emphasis to encouraging freedom of expression if 'used responsibly'. Finally, in 1968 the Code was abandoned and a ratings system introduced – films no longer had to be suitable for all audiences.

With progressively greater freedom, American film represented sex more openly, including prostitution. *From Here to Eternity* (Fred Zinneman, 1953) had a brothel scene; in *East of Eden* (Elia Kazan, 1955), James Dean's tortured character discovers that his mother is a 'madam'. In Charles Vidor's 1957 remake of *A Farewell to Arms*, the word 'whore' was heard for the first time in US cinema for decades. Elizabeth Taylor played a doomed call girl in *Butterfield 8* (Daniel Mann, 1960). Edward Dmytryk's adaptation of Nelson Algren's *A Walk on the Wild Side* (1962) is a complex portrayal of emotional and sexual power struggles focused on a New Orleans brothel called the 'Doll House'. An important film in the struggle for a more 'adult' cinema was Sidney Lumet's *The Pawnbroker* (1965), in which a young black prostitute (raising money to help her boyfriend escape from crime) bares her breasts to the central protagonist, reviving painful memories of the humiliations of a concentration camp. The film was refused a Seal of Approval until the producers appealed and won. In a more cheerful vein, Billy Wilder took advantage of the new freedoms to make romantic sex comedies featuring good-natured whores which poked fun at repressive morality – *Irma La Douce* (1963) and *Kiss Me, Stupid* (1964).

With less restrictive censorship and greater tolerance in society for sexual difference, film-makers are able to explore issues such as prostitution more easily. Explicit sexual acts on screen remain controversial, but no longer do censors or wide sections of the public demand automatic moral condemnation of sexual deviance.

The uses of this freedom remain subject, however, to the economics of the media marketplace: film-makers must consider box-office equations. Big-budget films target a global mainstream audience and require ingredients with mass appeal, demanding some combination of stars, generic familiarity, special effects and narratives that are 'high concept' and ultimately reassuring. Prostitution in its coercive forms – the trafficking of women, sex tourism – clearly threatens to be 'box-office poison'. Consequently, the successful commercial films that feature it are romantic comedies which employ prostitution to repair a 'hegemonic heterosexuality' battered by the gales of sexual revolution. In films such as *Night Shift* (Ron Howard, 1982) and *The Owl and the Pussycat* (Les Kaluza, 1971), uninhibited 'happy hookers' come to the rescue of sexually miserable men while themselves finding monogamy.

6.5 *Pretty Woman* (Garry Marshall, 1990)

Released at the end of the Reagan era, *Pretty Woman* was the top-grossing film of 1990, making $450 million worldwide. Julia Roberts won a Golden Globe (1991) and an Academy Award nomination for Best Actress (1990), and the film clinched her ascent to stardom.

From a downbeat script entitled *3000* emerged a film to which adjectives such as 'heart-warming' are commonly applied. As US critic Roger Ebert commented on his website: 'here is a movie that could have marched us down mean streets into the sinks of iniquity and it glows with romance'.

Disney, owners of Touchstone, deemed *3000* uncommercial, and Garry Marshall was employed 'to lighten it up'. The film demonstrates how contemporary Hollywood negotiates social change in a profitable way by invoking troubling issues

> Here is an example of commercial marketing of prostitution in Hollywood films:
>
> 'Twelve-year-old Frank Wheeler and his two best buddies are determined to solve life's biggest mystery – women! So they pool their piggy bank money and head for the big city. Their plan: to peek at a naked lady.
>
> The kids hit the jackpot when they meet V (Melanie Griffith), a gorgeous, warm-hearted "working girl". But when Frank looks at V, he sees more than just a beautiful body. He sees the perfect wife for his shy single dad (Ed Harris).'
> Video box description of *Milk Money* (Richard Benjamin, 1994, USA)

Pretty Woman: Vivian's masquerade as a prostitute will soon be dissolved by romantic love

but then re-signifying them in enjoyable, more reassuring ways. *Pretty Woman* is 'mythic' in anthropologist Lévi-Strauss's terms, as it works on social contradictions and magically resolves them.

The narrative of *Pretty Woman* is skilfully constructed to deliver emotional pleasure, while disarming anything that would undermine it. Like the conjuror who entertains guests at the party at the beginning of the film, it uses 'feints of hand' to hold us spellbound while encouraging us to disregard the textual 'tricks' at work.

The first scenes establish the diegesis on which the narrative will work (a world of sharp polarities), and announce a critique of monetary exchange. Edward Lewis is a corporate raider, an iconic figure of capitalism at its most rampant; his preoccupation with business leaves no time for relationships. The credits employ a crosscutting montage to set up a web of associations and tensions: hands exchange drugs for money, echoing the conjuror's trick, while two women coded as 'hookers' work a street; a shot of a plaque celebrating Carole Lombard evokes 'Hollywood' with all its connotations of success and glamour. But a siren signifies 'danger'. Inside a sleazy hotel a woman stirs in bed as a slow pan caresses her sensuous form. It is a 'body double', not only literally, but also as a body image that men might desire while women might wish to own (a shot for two gazes). The camera traverses photographs torn in half with men's faces scratched out. Vivian, a street prostitute, gets ready for work in a series of shots that emphasise her appearance as a constructed masquerade; blonde hair, red make-up and a top that highlights her cleavage. Wearing cheap jewellery and worn high-heeled boots which she touches up with a black felt pen, she looks like the stereotypical street whore. The song 'I'm a Wild One' completes our understanding that she is a social 'outlaw', the very opposite of Edward. She owes rent and has to avoid her landlord by taking to the fire escape. Like so many things in the film, this will ultimately be re-signified.

Before Vivian's fateful meeting with Edward, the film gives us a glimpse of the 'mean streets' of her world. Hollywood Boulevard is clearly a far cry from the glamour of 'Hollywood'. She weaves her way through 'low life'. She passes a crime scene in which a prostitute's body is recovered from a 'dumpster' while tourists insensitively look on. When she

▶ What are the iconic elements that constitute 'a prostitute'? ●

finds her friend Kit, who has spent their rent money on drugs, a Latino pimp tries to persuade Vivian to work for him. We learn that she is new, refuses to have a pimp and, unlike Kit, never uses drugs.

Everything is set for narrative alchemy. Edward is rich, but emotionally unfulfilled; she is a street prostitute, but does not 'really belong'. He is not looking for paid sex, but for directions to his hotel in unfamiliar streets, and is no snob about whom he asks. Vivian is offering paid sex, but we have not seen her with any other clients; we are spared any emotional work to overcome the distaste this might have provoked.

The opening street scenes signify the social depths she inhabits. It makes her narrative ascent all the more pleasurable. Needless to say, the film quickly forgets about the body in the dumpster – too much reality would seriously derail the film's ideological project. The characters are defended from the stigma associated with 'hooker' and 'john'. He asks her not for sex, but for help; she makes him pay, but is soon enthusing about the car and invoking her small-town girlhood. He talks politely of 'you girls'. She feels his crotch as part of a joke about her fee being 'stiff', but he retains an air of amused detachment rather than sexual desire. When he asks her to his hotel room, he is polite in a 'courtly' way consistent with the 'prince' he becomes in her 'fairy tale'. Crossing the lobby and taking the lift up to his penthouse is the first of several scenes in which the incongruity of a 'hooker' in 'high society' is played for comic effects.

In his room, she produces an array of coloured condoms, but he would rather talk. The scene is full of signs to defuse stigma. He is not an ordinary 'john'. Nor is Vivian a 'typical hooker'. She flosses her teeth; she sits on the floor laughing with childlike abandon at *I Love Lucy*, a quintessentially 'all-American' TV sitcom. He enjoys her spontaneity and sense of fun. In their first sexual contact he makes no demands and passively enjoys what she does for him off camera. Reversing traditional romantic narratives, in which sex is the intense culmination of a relationship, here sex is to be recolonised by love. The disappointments of the 'sexual revolution' in a harshly materialistic world are assuaged. Sex per se is no longer a 'big deal', but its meaning is.

Edward is transformed by Vivian's influence from a 'workaholic' financial predator into a 'caring capitalist'; their

Pretty Woman: Julia Roberts in Gary Marshall's hugely successful 'Cinderella story' of the 1990s

sex scenes are intimate therapeutic sessions. Vivian, on the other hand, is empowered by Edward's money to become the person she already was, but disguised by cheap clothes and a wig. Money is not everything, the film asserts (in Hollywood's version of sociologist Karl Marx's famous criticism of capitalism as dissolving human relations in icy waters of cash calculation), but beautiful clothes are nice! With the help of the hotel manager, she adjusts to the etiquette of wealthy living; she metamorphoses into a radiant social 'beauty' while retaining her 'naturalness'.

One of the most crucial tests occurs when Edward takes Vivian to the opera: will she love it and reveal her spiritual depth? She cries in all the right places.

Edward and Vivian recognise that their respective worlds are both based on monetary exchange. They both 'screw people for money', he says; she compares his business methods to her way of dealing with prostitution. The people in Edward's world are coldly materialistic. The film proposes love as its 'philosopher's stone' – matter (money, sex) is infused with life-enhancing meaning. Capitalism becomes humane, while sex is restored to its role in companionate relationships and rescued from monetary calculations. Having experienced love, Vivian refuses to become Edward's 'kept woman' if she cannot have 'the fairy tale' of rescue, and resolves to 'go back to school'. But she gets the fairy tale, to the sounds of *La Traviata*. Edward overcomes his fear of heights and, a bouquet of flowers in hand, climbs the fire escape to her 'tower' to rescue her. In a show of modern gender mutuality, she tells him that she will 'rescue him right back'.

It could have been a critique of contemporary society – the metaphor of prostitution is a potentially subversive trope – but it is neutralised by precisely the mechanisms it claims to criticise (a commercial calculation by a media conglomerate about the pleasures 'punters' will pay for). Vivian's motives for becoming a 'hooker' are vague and unconvincing. An earlier script hints that her father was abusive and contained a sequence where she describes the 'weirdos' she encounters doing street sex work. The disappearance of these wider references to men closes down issues of male violence. Neither is there a hint in the film of real economic forces – did not the industries and communities trashed by real-life corporate raiders in the 1980s produce real 'Vivian Wards' and drug-abusing 'Kits'? Dissing materialism is undermined by the film's masturbatory enthusiasm for shopping as nirvana; Edward takes Vivian into a fashion shop and reduces the manager to an obsequious jelly by saying that he is going to spend a 'really obscene' amount of money. To the sound of Roy Orbison's upbeat 'Pretty Woman' song, a fast-paced montage delights us with Vivian's 'fashion show', and any 'sisterhood' with 'Skinny Marie' (the girl in the dumpster) dissolves in an acid of designer labels. The film certainly does not envision women, sex workers and others working together to address our 'sexual fix'. As long as love tempers capitalism, and it produces good clothes, we should not lose hope for a more humane world.

Yet, for all its contradictions and evasions, it does at least treat its two 'hookers' as human beings. Some critics lambasted it for glamorising prostitution and for not being a 'horror story' of abuse and degradation. But the 'reality' of prostitution is not exclusively 'crack whores' and misogynists out to abuse them. Although her past is thinly sketched, Vivian's character does propose that there is no impermeable line between 'ordinary women' and 'prostitute women', and that 'whore' is not an essence but a situation. It undermines the 'otherness' of prostitution. Equally, one can deride Edward as 'unrealisitic', but assuming that clients are 'perverts' or 'misfits' is neither true nor constructive; research is unanimous that, while there are disturbed and even murderous clients, most are 'average men', often married, and they come from all walks of life.

6.6 Independent film

The 1950s and 1960s saw a significant growth in film-making outside of mainstream industries; this was partly due to cheaper equipment (16 mm, Super 8, video), but also linked to the social changes of the time. Working with small budgets and unknown performers, and driven by artistic and political rather than commercial motives, a number of directors (Maya Deren, John Cassavetes, Shirley Clarke) pioneered an important sector of films that aim at niche audiences of committed film-goers (sometimes self-identified subculturally such as gay and lesbian). These films can explore issues in a more uninhibited way than big profit-driven films. From this sector (and from directors whose sensibility is formed by it)

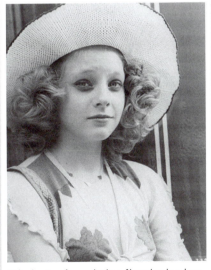

With relaxation of censorship laws, film-makers have been able to explore prostitution more freely. Jodi Foster plays a teenage prostitute in the Scorsese classic *Taxi Driver*

Films expressing their perspective on the sex industry have been made by sex workers, but these have received extremely limited distribution. Occasionally British TV documentaries have given opportunities for sex workers to articulate the meanings they attach to their work – for example, a recent documentary about Margaret MacDonald included interviews in which she described her career as a 'madam' and claimed that she, her team of well-paid 'escorts' and the clients did not suffer any harm from what were consensual transactions.

have come films in which prostitution and other types of sex work (stripping, phone sex) are treated in complex and exploratory ways: *The Naked Kiss* (Samuel Fuller, 1964), *Suspicious River* (Lynne Stopkewich, 2000), *The Center of the World* (Wayne Wang, 2001), *Dancing at the Blue Iguana* (Michael Radford, 2000), *Girl 6* (Spike Lee, 1996) and *Claire Dolan* (Lodge H. Kerrigan, 1998). Some independent films choose to depict sex work as exploitation with unprecedented visceral impact. It may be the central focus of a film (as in Lukas Moodysson's harrowing *Lilya 4-Ever*, 2002) or an element in portrayals of modern urban 'infernos'. In Scorsese's *Taxi Driver* (1976) child prostitute Iris becomes the catalyst for Travis Bickle's violently cathartic 'rescue'. In these narratives, the social circumstances that breed poverty, drug abuse and teenage alienation stand accused – economic collapse, urban decay, adult neglect of young people's needs and the predatory behaviour of men. But the prostitute characters, whatever their fate, are not represented simply as victims; they have inner lives. Other films, such as *Dancing at the Blue Iguana*, focus on the 'mundane' world of sex work as work. In *Iguana*, the club is a site of self-discovery, companionship, courage, good times as well as boredom, and love as well as hurt. Some films are interested in the 'theatre of sex' as a whole, refusing to draw neat boundaries between 'sex work' (bad) and 'real sex' (good). Rather than positing sharp dichotomies, independent films such as *The Centre of the World* restore prostitution to a continuum in which all sex is 'work' – performance, negotiation, a field of power and control, selfhood and alienation – and 'prostitution' a dimension of all sexual interactions.

The following films are two contrasted examples.

6.7 *Stella Does Tricks* (Coky Giedroyc, 1996)

'*£140,000 of lottery cash for more vice on Four.*'
(Daily Mail, *22 April 1996, commenting on the financing of* Stella Does Tricks)

There are no 'pretty women' in Coky Giedroyc's debut film about prostitution, but there is haunting poetry. Based on a script by Scottish novelist A. L. Kennedy and produced by the BFI Production Board, in S*tella Does Tricks* Kelly Macdonald plays a teenage prostitute working the streets of contemporary

The brutal reality of street prostitution is exposed in the low-budget independent British film *Stella Does Tricks*

London. Like many low-budget films produced outside of the mainstream industry, it had only limited distribution.

Whereas *Pretty Woman* veils Vivian's past, and only perfunctorily sketches the nature of street sex work, *Stella Does Tricks* is a complex weave of her life as a prostitute, sudden flashbacks to her Glasgow childhood, and sequences in which realistic situations suddenly segue into scenes from Stella's inner life. She struggles with an abusive past and a bleak present to find a liveable future.

The opening scenes establish the film's tactics: dressed as a schoolgirl, Stella buys ice creams from a van; she takes them to a middle-aged man on a park bench – father and daughter? He holds the ice creams while she covers his lap with a newspaper so as to masturbate him discreetly. This is Mr Peters, her pimp, a cut-rate Machiavelli who senses that she eludes him in 'flights of fancy' and tries to control her dreams. Suddenly the scene is interrupted, without any textual markers (such as a dissolve), by what we realise must be a flashback of a young girl watching an inept performance by a stand-up comedian; it is Stella as child and her father. The juxtaposition opens up a 'forcefield' between her childhood memories and her present. After leaving Mr Peters, Stella joins other 'working girls' in a cheap café; she tells them a story – 'Edward wants extras again' – in which she plays a trick on a client. The 'girls' are amused, but predict that Peters will be furious when he hears. They are right; later he finds her and burns her arms with cigarettes.

Next day we witness another of Stella's 'tricks'. With obvious experience, she undresses a nervous middle-aged man and tells him to get into bed. He turns off the light, but she immediately switches it back on. She is in control, it seems, but when she goes into the bathroom she hallucinates her father and unsympathetic Auntie sitting in a living room waiting to question her. Suddenly we are back in the present; it was one of Stella's 'flights of fancy' and, as she looks at herself in the mirror, Donald comes in to say to her that she's a 'grand little fuck'. Perhaps he thinks she will be pleased, but it exemplifies what Hannah Arendt, writing of the apparent ordinariness of Nazi war criminals, called the 'banality of evil'. He's a 'monster' who does not look like one. Later, Stella vents her rage by breaking off windscreen wipers from parked cars, kicking in the cars' headlights before another flashback takes us to a rickety wooden pigeon loft. The child Stella is full of innocent enthusiasm as her father shows off his birds.

Stella is trapped in an abusive present, and haunted by her past. Rather than unfolding chronologically through a series of scenes logically consequent on one another, the plot illuminates her uncertain but persistent efforts to escape Mr Peters through these flashbacks which progressively unveil her relationship to her father and aunt. The final revelation, that she was sexually abused as a child, comes in the middle of a harrowing scene in which Mr Peters organises a gang rape as a punishment for Stella's determination to leave him. This flashback is all the more powerful because earlier flashbacks have shown her love for her father and his 'love' for her. But his 'love' was a dangerous thing; we see her struggling in his arms in the very pigeon loft where she had trusted him. Her troubled past frames her vulnerability and her resistance to the 'paternalism' of Peters. Realism is made subjective.

Can she escape? After her rape, she makes an attempt to start a life with Eddie, a young drug addict, moving into his

One of the men involved in Stella's rape is played by Shaun Williamson, an actor well known for his time in popular soap EastEnders; when I screened the film to a group of students, his presence clearly affected their response to the scene; in discussion afterwards it was obvious that it partly undermined the realism of the filmic event. This illustrates how performers can bring specific meanings to a narrative. It is an example of intertextuality.

shabby room and trying to cheer it up with plants, and she decides to exorcise the past by going with him to Glasgow to confront her father and Auntie. In a rare moment of comedy, they tease her aunt with inflated condoms (sternly puritanical, her aunt had nonetheless failed to protect her from her father); finally, surprising her father after another one of his dismal nightclub performances, she burns his genitals with lighter fuel. Back in London, she gets a job as a flower seller; one afternoon, she sees Peters with a young girl about to repeat the ice cream routine in the park. She calls the police, watching as he is arrested.

But Kennedy's script refuses a happy resolution. Eddie is weak and, despite his affection for Stella, 'pimps' her to a mate in exchange for drugs. Afterwards, while Eddie lies comatose on the bed, she sits in a chair and her father and Auntie 'appear' in the room to advise her to 'Take a pill' and 'It's for the best'; she commits suicide. In a coda, Stella is dressed in her father's clothes and, sitting on a stage, begins a stand-up routine; she says that she has not been having any dreams, but that 'nightmares count … I'm here to tell stories … picture the scene …'

Kelly Macdonald invests Stella with wit and mischief, a spirit of revolt which, despite everything that happens to her, makes her more than a victim. She is a survivor – of child abuse, of Peters and of unthinking men who think that she's a 'grand little fuck' – and only Eddie's betrayal, his 'intimate terror', finally breaks her will.

Some critics have wished for a more hopeful ending, but the film's 'poetic realism' is subjective and provisional rather than polemical. *Stella Does Tricks* is not a 'case study' despite the fact that there are real 'Stellas' in the streets of our cities; her fate is not asserted as an inevitable outcome. She made a decision that the audience has to reflect upon. Moreover, the coda disrupts the apparent closure of her suicide – Stella takes the stage as narrator. This device subverts the habitual coding of fictional scenes into 'real', 'subjective', 'present', 'past', 'cause', 'consequence', etc. Where is Stella meant to be? Hasn't she just died? Are these her final 'flights of fancy' as the overdose takes effect? Surely it is not supposed to be heaven? Is she about to tell us what we have just seen or another story?

Working Girls is an intimate portrait of a brothel by feminist Lizzie Borden

6.8 *Working Girls* (Lizzie Borden, 1986)

In contrast to *Pretty Woman* and *Stella Does Tricks*, both of which feature street prostitution, *Working Girls* is set in a middle-class brothel in New York. Choosing to avoid the extremes of either fairy-tale romance or grim abuse, it attempts to represent the 'mundane' world of sex work – a 'day in the life' of women who are neither coerced nor entertaining hopes of romance with the clients they meet. They know that what they do is work, in which their skills can earn good money, but which can also be stressful and hazardous; the extraordinary thing about them is their 'ordinariness'.

Made on a budget of $110,000, *Working Girls* was directed by US 'independent' film maker Lizzie Borden with a predominantly female crew. Borden is a self-identified lesbian-feminist who became interested in making a film about sex workers while working on her debut *Born in Flames* (1983). She learned that some of the women she was working with were doing sex work, and she began to talk to them about their experiences. During the 1980s, feminists were having fierce debates centred on sexuality, pornography and prostitution, and she was keen to contribute. For her, sexuality is 'the main arena of power and control between men and women', but she rejects what she sees as the attempt by some feminists to impose an orthodoxy.

Working Girls opens with a shot of Mollie (Louise Smith) in bed with her black girlfriend. She gets up to help a child prepare for school and does some work in a professional-looking darkroom, before cycling through traffic to work; she is dressed modestly and might be going to an office, library or school. There is no music to code the scene and the visual style is low-key, almost documentary in approach.

But Louise is not a photographer or a schoolteacher; she works in a brothel to support herself until a photographic career becomes viable. Her colleagues for the 'day shift' are Dawn, a young blonde who is working through college, and Gina, a reserved black woman. None of them is distinguishable from 'ordinary women' in either dress or mannerisms. They share a work situation and are mutually supportive, but are not friends; the only thing they have in common is their work. The brothel is simply a two-level modern apartment with a sitting room where they spend much of the time waiting for clients, a number of 'themed' bedrooms and a kitchen. They have a stock of towels, and Mollie has to go out occasionally to stock up with condoms, dental dams and other tools of the trade. The telephone rarely stops ringing.

The rhythm of the film is the rhythm of their day: boredom can easily set in as they wait, and to pass the time between clients they chat about this and that, including the job and the brothel's 'madam', Lucy. In one conversation Mollie expresses her dislike of terms such as 'whore' and 'prostitute', she prefers 'working girl' because that is what she feels she does; she needs the money and appreciates the time flexibility. Dawn announces unselfconsciously that she wants to be a lawyer, which makes the others smile affectionately because she does not appear to see the irony. We learn that Dawn and Molly do not tell their partners what they do, for fear of their reactions. Gina, on the other hand, was honest with her boyfriend, but feels that it ended their relationship because he seemed to accept it too easily; she felt that, if he really loved her, he ought to have wanted her to stop. On gender relations, Mollie muses that sex work has cured her of her fear of men. As long, she says, as you know what their 'sexual trip' is, you can deal with them. These 'working girls' are neither coerced nor 'free'; prostitution is not their life, and they reflect on it with the ambivalence that most people feel about their jobs.

Similar to any workers, there are tensions between them and with their employer over working conditions, pace of work and remuneration. Lucy, who turns up to keep an eye on business, clearly has middle-class pretensions; she is outraged at what she thinks is Dawn's lack of sophistication in deportment and speech. As an entrepreneur, she wants to work the 'girls' hard, and to maximise profitability, even if it puts them under strain as the day wears on. Like any workplace, there are crises when an employee is late or is ill.

Other women turn up for shifts, which allows the film to broaden its perspective. Mary, a new girl who is obviously nervous, is upset when she gets a phone call from her child and realises that the baby-sitter has let her down. Lucy is angry because some of the clients are there, and tells Mary that 'men don't want to know about problems', so evoking a world of single mothers struggling to make ends meet. April is experienced, but has been away for a while having been robbed and beaten; she feels that Mollie looks down on her

French philosopher Michel Foucault argued that all human interactions are traversed by relations of power; or, as feminists have said, 'the personal is the political'.

and, in a tense exchange, calls her a 'college girl', implying class differences in the options that women have. The importance of 'race' is painfully signalled by the arrival of Debbie, a black woman with much darker skin than Gina; none of the men chooses her, including a black client who looks at her with especial disdain. 'Double standards' are more complex than one realised – the virgin/whore, good girl/bad girl structure intersects with differences in age, class and race.

A central feature of *Working Girls* is Molly's sexual transactions with her clients, encounters which Borden clearly intends us to see as 'typical' rather than 'exceptional'. The men are middle-class individuals who, for the most part, know exactly what they have come for and expect an efficient service for their money. They would pass unremarked in a prosperous doctor's surgery. Some have been before and know the woman they want to see again; others would like variety. Like any group of men, they vary in self-confidence and in their attitude to women. Some are friendly and easygoing; others are more demanding and self-centred. Having said this, the 'ordinariness' of the men far from legitimises them, and focusing on the typical rather than the unusual allows the film to convey a powerful sense of the 'micro politics' of sex.

The importance of the encounters is emphasised by Borden's decision to treat them differently from the other scenes. While the conversations are filmed in a relaxed, observational way, the bedroom scenes are 'stylised' both visually and aurally. Roma Baran's arhythmic and atonal music effectively 'triggers' a heightened mode of attention to what is on the screen (it is not conventionally 'dramatic', but codes the scenes as important), while the editing abbreviates the scenes into a set of 'emblematic' moments ('snapshots') as well as, in their 'clipped' pace, underlining Mollie's attempt to maintain a tight control over what takes place.

Once in the bedroom, Molly is pleasant but coolly professional, almost ritualistic. The music adds to the sense that one is in a 'theatre'. All of her actions are precise, and convey a sense of the importance to her of control and detachment. She is not 'selling her body', but giving conditional access to it for a restricted amount of time.

Some of her clients are easy to deal with: Bob is polite, enjoys posing with her in front of a mirror, and we see them briefly have intercourse, while Neil is shy, a teacher, and has brought her a gift. An older man, Joseph, is a highly educated university administrator and recognises that Molly is intelligent; he enjoys being dominated by her for the precise time he has paid for before resuming his social role. Even 'Fantasy Fred', despite his rather unusual requests for Molly to pretend to be a blind virgin, is harmless. Other clients are more difficult: an elderly Asian man, one of three men who have never visited the brothel before, refuses to shower and Molly has to wash him. He tells her to 'suck me' with 'no rubber', and she has to retain her composure while refusing to comply. She masturbates him, cleans up the semen and gets rid of him, but her stress level has risen.

The film suggests that the most wounding clients of all in Molly's experience are not the ones with whom she has the most anonymous relationships (where she is closest to being a 'sex object'), or even the obviously awkward ones who ask for things she will not do. Rather, they are the men whose demands are the most 'psychological' and who, either inadvertently or deliberately, cross the boundary she tries to maintain between her sex-worker role and herself as a complete person. These encounters in the film are the most provocative ones: Jerry is a 'construction boss' and flush with money; he clearly enjoys the power to pay for sex and likes, he reminds the 'girls', 'to be the centre of attention'. He tells 'hooker jokes' and jokes about bloody tampons. He can afford a 'threesome' with Molly and Gina; Molly finds it hard to resist trying to 'put him down' – which is understandable, but a weakening of her control. Elliott, on the other hand, is 'nice' and tells Molly that he really likes her, hoping they can have a real relationship. 'Can we meet outside here?' he asks, and gives her his card. He also wants her to have a real orgasm during their session ('There's always a first time.'). Not satisfied with paid sex, he wants to buy Molly's real feelings and respect. He makes a 'category mistake' which she finds unsettling.

Most troubling of all her clients – her resistance is reduced after a harder shift than usual – is Paul. He is a good-looking and articulate musician who has just returned from a concert tour; intelligent and cultured, he would appear to have more in common with Molly than her other clients. Like Elliott, he too tells her that he would like to 'get together on the outside', but is more insistent: 'You're not like the others … you're

In interviews with sociologists and in autobiographies, sex workers describe various psychological strategies and routines which they may employ in order to distance their work role from the rest of their lives. These include refusing to kiss, using a professional name, the use of condoms as a symbolic as well as health barrier, washing and changing clothes.

Karl Marx proposed that the basis of capitalism is the extraction of more economic value from a worker than that person is paid in wages – he called this 'surplus value'.

intelligent …. we could be brother and sister.' She deflects him politely, but he will not let go and challenges her: 'Why are you afraid to see me on equal terms?' This emotional invasiveness finally subverts Molly's detachment and she lets her role mask slip to tell him that she feels he does not like women and cannot see them as equals. A real relationship between them would not work. Stung, he calls her a 'whore', and when she objects he insists, 'For 50 bucks you're a whore.' Later she cries; he has succeeded in getting 'under her skin' and one feels that this was what he wanted to do, what he had really paid for.

At the end of her shift, Molly adds up her money and prepares to go. She asks Lucy, 'Have you ever heard of surplus value?' and announces that she will not be coming back. Cycling home, she is smiling; she buys some flowers for her girlfriend; the last shot shows her in bed with her lover. One is left wondering whether she will ever change her mind, and what Dawn and Gina will make of their lives.

Working Girls successfully break downs any rigid ontology of 'prostitute' as a special type of person, to undermine 'whore stigma', and to put the men who pay for sex into the frame. Prostitution, the film asserts, is not about an unusual type of woman, nor about two special types of women and men, but about an encounter between women and men which, although a specific type of encounter, is not in some other dimension from supposedly 'normal' sexual relationships. All sexual relationships involve expectations and negotiations; sex is often embedded in other forms of exchange, sometimes coercive ones; sex can be casual and anonymous, or just a chore, outside of sex work. Unsafe sex can be as common outside of sex work as within it.

Sex workers' rights activists welcomed the film for its representation of Molly, Dawn and Gina as real women. They applauded Borden's endorsement, in interviews she gave at the time of the release of the film, of the decriminalisation of prostitution in the United States. Sex workers should be treated as workers who require health and safety protection, not police records, she was quoted as saying.

Reading representations is never neutral. All criticism is made from a specific point of view, on the basis of assumptions one makes about the world. Interpreting films about prostitution depends on answers to many questions: Is it a form of slavery? Is it morally degrading? Is it an indictment of society? Of men? Can it be consensual? Is it a form of work? Should it be decriminalised? Are consensual sex workers pioneers of sexual freedom? I would argue that, at a minimum, one should recognise that prostitution is a highly complex phenomenon and that no one representation can be the 'truth'. In my view, the most socially constructive representations are those which encourage us to challenge the 'otherness' of prostitution. McKeganey and Barnard (1996) express it well when they criticise those who assume that:

> ... the woman who sells sex is never our mother, our daughter, or our sister but some anonymous other who is infinitely more desperate than those we love ... the man who buys sex is never our father, brother, husband or boyfriend, but another whom we do not know and may not even wish to know.

We should have the courage and honesty to recognise ourselves in the 'others' ...

References

McKeganey, Neil P., & Marina Barnard, *Sex Work on the Streets* (Oxford: Oxford University Press, 1996).

MacLeod, Eileen, *Women Working: Prostitution Now* (London: Croom Helm, 1982).

Pascall, J., & C. Jeavons, *Pictorial History of Sex* (London: Hamlyn, 1975).

Roberts, Nicki, *The Front Line* (London: Grafton, 1986).

Rosen, Marjorie, *Popcorn Venus* (London: Peter Owen, 1973).

Selected further reading

Chapkis, Wendy, *Live Sex Acts* (London: Cassell, 1997).

Jacobs, Lea, *The Wages of Sin* (California: University of California, 1995).

Leff, Leonard J., & Jerold L. Simmons, *The Dame in the Kimono: Hollywood, Censorship and the Production Code* (London: Weidenfeld & Nicolson, 1990).

Phoenix, Joanna, *Making Sense of Prostitution* (London: Palgrave, 1999).

Ringdal, Nils, *Love for Sale: A World History of Prostitution* (London: Atlantic Books, 2004).

Scambler, Graham, & Annette Scambler (eds), *Rethinking Prostitution: Purchasing Sex in the 1990s* (London: Routledge, 1997).

7. Roughs and Respectables: Representing the 'Other'

WENDY HELSBY

There is a group of people who leave rubbish around encouraging scavenging rats. This group can be unruly, get drunk and fight. They make themselves homeless by arguing with others and not following the rules of society. They can be very smelly with uncivilised personal habits, such as leaving their bodily fluids around the streets. They may intimidate elderly and vulnerable people by their language, loudness and by acting as a group. Who are they?

In this chapter the convention of lower case 'g' is used for 'gypsy', but please note the comment on p. 153 by Richard O'Neill.

Did you think about groups such as football supporters? It could of course be a description of college students! This description is a gross simplification with the most negative aspects being selected. As with all stereotypes it has reduced complex cultural codes to simple and easily consumed negative signs that could be assigned to several groups whom society may use as scapegoats in particular situations.

Understandably, given the time and cost pressures on media producers, sometimes a shorthand is used that ignores the complexity of drawing boundaries and can limit representation of groups to a few cartoon-style strokes such as those above. This 'lazy' attitude means that there is a tendency in the media to use handy stereotypes that produce one-dimensional images. In this discussion we will be looking at how beliefs surrounding a group who are usually outside our experience are created through such media discourses.

If you belong to a minority or less powerful group you will be defined by images and language produced by more powerful voices. This was, for example, the case in the classic Hollywood period with groups such as African, Chinese and Native Americans. Here they were marginalised, and their very absence or invisibility was also a form of representation. Disabled people have also often commented about their absence on the screen. Stereotypes of a particular group can become the norm. Members will begin to believe the mediated version, even if they know that this stereotype is not the reality of their own situation. So through powerful forms of construction and repetition the image might appear to become a reality. The prophecy is fulfilled.

If we can so easily believe or play to our own stereotype, you can see then how we can easily believe the stereotypes of other cultures, particularly when they invade our space as in the terrorist activity of 9/11 and those they claim to represent. Ask any group to list words and images about the inhabitants of regions such as the Balkans, the Middle East and Africa, and they will probably come up with quite similar lists, most of which they have gained from the media because they will have had no personal experience of these people. Some cultures we may categorise in ways such as 'asylum seekers', 'terrorists', 'illegal immigrants', 'fundamentalists' and so on. But this is not a one-way traffic, from the West to a view of the rest. In other circumstances the West may be the minority or other, and experience stereotyping and scapegoating as the demonised group. This is certainly how African states have represented the Western imperialists.

Here, however, we are concerned with how powerful media agencies in the West can reproduce and confirm ideas of difference and allow difference to be defined against such norms as the WASP (White Anglo-Saxon Protestant), and how this has underpinned our understanding of the concept of otherness.

So, first, how do we view ourselves?

With the recent Gulf wars there have been many stories about the British in conflict. How do we see ourselves as a nation in time of war? The stiff upper lip, for example, has been a standard signifier of the British character in many texts particularly in World War II films and others such as *Zulu* (Cy Endfield, 1964). To such an extent is this recognised that it is also used to lampoon or satirise the British character, as in *Blackadder Goes Forth: Regeneration* (BBC1), *It Ain't*

▶ Draw up a list of attributes and attitudes of a stereotypical Briton. There are of course several stereotypes, depending upon the situation. Compare your list with others — you will probably find there are similarities. ●

Half Hot Mum (BBC1, 1974) and *Dad's Army* (BBC1). Do you believe it really exists? Or is it a construction and therefore ideological and mythic in its effect? Look at the language used in newspapers in recent conflicts. What image is conveyed through language such as 'Our Boys under Fire' (*Daily Express*, 21 March 2003)?

Such beliefs about us and others are mediated through many forms, including photographs, music, moving images, language and print. When they concern those about whom we know little, those whom we regard as 'foreign' or 'different' and who live outside our perceived boundaries, they can be powerful signifiers, as with the 'enemy' in war texts. But the 'other' can also include people within our own nation state; where a minority group is represented we can see a process of marginalisation, stereotyping and even exclusion. There are many within society who can be defined as marginal because of their race, religion, ethnicity or other grouping. When we look at how their diversity is represented we often see it reduced to 'like us or not like us'. How can we get a rounded and multifaceted representation that is a 'polyvocal', or a many voices, view? (An alternative view is explored in Chapter 9 on Beyond Britishness.)

In order to explore the way that such marginalisation works in a complex interaction of texts and ideas (intertextuality), this section looks at a diasporic group (a dispersed people with similar identity) who traverse national boundaries and who have an ambivalent relationship to the dominant (hegemonic) powers. This is the gypsy, or traveller, 'nation'.

Gypsies originated in the Punjab in northern India and migrated through Persia (Iran) to Egypt, hence the name 'gypsies'. They further migrated into Europe, some through Romania, and thus are called Romanies, Romani or Rom. Their reach extends over all of Europe from Scandinavian countries to the Iberian peninsula, as well as in Britain and the United States. The diaspora also exists in many other areas. They are traditionally a migrating people; however, many have permanent homes. Even within the gypsy diaspora there are often different languages and traditions, as they have been assimilated into local religions and cultures.

The gypsy as itinerant or irritant?

▶ Have you ever felt marginalised? Have you ever been in the position of being in the minority? What did it feel like? Describe the experience. ●

▶ It is possible that you have already attached images and beliefs to the group referred to as gypsies. Before reading further, try listing the ideas and images that your mind conjures up. Divide them into negative and positive groups. Write down any facts that you know about gypsies. After reading this chapter, come back and review your list and ask yourself whether you would change anything. ●

7.1 'Travellers are not people'

You may be asking the question: Why are these issues around a minority group of only about 100,000 in Britain important? 'Travellers are not people' is a quotation from an *Open Space* television documentary which showed video letters between two women – one a gypsy, the other a non-gypsy. Does this quotation remind you of the rhetoric of such regimes as Nazism? Half a million gypsies were murdered in the Holocaust because they were represented to the German nation as being not 'human'. Today there is still the whiff of this viewpoint even in 'civilised' societies. Martin Clayton (2002) reports a right-wing politician, Miroslav Sladek, as saying in the Czech Parliament, 'Gypsies should be subject to prosecution starting from the time of their birth because being born is practically their biggest crime.'

7.2 An outsider's view

What is the difference between race and ethnicity? Are gypsies an ethnic minority or a racial group? This is a real semantic dilemma. You can find detailed discussions about the ways such terms have been used both scientifically and ideologically in sociological books such as Robert Miles's *Racism* (1989). Robyn Wiegman concludes that the difference is as follows: 'Where ethnicity provides the means for differentiation based on culture, language, and national origins, race renders the reduction of human differences to innate, biological phenomena …' (p. 160).

What facts reaffirm or challenge the dominant views of the people we term gypsies as a race or ethnic group? This is particularly difficult to assess when there are many groups of travellers, such as the New Age traveller, who contribute in different ways to the imagery and beliefs surrounding those people who do not conform to society's mores. The images become muddied as each group blurs into the other. Professor Thomas Acton says, 'whereas most racism consists of complaining that people resemble too much various ethnic stereotypes when it comes to gypsies the most common racist complaint is that they do not resemble the historic stereotype of "the true gypsy". For example, Irish and Scottish travellers, or tinkers, are often regarded by some as inauthentic because they do not conform to the gypsy stereotype by wearing particular 'folkloric' clothes; however, they have in fact been recognised officially by the Irish state as an ethnic group in their own right.

Who do you regard as a true gypsy? Do you believe that most travellers you see on the roadside are 'not real gypsies', not authentic, but really vagabond scroungers? Where did your views originate? Possibly they come from local newspapers, word of mouth, television dramas or maybe from children's books and comics. I certainly remember a story about a gypsy girl being a featured series in the comic *School Friend*. Carla Stevens (1979) shows how literature aimed at young people begins to develop beliefs about others: 'it should be pointed out that one of the main sources of stereotypes is fiction in which gypsies play "minor" roles' (p. 78).

To counteract some of these assumptions here are some facts about the gypsy nation:

- Around half a million gypsies were murdered in the Holocaust.
- Between 50,000 and 100,000 gypsies live in North America.
- The British 1968 Caravan Sites Act said that councils must provide adequate accommodation for persons of a nomadic habit of life – gypsy, New Age, fairground travellers. (By 1989 only six local authorities had done this.)
- In Britain, under the 1986 Public Order Act Section 39 it is a criminal offence not to leave land or to return in three months when ordered off by the police (brought in to deal with New Age travellers, but used against gypsies).
- Britain's 1994 Criminal Justice Act has been used to eliminate gypsy meetings and sites.
- Between 1986 and 1993, 67 per cent of traditional travellers sites disappeared in the United Kingdom.
- Ninety per cent of gypsy children in France are illiterate (Carla Stevens).
- Sixty-two per cent of gypsy children were placed in schools for the mentally disturbed in the Czech Republic (K. Connolly in the *Guardian*, 19 April 2000).
- In the Czech Republic gypsy children often start school with little knowledge of Czech and with an oral rather than written culture. They are unable to succeed at IQ tests which do not take account of cultural and linguistic

▶ Here is an official Local Authority definition. Read it, then ask yourself what other groups it could refer to if the word 'gypsy' were taken out.

A gypsy is a person capable of being a member of a racial group:

1. Long shared history, with a conscious sense of distinctness
2. Cultural tradition, including family and social customs and manners; but not necessarily religious observation
3. A common geographical origin or small number of common ancestors
4. A common language
5. A common literature, including folk lore or tradition
6. A common religion. A number of gypsies are taking an interest in religion e.g. born-again Christians
7. A minority population
8. Membership by birth or adherence

Gypsy Law Part 1: The Meaning of 'Gypsy', Alec Samuels JP Barrister BA (Cantab), Local Government Review 13 April 1991 ●

differences. 'Romany children simply do not have a high enough IQ to manage normal schooling ... they stick together, they get married in those large families and they have children with genetic problems.' – Marta Tepla of the Department of Special Schools in the Ministry of Education ('Czech Gypsies Begin Test Case for Pupils Classed as Retarded', *Guardian*, 19 April 2000).

- Thousands of gypsies (called Roms in Eastern Europe) had to flee Kosovo, as they became scapegoats for the two warring factions during the Balkan conflict in the 1990s.
- Mob violence in Romania resulted in hundreds of Rom deaths in the post-Ceausescu period.
- The Society for Threatened Peoples based in Gottingen has documented twenty pogroms against Romanian Romanies in 1990 and 1991 ('Gypsy Road to Nowhere', *Guardian*, 2 October 1992).

These brief facts indicate both how gypsies are perceived and how they are widely marginalised. The reasons why these groups are marginalised lie in the history of society across Europe. Pre-sixteenth century Europe accepted the nomad, such as the wandering peddlers, troubadours and minstrels of the medieval period, as part of the commercial world. Gypsies were part of these groups welcomed for their skills as good smiths who repaired and made swords, blades, pots and pans. The creation of the European nation-state through the sixteenth century led to outlawing of this type of lifestyle. As a result gypsies often settled down into villages, especially in Central Europe. They developed their musical skills and were hired for celebrations and entertainment. This role is seen in films discussed later – *Black Cat, White Cat* (Emir Kusturica, 1998) and *The Crazy Stranger* (Tony Gatlif, 1997) – and also often referred to in literary texts. Others continued to travel and trade both within and across the boundaries of the nation-state; however, events in the twentieth century have made this way of life increasingly untenable.

7.3 The romantic and the demon: gypsies in stories

Stories about gypsies usually position them at the extremes – black or white, bad or good; there are rarely shades of grey. Negative representations of gypsies have a long literary tradition. In Jane Austen's *Emma* (1816) a young lady is harassed by a group of gypsies on the roadside. This is an example in adult literature of a minor role but a powerful representation of gypsies (remember what Carla Stevens said on gypsy minor roles in children's literature) and has continued as each new medium appeared. *Emma* and its description of the gypsies will not only have been read, but will also have been seen by millions of people in television and film adaptations.

One of the earliest and at the time most popular fictional films in which another negative image of a gypsy appeared was *Rescued by Rover* (Cecil Hepworth, 1905). Hepworth based his story on the nineteenth-century folk myth of gypsies stealing children. This film tells the story of the kidnapping of a baby by a gypsy woman. The baby is found by Rover the dog, rescued from the craven gypsy woman and restored to the family.

More recent representations of travelling groups were seen in *Snatch* (Guy Ritchie, 2000), which has a theme of a gypsy fighter (Brad Pitt) seeking revenge, and *Twin Town* (Kevin Allen, 1997), which is set in Wales and focuses on 'trailer trash'. Most British gypsies would not identify with either of the groups in these two films. Outsiders, on the other hand, would probably believe them to have similar backgrounds and traits.

But there are positive as well as negative connotations that coalesce around the image of the gypsy. In Britain we still have the romantic notion of the exotic free-wheeling life of the open road, rather as Toad saw it in the book *Wind in the Willows* (Kenneth Grahame, 1903). These images call upon the heritage and nostalgia of the painted gypsy caravan pulled by a horse along country lanes. They reflect the ideology of a carefree existence and of groups at one with nature, as represented in the BBC Children's Hour radio programmes based on the books in the series *Out with Romany* (Bramwell Evens). Today you can even buy this type of holiday.

'Meg Merrilies', a poem by John Keats and read by thousands of school children, was another one of the many other contributions to the romanticised image of the open road. Other references are the Hungarian gypsy violinist playing romantic tunes at restaurant tables; flamboyant dances around camp fires; men with earrings and scarves; women with full, colourful skirts and shawls; and fortune

The gypsy woman conforms to the stereotype and steals the baby in *Rescued by Rover*

Marlene Dietrich plays a fortune teller in *Touch of Evil*

tellers such as the famous Gypsy Rose Lee. In this vein local newspapers report positively on gypsy horse fairs such as Stow and Appleby Fair, while the Cirque Eloize based its *Nomade* (2003) performance on just such a gypsy theme. These images are powerful conveyers of 'mythic' representation, although today they are not the reality for most of the 100,000 gypsies living in the United Kingdom. There are, however, still remnants of this life style to be seen. Within a few miles of where I am writing there are traditional gypsies with painted horse-drawn caravans living on the grass verges of country roads. On the other hand, a few miles in the other directions there is constant aggravation between local town residents and 'pikeys' in their motorised caravans. A few years ago the story of the farmer Tony Martin and the killing of Fred Barras, who belonged to a settled travelling family, was headline news. This tells us something about the news values used by the newspapers, but also how the stereotyping through discourses which include words such as 'pikey' circulate and are constructed through the media.

It is these 'modern' groups with their large caravans, televisions, cars and lorries who regularly appear in local newspapers. It seems that for travellers it is wrong that they should be using the advantages of modern life, and it is rare that positive stories are circulated, except where traditional activities are reported such as horse fairs. Travellers are usually newsworthy only as problems. During the writing of this chapter, there has been at least one story a week in the local news about gypsies or travellers camping in inconvenient or illegal locations. In March 2005 the *Sun* mounted a 'campaign to end the gipsy [*sic*] camp free-for-all' ('Gipsies: 1,000s Join Our Fight', 11 March 2005), and in the same paper Richard Littlejohn claimed that 'Middle England is to be turned into a giant Soweto for wealthy gipsies.' This was illustrated by aerial shots of campsites. The issue has been taken up in television drama. The police series *55 Degrees North* had an episode about a land dispute involving Irish travellers (BBC1, 12 June 2005).

Another example of selection and bias in the media was a programme broadcast on American Public Radio in the United States in February 1997. It was called *Sound and Spirit of the Gypsies*. The programme played to the stereotype of the romantic musical but illiterate gypsy with special magical

'Pikey' is one of the negative words associated with gypsies that has an historical root. Geoffrey Chaucer used the word 'piked' to mean 'stole' in 'The Legend of Good Women'. About 700 years later the word was also used in an article about the Gulf War, 'There'll be more fighting than at a Pikey's wedding' ('Countdown to Battle', *Mail on Sunday*, 16 March 2003). This shows how meanings of words can be used to stereotype. In this case, people who fight and steal equals 'pikeys'.

powers, but it also pointed out that they were well known for stealing chickens. This item led to a complaint from the Romani organisation in the United States. 'There are roughly one million Roma living in the USA … would you … hire a person you thought had such different ethics that they thought it OK to steal … How do you think your program will affect their prospects? We are not fictional characters, we are real human beings …' (www.romani.org/local/ rom_stereotype.html).

It is not often we hear how it feels to be one of the marginalised or 'deviant' group. Here Richard O'Neill, a gypsy from the North of England, gives an insider's view:

> Gypsies have always been quick to change and develop as a group. My dad was born in a horse-drawn wagon in 1925. He learned to drive and got an aluminium caravan as soon as he could and then a house when that was a better option for his business. We are not seen as the rapidly changing people that we really are with many of our kids at university, settled in houses with professions and established businesses (some of which employ many non-Gypsies). Instead we are seen as deeply sentimental noble savages adrift in a modern world which we don't understand; or outlaws and self imposed outcasts who move around and illegally camp leaving large amounts of rubbish and crime in our wake. (Richard O'Neill, Internet interview, 22 May 2003)

As the gypsy woman in the *Open Space* programme said, 'We get blamed for everybody's rubbish.'

Why is this group perceived as such a pariah in a society such as ours where, unlike other areas such as the Balkans, there are no major disturbances and less need to scapegoat? Fred Barras died because he had illegally entered the farmer's house and was shot by the owner. The death of another young boy, Johnny Delaney, reported in the *Guardian* as the 'Brutal Death of a Travelling Child', shows the tragic consequences of stereotyping where no crime was being committed. The report included this quotation:

> 'We can't think why anybody would attack him except because he was a traveller. No matter how much we have, we are still dirty Gypsy bastards. No matter how good you can be

The UK Press Complaints Commission guidelines say that newspapers 'must avoid publishing details of a person's race, colour, religion, sexual orientation, physical or mental illness or disability unless relevant to the story' (www.pcc.org.uk). The Commission for Racial Equality (CRE) has produced a leaflet *Travellers, Gypsies and the Good Practice Guide from the Commission for Racial Equality* (1998). Many newspapers avoided using the word 'gypsy' or 'traveller' in their reporting of the Martin/Barras case, but on Martin's release the gypsy revenge story became a main angle for the tabloid newspapers.

to people, they still treat us the same way … People pick on us because of where we come from … They don't want to know you. It's just like being a racist against a black person. You can't blame everyone for what someone else has done. It's all true hatred. But if you cut one another you will bleed and we all bleed the same stuff …' (Guardian, 10 June 2003)

Those people who read the March 2005 editions of the *Sun* would undoubtedly believe the 'sprawling … squalid … sewage' image. Of the many opinions quoted, not one appears from the side of the gypsies; we are not asked to identify with their problems.

In the 1990s there was major concern about the plight of gypsies in Eastern European countries, and Western newspapers ran sympathetic stories about them. But negative national coverage began to occur when they became more visible in our cities and invaded our 'space', such as with incidents of begging by European gypsy families. Andrew Marr, in an article entitled 'Our Ugly Intolerance' (*Observer*, 19 March 2000), compared the treatment of two women singing for money in public spaces in London. One was singing in the street in Covent Garden, accompanied by a tape and being showered with coins; the other was dressed in richly coloured skirt and headscarf and singing in the Tube train. She was told: 'Oh, shut up and leave us alone.' Marr sees the difference as one of culture and isolationism. With one we were being entertained; with the other we were being made aware of a social conscience. We find the first easier to live with than the second. The Roma singer stood 'for an uncountable army of the poor'.

More recently the *Daily Express* (20 January 2004) had the following story about Romanian gypsies: '1.6 million gipsies [*sic*] ready to flood in … Gipsies prepare to invade Britain.' What do English gypsies feel about this type of reporting? Richard O'Neill, as a member of the gypsy community, states: 'Anytime the word Gypsy is mentioned then it affects us and interests us. The bizarre upside to all of the illegal immigrant and migrant coverage means that English Gypsies appear more attractive, the lesser of two evils.'

Once we start to look at a minority group such as gypsies in a more rational way we can see that there are probably many factors that coalesce to create such discourses. Gypsies are not an organised group with a leader and hierarchy that accords with our views of how society should be regulated. They are often mobile and dispersed, and therefore do not become numbered and accountable by institutions. Their mobility means that they have often been associated with marginal groups such as refugees and immigrants. As we have already noted there is also a confusion between different travelling groups and their names – New Age travellers, 'horse-drawns', 'crusties', pikeys and tinkers. Often names are used generically connoting a travelling lifestyle, and this conflates groups who do not have the same ethnic background as the gypsy and who may have taken up travelling for other reasons, such as economic or lifestyle, rather than as an inherited way of life. Whatever their reasons, in effect all these people are all tarred with the same brush of difference.

One of the key images circulating around these travelling groups is that of scroungers or spongers who get something for nothing because they work outside of the economic systems. In the rural past, however, farmers welcomed gypsies as itinerant labourers, as they provided an additional workforce without the problems of accommodation and employment contracts. They moved seasonally across the country working on the harvests. Today this work is more often done by itinerant labour from Eastern European countries and other areas. Householders who needed knives sharpening and pots mended – the old smithy skills – and other odd jobs used their services. In a pre-motorised era they provided horses. It is obvious that roles such as knife sharpening, itinerant labouring and horse trading have disappeared. The traditional roadside sites have also been built upon or made into dual carriageways and subsequently, rather like the urban fox, gypsies have been forced to move out of their natural environment and 'invade' other spaces. The woman in the *Open Space* video letter said that the gypsy woman should go back to the country where her 'kids can go wild'. Do gypsies really want their kids to 'go wild'? Even where they have bought land they have often been denied the right to build on it because of planning laws. Today their activities include collecting scrap metal, which can be unsightly, but may also be regarded as an important recycling activity for our wasteful society.

When asked how he would define himself as a gypsy, Richard O'Neill said:

> This is incredibly tricky for a whole host of reasons. For example, the Irish Traveller is a distinct ethnic group which whilst similar is not the same as English Gypsies. To use one term would be detrimental in certain circumstances as you may be taken less seriously. If I was talking to others as in this book I would use Gypsy with a capital G. But if I was doing something with my own people I would use Traveller. If it was abroad I would use Anglo or English Romani.

Scrap is certainly the image that is conveyed in *Snatch*. The gypsy campsite is littered with old washing machines and other detritus. The aggressive nature of the character played by Brad Pitt and the questionable honesty of the children, not to mention the adults, are immediately foregrounded. Whenever the group is referred to by one of the other characters they say something that confirms that 'pikeys' are not to be trusted. Given that this is said by characters who are themselves violent liars and cheats the irony is obvious.

7.4 Insiders and outsiders

Apart from Richard's comments much of the material that has been referred to here so far has been from the outsider's view. The voice of the gypsy is hardly heard in public. The opportunity to hear views such as those of Richard O'Neill, and the insights he gives, is rare. How would our ideas be changed if we heard more of these insider's viewpoints, from the position of the 'other', as though we were in the position of the Native American outside of the wagon circle or in this case from inside the gypsy 'caravan'? Even in the Balkans where gypsies are a substantial minority their impoverished situation is almost invisible in the media.

Rarely do we hear genuine voices and often these are mediated through the agenda of the programme makers. It is important to remember who is representing as well as who is being represented. There have, however, been some examples of trying to give voice to these people, such as a document on the plight of European gypsies published by the Minority Rights Group (1973). In this country there have also been television documentaries looking sympathetically at issues relating to policing and travellers such as *Seven Days at Stoney Cross* (BBC2, July 1986). In thinking about this compare your response to the way that the police are represented in crime programmes and documentaries such as in *Crimewatch UK*, which were discussed in Chapter 3. Photographer Jo Spence, in her work *Putting Myself in the Picture* (1986), also tried to redress the imbalance. She visited and photographed gypsies: 'I was both privileged and upset to be allowed to look at a world where people worked so hard to survive, whilst labouring under such terrible disadvantages.'

Open Space also attempted to give voice to the gypsy community. This viewers' access programme, which has

Richard O'Neill commented that 'Snatch was about Irish Travellers, a distinct ethnic group. But I think any film like this not only perpetuates myths but can cause harm. I dread to think that a number of young men who went to see this film if asked to describe a Gypsy man would have a picture in their mind of one-punch Mickey O'Neill.'

Happy campers or social menace?

already been referred to, was one in which the views of two women on opposite sides of a dispute over a gypsy site were shown. They spoke to each other via video letters, and this gave the opportunity to hear an ordinary gypsy voice rather than only that of the non-gypsy. But these programmes are outweighed by other images on television. A documentary on the travellers' site issue in Avon had an opening sequence of caravans appearing over the horizon from a very low viewpoint. It was an image of invasion. The viewer was positioned to feel afraid.

Television dramas occasionally use the gypsy as a subplot within the narrative. For example, *The Bill* has used a gypsy encampment plot line with a mentally retarded gypsy boy. We are meant to feel sympathy with the young boy who is wrongly accused, but what the episode does is to confirm the stereotype of the illiterate and simple-minded gypsy. Children's television drama has also used the romantic, exotic, untrustworthy images, as in *Gypsy Girl* (ITV, February 2001). All of these confirm negative and stereotyped representations. In February 2005, BBC2 broadcast a documentary, *Gypsy Woman*, charting a traveller's legal battle against the town councils that keep forcing her to move on every few weeks.

7.5 The cinematic gypsy – Eastern Europe

Those who have studied films from Eastern Europe, whether with Roma protagonists or, more usually, used as subplots, see the representation of this marginalised group as a projection of the Balkans in the European context. In films from this area their representation works as a metaphor for the general Balkan situation. Just as the Roma are marginalised in Balkan society, so the Balkans feel that they are marginalised in Europe. Dina Iordavana (2001) refers to this as 'projective identification'.

As in the West the Roma are admired for their free spirit, their exotic natures and 'savvyness', and they represent a contrast to the rigidity of organised society. On the other hand, gypsies are 'exemplary pariahs, outcasts, the very bottom of internal hierarchies throughout Europe' (Zivkovic, quoted in Iordavana, 2001, p. 217). They are not seen as a 'full' member of the nation-state because they are transnational. They are without an organised power base, and they are

The gypsy 'godfather' in *Black Cat, White Cat* ironically repeatedly watches the ending of the classic Hollywood film *Casablanca* ... 'I think this is the beginning of a beautiful friendship.'

therefore normally a group who are not seen as a threat to the state's hegemony and can be easily used as scapegoats. When the two cultures do collide, the Romani usually come off worst. In the film *Black Cat, White Cat* (Emir Kusturica, 1998), the gypsy father is cheated by the Russian bargemen, and in *The Crazy Stranger* (Tony Gatlif, 1997) the Romani village is burned and the leaders killed, and the inhabitants flee, dispersed by the surrounding group.

The plight of the Romani deteriorated rapidly in the Balkans after 1989, and this forced migration led to many of the illegal immigration problems across Europe and the consequent moral panics and scapegoating of these groups in Western European countries. David Blunkett, the then Home Secretary, stated that immigrant children were 'swamping' our schools, and he suggested setting up special schools for them ('Blunkett Defends "Swamping" remark', *Guardian*, 25 April 2002). 'But in terms of moral imperative, a human tragedy and a continent's shame, the treatment of the Roma, Europe's largest and fastest-growing ethnic minority, stands out' (Younge, 2003). This migration has exacerbated and confirmed the negative view of travellers. The asylum seeker, illegal immigrants and economic migrants issues have been conflated with the plight of the Roma.

In Britain these groups have been labelled as criminals or leeches. There have been unsubstantiated reports of shoplifting sprees and other antisocial activity. It has been an image of invasion in which the Roma appear to be the leaders. There has been a failure to acknowledge that they are the victims of persecution and institutional racism in Eastern Europe. Many of the documentaries, mostly Western-made, and news features which covered the plight of the Romani in Central Europe during the 1990s did not address issues from inside: 'they [the gypsies] somehow remain absent from the public discourse. Sidestepped as audiences, they are unable to enter the public spotlight to react to their representations' (Iordanova, 2000, p. 230).

This fear of invasion – 'Britain Here We Come' (*Daily Express*, 20 January 2004), which warned of hundreds of thousands of gypsies entering the United Kingdom and was hyped for 1 May 2004 with the expansion of the European Union – was revealed later to have been inaccurate and scaremongering. In August BBC News reported that what had actually happened was that a small group of educated and relatively wealthy gypsies had migrated to other countries such as Britain.

In this discussion you will have noticed that the representation of this group follows two opposing poles. On one side there are the deceivers living off the hard work of others; on the other side the gypsy has been admired as a romantic contrast to ordered civilisation. They represent the rural idyll as opposed to urbanisation; the free life contrasted to the controls of the state. This is certainly how Emir Kusturica represents the Roma lifestyle in *Black Cat, White Cat*. They are romanticised and exoticised. The gypsy family is seen sympathetically as the 'innocent' who is duped by gangsters. As the head of one of the gangster families says, 'I have no racial prejudice.' But in representing the gypsy as the romantic free spirit the media can suffer a:

> ... *cultural amnesia in the way that they have treated gypsies and the way that society has treated this marginalised group: decades after the persecution of the gypsies under the Third Reich, gypsy life remains in the popular imagination as a carefree, defiant, disruptive alternative to a Western culture ... outside of historical record and historical time, outside of Western law, the Western nation state, and Western economic orders, outside of writing and discursivity itself.*
> (Trumpener, 1992)

How do we reconcile such opposing beliefs?

As Kate Trumpener's quotation indicates, in spite of the sizeable minority in the Balkans, there has been little or no self-representation of Roma life, particularly in cinema. The nearest have been some ethnographic films made by Roma groups. The one film-maker who can claim to have insight into the life of the Roma is Tony Gatlif, who is part Roma. (His work is discussed more fully in Iordanova, 2000.) His first film, *The Princes* (1982), made in France, was a bleak view of gypsy life in a Parisian suburb. In 1993 he produced a feature-length documentary *Latcho Drom*, exploring Roma culture through music and dance. Gatlif said about this film: 'I wanted to make a film the Roma people could be proud of, not something to exhibit their misery' (Clayton, 2002). The film is about an oral culture and moves in a musical odyssey through Europe. 'After all, our identity is the only country the Rom people possess' (Gatlif, ibid.).

Gatlif also made *The Crazy Stranger*, set in Romania and about the Balkan gypsies. Ironically even this sympathetic portrayal has a non-Roma protagonist with whom we identify. Stéphane is assimilated into the Roma culture as he discovers the closeness and honesty that is missing in the competitive bourgeois world. The camera follows his (and our) discovery of the world behind the stereotypes. The film can be read as a negative portrayal of the Romani whose desire for revenge, a theme also seen in *Snatch*, precipitates the final tragedy of the burning of the Romani village and the occupants' flight. On the other hand, with the end of the film Gatlif appears to be showing the hypocrisy of the outsider where the romantic or ethnographic view keeps the Roma separate from us in a sort of mythic no man's land. Once they try to integrate, we feel our society is threatened by the very values that we admire and we react with violence. Such integration is seen in the current issue of gypsies buying land and attempting to create their own settlements – 'Gypsies Battling to Stay in Swanmore' (*Hampshire Chronicle*, 7 May 2004).

*Black Cat, White Ca*t, made by Emir Kusturica, who is not Roma but who has run a gypsy band and made several films based around the Roma, conveys the romantic free spirit of the Roma lifestyle in a comedy of black marketing and romance. The film shows the gypsies as victims of exploitation, but as also willing to exploit. Although

Still from Emir Kusturicka's *Black Cat, White Cat,* a film which centres on the Roma lifestyle

apparently apolitical the film at the end unceremoniously dumps the powerful and crooked gangster into a filthy latrine. Such ridicule is perhaps the only way that the weaker Romani can show their rebellion.

Black Cat, White Cat provides the classic end: that love conquers all. But the film is full of ironic comments about such ideologies. Prince Charming finds the slipper and his Cinderella, but they are the least likely of romantic heroes as both are regarded as physically ugly. There is also an ironic subtext about cultural imperialism in the constant playing of the end of the film *Casablanca* (Michael Curtiz, 1942) by the dying head of one of the family gangs. *Casablanca* is the epitome of the classic Hollywood film and its ending encapsulates ideologies about romantic love and national duty. The contrast between *Casablanca*'s highly controlled, sophisticated structures and formality and the chaotic carnivalesque atmosphere conveyed through the mise en scène and camerawork of Kusturica's film symbolises eloquently the cultural, social and ideological distances between the two 'worlds' inside the film.

The irony that was highlighted in the introduction to this chapter is that the stereotype can be self-fulfilling. The Roma actors had to perform within the stereotypes acceptable to the producers of the texts. 'It is an irony, indeed, that the Roma have no other choice but to conform to the existing stereotypes. In such a context Roma film-makers are also compelled to comply with existing representations' (Iordanova, 2001). Alaina Lemon has written about how in Czech films the director has taught Romani actors to be 'proper Roma'!

7.6 The cinematic gypsy – Western films

You may feel that films produced and representing Eastern Europe are not directly relevant to your view of the world. So let us look at how gypsies have been represented in films from the West. In *Black Cat, White Cat* Kusturica used the beliefs about family, tradition and loyalty in the gypsy community for comedic purposes. We can see this belief referenced in a Western mainstream film such as *Snatch* (2000, Guy Ritchie). *Snatch* is a gangster film in which the Brad Pitt character is a bareknuckle fighter who takes bloody revenge upon the men who have killed his mother. Behind him both in the frame and in the action stand the gypsy male 'family' group.

Kusturica was also the director of Time of the Gypsies *(1988), which focused on the illegal trafficking of gypsy children into Italy from Czechoslovakia. (This film was partly financed by David Puttnam as head of Columbia studios, with a guaranteed American distribution.) It is one of the few films shot in the Romani language and had to be subtitled in every country in which it was released.*

This is exactly the problem that women film directors from Tunisia were having with producers from outside the Arab world. What the producers wanted was a representation of Arab women that conformed to the Western stereotype. See Chapter 9, p. 202.

▶ *In American films the itinerant Mexican worker, often seen in the classic Western but also appearing in many other genres, such as in the opening of* Men in Black *(Barry Sonnenfeld, 1997), probably serves a similar function to the itinerant gypsy in Europe. What is this function?* ●

▶ If you have seen *Snatch*, think about how the family groups are represented and compare this with families represented elsewhere. Chapter 2 may help with this. ●

▶ What was the first film you remember seeing in the cinema or on video as a child? Most people remember an animated film; often it is a Disney film and one which works on stereotypes. ●

When it was being made the makers visited a gypsy family. A report in the *Sunday Mirror* ('You're a Brad Boy', 30 April 2000) focused on Brad Pitt as star, but at one point it reports a gypsy taking Brad Pitt on a tour of the site. "'During a quiet moment I said to him. Don't take the p*** out of us when you make this film. You have seen for yourself how we really are.' He said, 'Man, I'm doing the film and I wouldn't let that happen.'" If you have seen the film, do you think it happened or not?

Disney films are some of the most powerful conveyers of ideologies in children's entertainment. How does Disney represent gypsies? Disney's *Hunchback of Notre Dame* (1996) is based around the gypsy community in Paris. In the film's opening Cleopas, a gypsy entertainer signified by his gold earring, tells the story of a group of gypsies trying to enter Paris. A gypsy woman seeing her husband captured attempts to flee with her child. Frollo kicks her to death, and for atonement is ordered to bring up the child. This infant becomes the deformed Quasimodo. In the opening sequence there is a sympathetic drawing of the female character whose iconography has the tinge of the exotic, particularly for the male voyeur; however, the male gypsies are characterised by extended features such as large noses and are physically unattractive.

Esmeralda is the beautiful gypsy dancer who entertains the crowds and whom Quasimodo loves. But Esmeralda loves the handsome (and blonde) French Captain. Quasimodo is both brown-skinned (remember he is also a gypsy) and disabled. He also represents the horror of male other sexuality often represented by the monstrous, such as King Kong, and inevitably fails to win the 'princess'. The story is scattered with dialogue such as 'They're gypsies. They'll steal us blind'; 'Gypsies don't earn money. They steal it'; and 'such a clever witch' when referring to a gypsy woman, referencing the link between gypsies and magic.

You may regard a Disney animation aimed at children as harmless in its simplicity of characters. There have, however, been several studies on Disney films that reveal the conservative nature of the stories (UWIC, 2000). It is also worth remembering the strength of the influence of literature, including fairy and folk stories, in the role of delivering ideologies. Edward Saïd (1994), for example, has written critically about Daniel Defoe's *Robinson Crusoe* as an imperialist text where the native character, Man Friday, is treated like a pet dog.

There have been other films aimed at younger age groups where there are 'gypsy' characters, such as *Into the West* (Mike Newell, 1992) and *Danny, the Champion of the World* (Gavin Millar, 1989). In films aimed at adults Marlene Dietrich has appeared in *Golden Earrings* (Mitchell Leison, 1947) as a gypsy, and she played a similar character in *Touch of Evil* (Orson Welles, 1959). In both these films Dietrich exemplifies all that we have said about the exotic use of the minority group. Of the same period was a British film called *Madonna of the Seven Moons* (Arthur Crabtree, 1944), where the demure female protagonist lives a secret sexually active life as a gypsy, so distancing her from the moral world.

7.7 Conclusion

It has been argued that we need to think not just about the opposition between margin and centre in terms of the way we study texts, 'but as a de-centred polyvocal multiculturalism' as well (Wiegman, 1998). As with any discussion on representation, it is essential that the context both social and historical is part of that discussion. This entails looking at a minority group both in the micro sense of the texts under discussion and in the macro sense across the media and the context in which they are produced. Unlike the large issues of race and gender, such minority groups as gypsies may appear to be unimportant, but it is in these less politicised groupings and minority representations that we can see the assertion and indexing of innate physical differences as conveyers of beliefs or ideologies. We can note the fetishism of physical qualities such as skin colour or nose size, or iconography such as earrings and scarves, which help to maintain these beliefs and the associations of words such as 'swamping' when discussing their appearance.

It is perhaps now time to go back to the original list of ideas that you were asked to make at the beginning of this chapter (p. 146). You may not have changed your views or your list, and this is not the purpose of this section, but perhaps you now understand how and why the list looks like it does. As has been pointed out in other chapters,

▶ Compare the image of Esmeralda near the beginning of the film where she is dancing in the square in front of Notre Dame (DVD – 22' 03" approx.) with the one of her as she appears in the final frame on the steps of Notre Dame. What are the differences in the way she is represented?

In the first scene she is exotic and alluring. The angle of her body suggests sexuality and danger. Her clothes are bright and tight-fitting. She is wearing a gold earring which signifies 'gypsy' with all its exotic connotations. At the end of *Hunchback of Notre Dame* Esmeralda has lost her earring and her gypsy clothes have been replaced by a plain white (virginal) shift. She stands demurely on the steps of the church holding the hand of her 'prince'.

Is Esmeralda still a gypsy at the end of the film, or has she become something else? How do these representations of 'Romani' culture collude with the outsider's stereotypes? ●

how groups are seen and how audiences read texts are fundamental to the discourses of representation.

Nineteenth-century French novelist Gustave Flaubert sums up the view of gypsies that perhaps still exists today:

> 'A week ago I was enraptured by a camp of gypsies that stopped at Rouen … They had aroused the hatred of the bourgeoisie even though they were harmless as lambs. This hatred stems from a deep and complex source; it is to be found in all champions of order. It is the hatred felt for the Bedouin, the heretic, the philosopher, the recluse, the poet, and it contains elements of fear. I who am always on the side of minorities, am driven wild by it.' (quoted in Esty, 1969)

References

Acton, T. (ed.), *Gypsy Politics and Traveller Identity* (Hatfield: University of Hertfordshire Press, 1997)

Acton, T., 'Authentic, Expertise Scholarship and Politics: Conflicting Goals in Romani Studies', inaugural lecture, Greenwich University, 1998.

Bramwell Evens, G., *Out with Romany: Adventures with Birds and Animals* (London: University of London, 1937).

Chaucer, G., *The Complete Works of Chaucer*, Walter W. Skeat (ed.) (Oxford: Oxford University Press, 1965).

Clayton, M., *Roma: A People on the Edge* (Braiswick, Suffolk: Author Publishing Co., 2002).

Flaubert, Gustave, in *The Gypsies: Wanderers in Time*, Katharine Esty (New York: Meredith Press, 1969).

Iordanova, D., *Cinema of Flames: Balkan Film, Culture and Media* (London: BFI Publishing, 2001).

Iordanova, D., *Emir Kusturica* (London: BFI Publishing, 2002).

Kenrick, Donald, & Gratton Puxon, *The Destiny of Europe's Gypsies* (New York: Basic Books, 1973).

Miles, Robert, *Racism* (London: Routledge, 1989).

Saïd, E., *Culture and Imperialism* (New York: Vintage, 1994).

Spence, J., *Putting Myself in the Picture* (London: Camden Press, 1986).

Stevens, C., in *Racism and Sexism in Children's Books*, Judith Stinton (ed.) (London: Writers and Readers Publishers Co-operative, 1979).

Stinton, Judith (ed.), *Racism and Sexism in Children's Books* (London: Writers and Readers Publishers Cooperative, 1979).

Taylor, R., N. Wood & J. Graffy (eds), *Eastern European and Russian Cinema* (London: BFI Publishing, 2000).

UWIC, *Guys and Dolls* (Cardiff: Media Education in Wales, 2000).

Wiegman, R., 'Race, Ethnicity and Film', in *The Oxford Guide to Film Studies*, John Hill & Pamela Church Gibson (eds) (London: Oxford University Press, 1998).

Readings/cuttings

Clayton, M., 'Time to Move on', Traveller Education, *The Teacher*, December 2002.

Connolly, K., 'Czech Gypsies Begin Test Case as Pupils Classed as Retarded', *Guardian*, 19 April 2000.

Gillan, A., 'Brutal Death of a Travelling Child', *Guardian*, 10 June 2003.

'Gypsy Road to Nowhere', *Guardian*, 2 October 1992.

Kempster, Doug, 'You're a Brad Boy', *Sunday Mirror*, 30 April 2000.

Littlejohn, R., 'Two Jags Is Doing to Britain What the Travellers Are Doing to the Countryside', Opinion (Features), *Sun*, 11 March 2005.

Marr, A., 'Our Ugly Intolerance', *Observer*, 19 March 2000.

Orr, D., 'When Humans Behave Like Animals', *Independent*, 25 August 2000.

Trumpener, K., 'The Time of the Gypsies: A "People without History" in the Narratives of the West', *Critical Inquiry*, vol. 18, Summer, 1992, pp. 843–84.

Younge, G., 'Shame of a Continent', *Guardian*, 8 January 2003.

Wrathall, John, 'Gypsy Time', *Sight and Sound*, vol. 7, no. 12, December 1997, pp. 10–13.

Broadcasts

Gypsy Girl, C-ITV, February 2001

Gypsy Woman, BBC2, February 2005

'Love Like a Gypsy', *Something Understood*, Radio 4, 27 July 2003

'The New Age Traveller', *World in Action*, Granada Television, July 1992 – gypsy sites and council problems with New Age travellers

Open Space, Forum Television, Channel 4
Seven Days at Stoney Cross, BBC2, July 1986 – New Age
    travellers

Films
Rescued by Rover (Cecil Hepworth, 1905)
Madonna of the Seven Moons (Arthur Crabtree, 1944)
Golden Earrings (Mitchell Leisen, 1947)
Time of the Gypsies (Emir Kusturica, 1988)
Danny, Champion of the World (Gavin Millar, 1989)
Into the West (Mike Newell, 1992)
Latcho Drom (*Safe Journey*) (Tony Gatlif, 1993)
The Hunchback of Notre Dame (Gary Trousdale & Kirk Wise,
    Disney, 1996)
Gadjo Dilo (*The Crazy Stranger*) Tony Gatlif, 1997)
Twin Town (Kevin Allen, 1997)
Black Cat, White Cat (Emir Kusturica, 1998)
Snatch (Guy Ritchie, 2000)

Useful websites
Gypsy travellers have built communities on the Internet:
www.ercomer.org/ – European Research Centre on
    Migration and Ethnic Relations
www.gypsy.ukgateway.net – Romany Gypsy Photograph
    Collection
www.romani.org – Romani organisation
www.geocities.com/~patrin/ – The Patrin European site
www.romnews.com – The Rom news agency
www.romaniworld.com – European Committee on Romani
    Emancipation

Part Four
Images of
National Identity

Introduction

Our sense of national identity, or rather our identification with a nation to which we feel we belong, is the subject of this section. This topic forces us to reconsider not only our own national identity, but also how we choose to represent ourselves and others as members of a national group. Globally groups and nations can be labelled in many ways. An example is George W. Bush's 'axis of evil'. Groups attacking the dominant power are often regarded as 'terrorists' and condemned. The weaker you are, the more likely you are to be called a terrorist – although you would believe yourself to be a freedom fighter. If you have more power and the ability to deliver violence through sophisticated weaponry you might term yourself 'defender of the peace'. These oppositional views are certainly how groups have been represented from different sides of world conflicts, for example in the Arab–Israeli conflict.

Such views are reinforced in many ways and become embedded in our cultures as ideological truths through iconicity, linguistic patterns, semantics and mediation. Representations of nation are also highly politicised and therefore deeply problematic. They are found in the mass media as a reflection of cultural production and behaviour: history and traditions; body language and sex; food and drink; art and architecture; sport and customs. Clearly, though, a nation is more than a sum of its parts.

This section looks at the concept of nation through two different foci. First, it looks at how the game of football could be regarded as a new nationalism. The game has a huge following both nationally in the United Kingdom and internationally. It has become a major commodity and contributes to the economy, with clubs and players being bought and sold on the international market. Footballers no longer play for their local team, but for whomever has bought them, and this does not have to be within their own country. But when the national teams come out on the pitch the idea of nationhood takes centre stage. The films chosen explore these ideas, but also look at how football is a site for other issues such as race and gender which intersect with the concept of nation.

The next section tries to bring together the issues of how nations are represented and how they represent themselves through narratives. To explore the complex area of cultural representations in storytelling, the next chapter offers a comparison between two films. As the language of film, cultural, symbolic and semiotic codes begin to work, their narratives develop alternative styles. These two texts allow us to see how many issues that have been raised earlier, particularly the family, gender roles and the issue of sexual exploitation, can be integrated into the study of a single text.

This is the last of the discussions. The final chapter brings together many of the issues raised in this book and roots it in the reality of making texts, through an interview with one of the actors in the film *East Is East* (1999).

8. Football and Film: Representing Nationality

MARK RAMEY
In loving memory of my mother, Constance Ramey

The narrow theme of 'football films' will enable us to focus on a significant area of national identity. I will explore what we mean by national identity first, then focus on 'football films' and their representations of nation through a short analysis of three contemporary football-themed films: Mike Bassett: England Manager *(Steve Barron, 2001),* Bend It Like Beckham *(Gurinder Chadha, 2002) and* The Football Factory *(Nick Love, 2004).*

My argument consists of two ideas. The first concerns the position football holds in our society. I maintain that football is an area largely unexplored by academics despite its cultural currency and links with so many social identities. Academic indifference means football films are often seen as cinema's impoverished relations, yet football-themed texts can yield insights into the contemporary 'representation of nationality'.

My second idea is more controversial and comes from applying postmodern philosophy to the exploration of nationality. I argue that advanced Western cultures are in a postmodern era. This is characterised by a playful but never painless reassessment of all values – a reassessment which never goes beyond the surface in search of deeper, more essential truths. Thus, at a time when essentialist ideologies seem increasingly redundant and consumerism is rife, it is becoming ever harder to represent nationality as anything other than a lifestyle choice.

8.1 Nationality in crisis

Readers may recall their discomfort when using the proper nouns and adjectives 'Britain/British', 'England/English' 'Europe/European' to identify themselves and others: the words seem awkward and can carry unwanted connotations. This descriptive dilemma is indicative of the changing face of national identification. Who are we?

'We're all Americans now,' wrote the *Sun* columnist Richard Littlejohn (2005), in response to the 'Twin Towers' tragedy in New York. Although perhaps not meant literally, the statement perfectly illustrates how ideas of nationality are challenged and redefined in times of crisis. The same statement written a day before could have been read as a critique of American globalisation.

Ernest Baker (1928) writes: 'Not only is national character made; it continues to be made and remade.' This process accelerates during times of social change, and 'war' provides the clearest example. War necessarily polarises national identity; a war without an enemy is, after all, nonsensical.

The British have nostalgia for World War II because it represents a 'golden age' of national unity. Images of the war remain iconic reference points of national identity: Churchill, Spitfires, the dome of St Paul's rising above a sea of smoke. Even Sven Goran Eriksson, the English football manager, invoked in 2002 the Dunkirk spirit: 'Your country won two World Wars. In my squad I see the same fighters, players who will not give up …' Wars emphasise national identity and national difference. Their representation in the media very clearly informs us both who we are and what makes the enemy so different. Even old wars define new ones. Agincourt, the Armada, Waterloo – all have been spun and recycled into morale-boosting examples of national triumph over adversity. As George Orwell remarked in his novel *Nineteen Eighty-Four* (1949): 'He who controls the past, controls the present…' By 'controls' Orwell meant 'represents', noting that the political results of such representations are often socially disastrous.

But why are notions of national identity so potent? A. D. Smith (1991) conservatively observes, 'Of all the collective identities which human beings share today, a national identity is perhaps the most fundamental.'

Yet developments in niche markets, globalisation, political devolution and information technologies such as the Internet

▶ Perhaps we define ourselves by 'who we are not' rather than by 'who we are'. Who aren't you? ●

are eroding such ideas. Personal identity is not simply about national identification any more. It may be that a sense of national identity is becoming increasingly inappropriate for Western industrialised nations, but that is not to say that it is becoming irrelevant in other areas. Issues of nationality are of fundamental importance in 'disputed regions' such as Chechnya, Palestine, Northern Ireland, Iraq and Tibet. Closer to home the recent rise of the BNP in Bradford and the racist far right across Europe are dramatically indicative of the fight for national status.

My point, however, is that the discourse is ongoing and dynamic; national identity is in a state of flux. As Jeremy Paxman (1999) observes, 'Once upon a time the English knew who they were.' Ziauddin Sardar (2002) notes: 'We are in the middle of an identity crisis ...' If both commentators are right, then any representations of a unified nation (a recipe for national identification) must be treated with suspicion, for in such cases national identity is not about who we are; it is about who we are told to be.

The media clearly play a massive role in the dissemination of national ideologies: the largely political and media-generated debates over economic migrants and asylum-seekers is a good example of this (see Chapters 7 and 9).

Sporting events, especially where national teams compete, are very interesting indices of national identity, barometers measuring a nation's sense of self. And in this country, a country whose sense of national identity is shifting, national sporting conundrums abound. For example, in the Olympics we enter a squad that represents the United Kingdom ('Team GB' in 2004), but in the Commonwealth Games England distances itself from all colonial appendages and stands alone: England dominates the Commonwealth just as it dominates the United Kingdom.

The violent struggles for independence that characterised the partition of India in 1948 are still going on in Northern Ireland, where the Loyalists are now paradoxically more British than many Britons. Even the Union Jack, an iconic representation of our United Kingdom – which is now as much a fashion brand and design commodity as it is a national standard – reveals ideological positioning.

The process of political devolution that began in the late 1990s has therefore served to highlight differences within our

▶ If I took an extreme, postmodernist view I could argue that national identity is (or soon will be) merely another lifestyle choice. And if a 'national identity' is a brand battling for survival in the global market place, then why not re-brand when times are tough and invade other markets when times are good? Indeed, does this happen now? Has the crumbling British Empire finally succumbed to rampant American imperialism? Are we the 51st state of the United States? By buying the products of a culture do we also literally buy into that culture? Are we becoming Americans? Could we change brands?

Footballers seem to be doing this right now by claiming 'national status' through distant relatives and thus securing themselves a place in a national squad unconnected with their birthplace. Vinnie Jones, ex-football hard man, now Hollywood celebrity, was born in London, but went on to play for Wales! Are nations going to merge into super-brands such as 'Europe' and 'The Americas'? (Another echo of Orwell's *Nineteen Eighty-Four*, in which he posited the power blocs Oceania, Eastasia and Eurasia.) ●

Flags are useful indices of national feeling. They invoke passion and pride; they are symbols of identity, conformity, tradition and power. When the Union Jack was initially devised in 1707 some Scots flew their own version with the Scottish cross of St Andrew dominant over the English cross of St George. It is therefore not only flags, but also their meanings which are fought over.

The Union Jack is an amalgam of three national emblems (Scotland, England and Ireland) and was developed in 1707 as a symbol of the newly formed United Kingdom of Great Britain. It was around this time that 'Britannia' made her first appearance on our coinage and that 'Rule Britannia' (the national anthem) was devised.

For Britain, at the dawn of the modern industrial age, the Union Jack became a symbol of imperial dominance and militaristic might. But it was still a fiction, a device used to create a sense of solidarity among a notoriously diverse people. Even today the process of Scottish, Welsh and Irish political devolution is operating in tandem with European unification. It seems that the United Kingdom has always been a fictional entity.

Consider how you would feel about a move to substitute the Union Jack with a more up-to-date representation of our country. This is something being considered by the Australian government if Australia were to become a republic. It is also significant that the Union Jack is the only national flag to appear on other national flags such as those of Australia and New Zealand.

▶ List the values that you associate with David Beckham. How would you represent those values in a photograph or moving image? How long does it take you to find such an image? ●

own supposedly united nation. The conclusion must be that not only is our kingdom (queendom!) disintegrating as a natural consequence of the end of Empire, but also that the divorcing nations are keen to re-establish their own identities – the English being no different! The current popularity of the cross of St George was indicated by a sales peak during the 2002 World Football Cup finals and the apparent decline of the Union Jack as a populist flag (perhaps because of its imperial and racist connotations?) bear witness to this changing sense of national identity.

But national identity is also under siege from other areas such as: the European Union and the Euro; the Channel Tunnel; the increasing numbers of overseas tourists; immigration; Americanisation; the multicultural urban landscape; and the rise of postmodern cultural practices. What we can see therefore are profound shifts in the way nations identify themselves within the United Kingdom. Am I English, Scottish, Irish, Welsh or British? Am I European or American? Who am I? What is my 'brand'?

8.2 Beckham and branding

David Beckham places the ball just outside the Greek penalty area and retreats a few measured paces. He is a study of concentration and calm, the focal point of a nation's hopes and dreams. There are only seconds left on the clock and if he scores England qualifies for the 2002 World Cup finals. A nation holds its breath. The Greek wall stands firm as Beckham starts his run-up; his body arches, his arms pivot and his right leg swings back like a pendulum. Then the ball is sailing up and over the wall, arcing though the air, curling past the flailing hands of the Greek goalkeeper and thundering into the top corner of the goal. England has qualified for the World Cup. Beckham is a national hero. Nobody, but nobody, can bend a ball like Beckham.

Love him or loathe him, Beckham is clearly a global icon part of the 'global language of soccer' (Morrison, 2002) and so if we wish to understand the world in which we live both football and Beckham demand our attention. For example, the above-mentioned football match made it into the top twenty UK viewing figures for that year, and Beckham recently featured in a global Pepsi promotional campaign – to name but one of the many brands he endorses.

The subsequent World Cup finals were watched by a global audience of more than two billion – one-third of humanity! Coca-Cola would have us 'Eat, Sleep and Drink Football'. According to Claire Cozen, writing in the *Guardian* (2002), 'Football may be in danger of overtaking sex as the ultimate attention grabber.' Footballers are the new rock stars; 'Beckingham Palace' the new seat of royalty. Welcome to Planet Football – almost!

What is undeniable is that the game is now more popular than ever. One and a half million British women now take part in some form of the sport every week. Countries originally firmly resistant to football such as the United States and Japan are now competing and achieving at the World Cup finals. What this reflects is the increasing commodification of football, as Dave Russell (1997) notes: '… football as consumer cornucopia sits well with much current economic philosophy'. Footballers are now global superstars, akin to pop and film stars in their appeal and influence. This was seen in the Beckham 'Mohican' haircut of 2002 that rapidly infiltrated street culture. Football and its icons are a national obsession. On the eve of a crunch match between Brazil and England in the 2002 World Cup finals, the *Daily Mirror* produced a virtually blank front page with a small cross of St George and a low-key headline: 'Nothing Else Matters'. It was the so-called 'silly season' for hard news, but nevertheless it reflects the passionate national identification with the sport in certain readerships. Indeed, John Williams (1999) notes that the current Blairite administration has identified football as a key 'feature of a modern, regenerated and re-branded Britain'. He goes on to say that 'sporting heroes are also increasingly promoted and experienced as the new role models for the young in the late-modern societies where authority and respect no longer relate to some established and ethnically exclusive scale of hierarchy.'

This global footballing identity has certainly helped to fracture notions of national identity. During the World Cup of 2002 both Korean and Japanese fans turned out in their droves to support teams from other countries, in particular the glamour sides such as England. The cause of this phenomenon has in some way been identified by Williams: '… football has globalised in terms of the mobility of players and access via TV to coverage of top players all around the

At time of writing Beckham's biannual haul from endorsement deals alone amounted to £15 million. He endorses products globally and has even launched his own brand of clothing. Beckham's brands include Pepsi, Adidas, Police (sunglasses), Brylcreem, Vodaphone and Castrol (oil).

The Beckham transfer saga from Manchester United to Real Madrid received massive media coverage culminating in the surreal televising of his medical examination. There was a huge potential audience worldwide and so the live programme was scheduled late in Spain to fit in with prime time in the Far East. The event was, of course, sponsored by a leading medical company who paid Real Madrid £250,000 for the privilege of linking its products, however tenuously, to the 'great' man. The club's official presentation of the player resulted in as many as two billion fans worldwide tuning in to see the showbiz-style ceremony. In the space of a few days after the signing, Real Madrid's UK shirt sales rose sharply, making Real Madrid the most visible non-English club in England.

Nobody brands it like Beckham!

A foreigner as England Manager? Never.

An advertisement for Lipton Tea: Football represents more than just a sport – images of the nation are in play

world …' The enthusiastic Japanese and Korean support for the English side (as well as their own national sides) is therefore evidence of the game's global commodification: football is most definitely a brand. As Martin Jacques (1997) notes, 'Nike and even Manchester United are, as much as Coca-Cola, the commercial brands of the age.'

National football can then, in some way, be said to represent the state of the nation. As Chas Critcher (1982) notes:

> In 1953 a new queen was crowned [and] an Englishman was one of the first to climb Everest … All seemed right with the world. But in the same year England were soundly thrashed 6–3 by Hungary at Wembley, the first national side from the continent to beat England on their home ground … this defeat [and the subsequent return-leg 7–1 rout] reproduced within the game a more general crisis of British Imperial philosophy …

Dave Russell (1997) provides a more refined 'class' reading of this argument: 'Football's position within the wider national culture has always been a barometer of elite attitudes towards both popular culture in general and the political and moral health of the working class in particular.'

This referencing of 'elite attitudes' can be found in academic circles where the old classical mind/body dualism has elevated 'artistic' achievements above 'sporting' ones. Sport is one of the most popular cultural practices in the world, so it is significant that so little academic energy has been directed towards understanding it. Football is indeed an ideological battleground, often dismissed by elitist intellectuals and radical feminists as evidence of a lowbrow working-class activity and a crude celebration of machismo. It is clearly more than that and has always been so.

8.3 Films and national identity

The issue of national identity is so important that it is therefore no surprise to find it being dealt with in British films. As Moya Luckett (2000) notes: 'Nineties films articulate [an] awareness of a national identity in flux…' and '… British national identity has become increasingly fraught, threatened by European federalisation and the imminent break-up of the United Kingdom. Ironically this same period has seen British cinema enter one of its upward cycles.' Luckett also comments on the formation of an alternative British film canon, a canon including such films as *Trainspotting* (Danny Boyle, 1996) that counters traditional 'heritage'-centred ideas of British cinema. I would argue that football films should also find a home in this 'alternative canon'.

But what is the 'heritage film'? What is our heritage? Once again we must enter the slippery world of words and use a term which implies continuity and a shared sense of belonging, and yet which fails to capture the nature of the multicultural postmodern experience.

8.4 Heritage films

Our heritage is our shared historical and cultural identity, and the study of so-called 'heritage films' is a conventional but revealing route into a study of nationality. For example, we could explore how royalty is referenced in *The Madness of King George* (Nicholas Hytner, 1994) and *Elizabeth* (Shekhar Kapur, 1998). We could watch representations of World War II as in *Hope and Glory* (John Boorman, 1987) and *Charlotte Gray* (Gillian Armstrong, 2001). We might even explore modern adaptations of works by Charles Dickens, Jane Austen and William Shakespeare – respectively, *Great Expectations* (David Lean, 1946), *Bride and Prejudice* (Gurinder Chadha, 2004) and *Richard III* (Richard Loncraine, 1995).

These familiar representations of British cultural life can be crudely summarised as being part of the 'heritage tradition'. In some sense the British national identity is a mainstream construction of these subjects: royalty, military and the literary. This tradition has frequently provided British and foreign film producers with a rich seam of material to mine.

Heritage films construct a glorious past and reveal a desire to connect with tradition. The Britain represented in these films is one of nostalgia and reverence for the past. It is essentially a postcard representation of nation; something to appeal to traditionalists at home and tourists overseas. Stereotypes will be used to anchor the film's sense of time and place, and a nation will rise up from the myriad images of London buses and country houses, cups of tea and bumbling aristocrats. Films of this nature tend to be made in the Hollywood model, for a global audience (see sidebar).

Hollywood's love of the UK heritage film is clear when we consider which films have excelled at the Oscars. The first Oscar awarded to a British production was in 1933, when Charles Laughton won Best Actor for his eponymous role in *The Private Life of Henry VIII* (Alexander Korda, 1933). Our first Best Picture award was in 1963 for Henry Fielding's literary classic *Tom Jones* (Tony Richardson), and our much-vaunted triumph in 1982 ('The British are coming!') was *Chariots of Fire* (Hugh Hudson, 1981), which was set partly at Oxford University.

Like any generic term, 'heritage film' disguises a variety of cinematic shades. Some heritage films can be profoundly subversive, such as Tony Richardson's anti-Establishment *The Charge of the Light Brigade* (1968) or Peter Greenaway's avant-garde *The Draughtsman's Contract* (1982). Even royalty can be challengingly portrayed – radically as in *Orlando* (Sally Potter, 1992) or more gently as in *Mrs Brown* (John Madden, 1997).

It is perhaps significant, however, that *Four Weddings and a Funeral* (Mike Newell, 1994), *Notting Hill* (Roger Michell, 1999), *Bridget Jones's Diary* (Sharon Maguire, 2001) and *Bridget Jones: The Edge of Reason* (Beeban Kidron, 2004) all feature American actresses falling for bumbling English gentlemen in the shape of Hugh Grant or Colin Firth. These films very clearly trade in highly conventional national stereotypes with an international audience in mind.

Professor Andrew Higson's postmodern reading of the heritage tradition will reward readers who wish to explore the area of heritage films more thoroughly. See in particular his seminal text Waving the Flag: Constructing a National Cinema in Britain (Oxford: Oxford University Press, 1997).

A comparison of UK box-office figures with Premier League attendances is revealing. The total attendance for the 20 English Premier League sides in the season 2002–2003 was 13,476,455. The total UK box office for 4000 screens was 175.9 million.

▶ What adjectives would you use to describe other international teams such as Argentina, Germany, Japan, France and Brazil?

Are you really describing a football team or merely representing a list of cultural stereotypes? ●

Sky's audacious bid for the rights to the newly formed Premier League in 1992 now costs it £1 billion for a three-year deal. Its coverage helped to glamorise the 'new look' football which had emerged from the influential Taylor Report. The report was a reaction to the Heysel and Hillsborough stadium disasters of the late 1980s that lead to a three-year ban on English clubs in Europe and changed the old terraces into all-seater grounds.

The TV boom is now over, as witnessed by the collapse of ITV's OnDigital package with Division One and the debacle over ITV taking the highlights package away from the BBC and into a Saturday prime-time slot. Football remains a priority at Sky, however, dovetailing very nicely with another Murdoch enterprise, the *Sun* newspaper, which also devotes itself to football and, in particular, the cult of the celebrity player.

So an alternative film canon that includes contemporary and popular culture needs developing to do full justice to the rich textures of modern life. Football is now so central to our culture that films which deal with it must necessarily engage with a discourse on national identity.

But what of football's relationship with film? What can an exploration of contemporary English football films tell us about the English national identity? In what way will contemporary cinematic representations of football (the game, the players and the fans) reveal about us as a nation?

8.5 Football, film and television

Football as either a main subject or a theme can be found in a wide variety of British films, as well as films from other nations. *The Cup* (Khyentse Norbu, 1999, Bhutan); *Le Ballon d'or* (Cheik Doukoure, 1994, Guinea) and *Shaolin Soccer* (Stephen Chow, 2001, China) are just three examples from outside Britain. From Britain, we have the macho professional rediscovering his soft side in *Mean Machine* (Barry Skolnick, 2001). This film (a remake of a 1970s American football movie) ironically stars Vinnie Jones, a real-life ex-pro turned actor. Then there are the social-realist 'feel-good' dramas that depict Northern boys and men situated in and around real football clubs: Manchester City in *There's Only One Jimmy Grimble* (John Hay, 2000); Newcastle United in *Purely Belter* (Mark Herman, 2000) and Sheffield United in *When Saturday Comes* (Maria Giese, 1996). More reflective of broader cultural interests in football there are biographies of old stars such as *Best* (Mary McGuckian, 2000); literary adaptations such as *Fever Pitch* (David Evans, 1997); and explorations of hooliganism such as *I.D.* (Philip Davis, 1995). Earlier films such as *The Arsenal Stadium Mystery* (Thorold Dickinson, 1940) and *Gregory's Girl* (Bill Forsyth, 1981) show that the theme of football is not a new one. Even television has jumped on the football bandwagon with the hugely popular drama *Footballers' Wives* (ITV, 2002) now in its third series and the critically acclaimed play *The Firm* (Alan Clarke, BBC, 1988). The jewels in sports broadcasting's crown, however, are Sky's live football and BBC1's long-lived highlights package *Match of the Day* (1964 to date).

It is this link, the link between football, film and representations of nationality, which I wish now to explore.

The focus will be on three relatively recent British films: *Mike Bassett: England Manager* (Steve Barron, 2001), *Bend It Like Beckham* (Gurinder Chadha, 2002) and *The Football Factory* (Nick Love, 2004). What can these films tell us about the shifting character and ideological roots of English national identity?

8.6 *Mike Bassett: England Manager* – first half

Mike Bassett: England Manager concerns the rise, fall and rise again of the eponymous Mike Bassett, an 'old school' manager with little tactical sense who each week writes his team out on the back of a cigarette packet. This particular foible leads to the hilarious accidental selection of two overweight and untalented players from the lower divisions, 'Benson' and 'Hedges'!

The Football Association selects Mike for the post of England manager because no other suitable candidate is available. The FA is ruthlessly parodied as an inaccessible, out-of-touch clique from a patrician era of football administration. Mike is a forthright, passionate man from working-class stock and, although clearly out of his depth, he is determined to do his best. Needless to say he selects a team of staff and players consisting of has-beens, yes men, psychopaths, egotists and party animals to represent the nation (or are they representative of the nation?).

In a series of crunch matches we see England progress to the World Cup finals in Brazil. This ill-deserved achievement is made courtesy of Liechtenstein's intentionally ludicrous victory over Turkey. (Postmodern apologies to Liechtenstein, who are no doubt very good, and Turkey, who have become the new Germany, the new enemy, the new 'other'.)

In Brazil the team performs disastrously and when Mike is photographed drunk and semi-naked dancing on a hotel bar, outraged journalists demand his resignation. Unrepentant Mike goes on to win a famous victory over the old enemy Argentina, involving a scene that parodies Maradona's infamous 'hand of God' goal in the 1986 World Cup finals. This victory leads to a semifinal clash with the host nation, Brazil, which Brazil wins. National pride is restored, however, and Bassett and the team return to England heroes.

Structurally the film is a postmodern comedy in that it ironically adopts the form of a documentary (a mockumentary).

▶ Explain how football and nationality are united in these marketing phrases:

- *Mike Bassett: England Manager* DVD tagline – 'He knows FA!'
- *Bend It Like Beckham* DVD tagline – 'Who wants to cook Aloo Gobi when you can bend a ball like Beckham!'
- *The Football Factory* DVD tagline – 'What else you gonna do on a Saturday?' ●

It anchors its sense of realism through a number of 'real' media and football celebrities: the journalist Martin Bashir, who famously interviewed Princess Dianna and Michael Jackson, supplies the voiceover and acts as onscreen interviewer, while a number of TV football pundits make cameo appearances. There is even a short role for the world's greatest ever player, Pele. The form of the film parodies the documentary style in a number of ways: the use of surreal computer graphics to illustrate football tactics; a hopelessly inept silhouette interview; and a series of scarily plausible tabloid front pages are but three examples.

8.7 Mike Bassett: England Manager – second half

Mike's plucky, amateurish underdog is in some sense homage to the old footballing world of fags, booze and oranges at half-time. He is an incongruous figure of fun, hapless but good-natured, and so someone we want to cheer on. He signifies the contemporary neo-middle-class Englishman, inadequately battling with his unreconstructed male demons and the rapidly changing world around him. The old certainties have gone and only his working-class dad's words of wisdom, courtesy of the quintessential Empire poet, Rudyard Kipling, seem to get him through the tough times. Mike Bassett is the stereotypical Englishman of old: clumsy and self-deprecating; loyal and honest; an underdog wary of new ideas; a pragmatist and a fighter. He is clearly a very conventional representation: a nostalgic figure of fun for a postmodern age where such certainties are to be gently mocked.

One scene defines this shift away from the wistfully nostalgic representation to a postmodern sensibility. Mike, in a fit of despair as his team, his career and his marriage near collapse, is persuaded by the 'Gazza' figure in his squad, 'Tommo', to 'have a Sambucca' to cheer himself up. The inevitable occurs and the next scene shows Mike and the entire squad roaring drunk. Here is the drinking culture that in some sense characterises one aspect of our own national identity. As Mike strips and dances on top of the bar we cut to a Portuguese journalist and the real Pele approaching the bar. Pele is urbane and charming, and pulls up short when he sees the scene before him. 'Oh no! It's the English,' he says, steering the interviewer away from the scene to a barrage of criticism and abuse from Bassett, who has recognised him.

'Gazza', or Paul Gascoigne, was an English midfielder who entered the game in the late 1980s and went on to become a national hero. Undoubtedly gifted on the field and known for his cheeky behaviour and wit, he came to typify the new 'laddism' of the early 1990s, as exemplified in print by *Loaded* and *VIZ*, and on television with *Men Behaving Badly*, *Red Dwarf* and *TFI Friday*.

It could be argued that football was an extension of this new breed of man – certainly sport was an important aspect of his lifestyle, along with booze and sex. This boozing side of the new lad turned hard-drinking Geordie Gazza into a cult figure. Predictably, Gazza's personal life fell apart, and he is now trying to rehabilitate and rebrand himself. Gazza can be seen as the George Best of the 1990s – a greatly loved but self-destructive and wasted talent.

Here we have represented a delight in our own infantilism and a lamentable sense of superiority over our more sophisticated foreign peers. As John Williams (1999) notes:

> The pitfalls facing each new England manager and his hapless squad seem to have been read by the press as a tale of nothing less than the failing state of the English nation itself. Not far below the surface in these media accounts is often an implicit racism or imperialism which charts how far a nation has fallen from grace as measured by football defeats suffered at the hands of nations who can barely be considered our 'civilised' equals, never mind our footballing betters.

But English racial superiority is lampooned and parodied in this film for, although we enjoy Mike Bassett's ludicrous behaviour, we cannot help but recognise that Pele holds the moral high ground.

In laughing at ourselves we are sugaring the pill of change. Mike Bassett is a cultural dinosaur, a remnant of the industrial age, trying to come to terms with a world of cappuccinos and computers. Mike is funny because he is harmless, but two other characters in his team are less acceptable: his captain, a testosterone-fuelled hooligan shown on television rioting alongside English fans on the streets of Brazil; and his assistant, a narrow-minded bigot, obsessed with cars and fearful of foreigners. Of course we laugh at these characters and the irony of their representations, but racism and male aggression still mar the world of English football as they do English culture at large.

One final aspect of the film that is of note is the very un-Hollywood approach to the narrative. The English team does not win the World Cup. In fact, apart from the fluked win against Argentina and a face-saving exit to Brazil, it is woeful. What does this tell us about the English nation? It shows that we are in some sense able to produce relatively mainstream products that are imbued with an ironic awareness of social change. We know that we no longer rule the world and that our Empire is over; we know that foreign footballers tend to be more cultured, better players and much more likely to win the World Cup. Yet we seem to rejoice in our rediscovered underdog status. World War II was one of Britain's last

▶ Are all the representations of World War II merely propaganda? If the greatest period of British national unity was constructed, then are we not also constructed by representations? If everything is a lie, how can you tell what is true? ●

moments of cultural unity, significantly coming about when confronting the threat of a Nazi invasion.

A new invasion is now under way. We are underdogs again, but this time the invading force is not an army but rather a whole host of competing ideologies. As our culture becomes more fragmented, more pluralistic and less homogenous, so too our national identity must become more multifaceted. In some sense Mike Bassett's clumsy attempts to deal with the postmodern world, a world of arbitrary and ever-shifting boundaries, is representative of the patriarchal nation stumbling into the post-industrial light.

8.8 *Bend It Like Beckham* – first half

Following on in the same comic vein, *Bend It Like Beckham* is a 'comedy about friendship, family and football'. This hugely successful film is representative of the current interest in Anglo-Indian culture. Mainstream films such as *The Guru* (Daisy von Scherler Mayer, 2002) and popular art-house releases such as *Monsoon Wedding* (Mira Nair, 2002, India) reflect this appeal and are further complemented by successful 'crossover' Bollywood films such as *Devdas* (Sanjay Leela Bhansali, 2002, India). *Bend It Like Beckham*, however, is striking not so much for its dramatic entry into the burgeoning UK/Indian film canon, but rather for its challenging representations of gender and ethnicity, and how these are integrated into concepts of nationalism.

In some ways the plot is a familiar one: Jess, a young English-born Indian girl, is in conflict with her traditionalist parents. The source of the conflict, however, is where the narrative shows some ingenuity. Jess is football mad, a passionate fan of David Beckham and a talented footballer in her own right. But the Indian community perceives football as a non-Asian and strictly male activity. Asian women are therefore effectively doubly barred from access to the sport. Football is then a catalyst for the conflict between Jess and her parents. They want her to be a good Indian girl, learn how to cook and marry a nice Indian boy. Football does not feature in their plans for their daughter.

Jess, on the other hand, is thrilled when she gets offered a place in a local women's football team – a team good enough to attract the interest of an American scout. As this film is a conventional 'feel-good romcom', it goes without saying that

In the United States, women's football is professional and high status. When America won the Olympic gold for women's football in 1996, Brandi Chastain became the world's most famous female player and received further endorsement from her sponsors, Nike.

This is no flash in the pan: 45 million people worldwide tuned in to see the 2003 women's FA cup final on television.

Jess wins a vital game for her team with a Beckhamesque free kick and is invited by the scout to California on a scholarship. Trying to get her parents to agree to this remains the last conflict to resolve. Jess's developing romance with a white Irish ex-pro further complicates the narrative. In a very modern way Jess chooses career and self-fulfilment over love and duty, and goes to the States, leaving both her new lover and her family at the airport.

8.9 *Bend It Like Beckham* – second half

In terms of the representation of nationality, this film clearly deals with a relatively modern phenomenon: multicultural Britain. The film's protagonists are a comfortably well-off, close-knit family group who live in a home typical of the pebble-dash prairies of suburban London. Their difference lies in their Asian ethnicity and cultural practices; a portrait of their patron guru gazes beneficently down at the family from the sitting-room wall.

Bend It Like Beckham challenges stereotypes of both race and gender

It is clear that this film is a study of Anglo-Asian culture and of the difficulties of belonging to two nations, but it is the phenomenon of 'female footballers' that acts as the main disrupting element in the narrative. As alluded to, Jess's family sees her fascination with football as unladylike. Her Anglo-Saxon blonde girlfriend Jules, on the other hand, is actively encouraged to play, but even this is problematic. Jules's mother becomes convinced that her daughter's fascination with football is in fact due to her confused sexuality – a reflection of the old cliché that girls who play sport are lesbians.

In both girls' cases football acts as a liberating force, enabling them to fulfil their ambitions without recourse to sex, men or tradition. Both girls challenge stereotypes that misrepresent their gender and ethnicity. That said, this is a light-hearted comedy and much of the narrative is interspersed with uplifting musical montage sequences and because of this there are very few downbeat references to racial tension. Indeed, aside from the friendship of the two girls, the only place where racial integration takes place on a consistent basis is in the team's changing room. The metaphor is clear: football is the more inclusive family.

Two scenes are worthy of mention. First, Jess is sent off in a match after she retaliates against a female opponent who racially abuses her. This is a not-so-subtle reminder that racism both on and off the pitch is still a problem in football. Secretly witnessing Jess's downfall, her father bans her from ever playing again – 'It is so unladylike!' We later learn, however, that on arriving in England as a talented, optimistic young cricketer he had tried to join a local team, only to come up against a racial bar. His disappointment and acquiescence in the face of this institutionalised racism eventually acts as the spur to let his daughter fulfil her dream, a dream he was denied.

Finally, in a scene intended to represent racial harmony and cultural tolerance, both girls' families bid them a tearful farewell at the airport and are thus united by their shared experiences and at one point a shared hanky. As the girls leave, Beckham (a lookalike) descends from an elevator walkway, like the modern-day god that he is, thus inadvertently blessing their venture.

A further scene of racial reconciliation is visualised when in the closing credits we see Jess's father and her new boyfriend, Joe, a marginalised Irishman, immaculate in cricket whites, having a knock-up in the park outside Jess's house. As the camera cranes upwards an ice-cream van jingles into the frame. What indeed could be more British than an Indian and Irish gentleman playing cricket in a suburban park!

The hooligan and racist minorities that still blight football's image would do well to consider this understated scene for it points towards inclusivity in sport which remains an issue to resolve for the world's sporting bodies.

8.10 *The Football Factory* – first half

The target audience for *Mike Bassett: England Manager* is 'football fans'. For *Bend It Like Beckham* it is 'women'. For *The Football Factory* it is 'men'. This is a film that follows the pointless life of a white male Londoner, Tommy Johnson. Tommy is involved with a gang of Chelsea-supporting football hooligans and does little else. He is nearing thirty and hence reassessing his life and values. His introspection is limited, however, consisting largely of a series of recurring nightmares. We accompany Tommy for a few months through a life that revolves around 'fighting' trips to football cities. At one point his grandfather offers him a free ticket to fly to Australia, but Tommy is unable to summon the moral integrity to start again in a 'new world'. The film concludes rather depressingly with Tommy answering a question he had posed at the very beginning of the film. 'Was it all worth it?' he asks himself, referring to the fighting and the subsequent life-saving hospital treatment he received. The answer: an unrepentant, 'Of course it was!'

8.11 *The Football Factory* – second half

Tommy introduces himself at the start of the film in a voiceover monologue, which clearly highlights the film's postmodern position:

> *'There's nothing different about me! I'm just another bored male, approaching thirty in a dead end job who lives for the weekend, casual sex, watered-down lager, heavily cut drugs and occasionally kicking fuck out of someone!'*

The monologue is part of the opening sequence which shows the film's protagonist first getting his 'head-kicked-in' by a rival gang of football fans, then meeting up with his own gang in Tottenham where they smoke-bomb a pub and brawl in the street. Music from the aptly named rock band Primal Scream accompanies the second scene: their even more aptly named song 'Swastika Eyes'.

During the street brawl, a young mum pushing her baby and pram, one of only three women in the whole film, stops and berates them for being so idiotic. Tommy has his postmodern reply to hand, even though he appears temporarily stunned into consciousness by her words:

> *'What else you going to do on a Saturday? Sit in your fucking armchair wanking off to Pop Idol, then try to avoid your wife's gaze as you try to come to terms with your sexless marriage. Then go and spunk your wages on kebabs, fruit machines and brasses [prostitutes]. Fuck that for a laugh! I know what I'd rather do: Tottenham away. Love it!'*

These monologues reveal a great deal about modern representations of English men for, as Tommy says, 'There's nothing different about me!'

Here we have the commodification of football taken to its logical limits. Tommy is a football fan who never sees a match. Significantly, the only football we witness in the film consists of extreme long shots of impersonal stadia, cathedrals to the sport, and a televised cup draw. Even football shirts are anonymous, Stone Island jackets and Burberry baseball caps being the preferred attire.

We do, however, briefly see a match between two schoolboy teams. While the boys are playing, two watching fathers – one a Millwall fan, the other a supporter of Chelsea – hurl abuse at each other from either side of the pitch. They eventually come to blows in the centre circle after one man suggests the other is a wife beater. As they fight, the kids and their adult referee, in disgust, take their game elsewhere, leaving the men, very pointedly, fighting over an empty pitch. The suggestion is clear: football attracts thugs who want to fight, but football itself is not responsible for the hooligan element.

If our representations of football can be linked with national identity, as well as with issues of race, sexuality, class and gender, then a representation of a 'typical' football fan is in part a picture of a 'typical' Englishman. If Tommy Johnson's brutal, loveless and empty life is anything to go by, we are all fighting for nothing. The football is an excuse to fight and that is an excuse not to think.

His lot is: pretend pop stars and reality TV; fast food and takeaway meals; prostitutes posing as masseurs; heavy drinking, gambling and drug abuse. All these elements are signposts to the postmodern in that they announce the commodification of life and the end of essentialism. What could be more postmodern than that!

Tommy's southwest London is peopled with characters who more broadly define national identity. His best mate runs a double-glazing firm and lives in a 'suburban nightmare' which, when fighting, he is somehow rebelling against. Here the old working classes have been suburbanised – England as *Brookside*. Significantly, the mate rejects his pretentious girlfriend and her super-suburban aspirations and reunites with the gang in time for the film's final punch-up.

Tommy's Granddad, Bill, and his friend Albert are self-effacing war heroes, widowers and neighbours. The film charts their farewell to 'old England' as they prepare to escape the estates of south London for the 'sun and surf' retirement culture of Australia. This is their swan song.

These two men both dignified and alone clearly connote

the end of, as Tommy says, 'What made Britain great'. They fought the racist Nazis and are now cruelly, ironically, lionised by racist nationalists at home. They live alone and forgotten. Their vision of England is as a cold, loveless, empty place. Their past is a nation's graveyard.

Two of Tommy's peers, Harris and Billy Bright, are gang leaders. Harris and Bright are forty-year-old psychotics who organise and lead the fights. Both men come from racist and violent families, but Harris is 'old school'. Bright, on the other hand, has embraced a re-branded, Blairite Britain. He made his money selling 'E' (the love drug) to thugs, hence 'thug drug', and his phone ring tone and house doorbell both play Wagner's bombastic 'Ride of the Valkyries' (Wagner was anti-Semitic and a nationalist). He now runs a florist, where Tommy Johnson also works. Some of the flower boxes hold bags of cocaine, which Bright is also selling. One customer is the leader of the arch-rival gang, Millwall. This man is Turkish, a no lesser crime than being a Millwall fan, but he is a customer and in the postmodern age cannot be sent away empty-handed. Drugs are the glue holding their relationship together, and so it is no surprise when they eventually fall out at the children's football match referred to earlier.

These representations concern men more senior in age and rank than Tommy. The younger generation, however, is represented by wannabe hooligan Zebedee and his comic side-kick who are, according to everyone, 'thieving little cunts'. Zebedee is a drug-fuelled teen, wired and wild, and his squalid demise at the hands of the only Afro-Caribbean in the film feels almost like a lifestyle choice. This is the postmodern run amok: high and hyper, uppers and downers, fighting and fucking. Zebedee is all surface, with only shadows for depth.

The only other character of any note is of course England itself. We travel north to Liverpool and name check Stoke and the cockney East End, home to West Ham. We glimpse the cross of St George in flags, insignia and bunting, and the 'ultra nationalist' Chelsea gang daub its team's name across the Union Jack. National identity is a badge to be claimed, adorned and adored. National identity is not a birthright; it is an ideological transaction. In other words, national identity is a construction rather than a given reality; it is now as much about consumer choice as it is about family and birthplace.

'Old England' is represented as a racially pure country, an

island race, a country without West Indians, Pakistanis and asylum seekers. It is a masculine place, where men seem redundant (sexual impotency is an occasional problem for Tommy and his mates) and women are invisible. This sense of a 'nation invisible' is further signposted by the numerous establishing shots of London Underground stations visited by the Chelsea gang.

Tommy's eventual realisation that the fighting is worth it as a 'lifestyle choice' is made clear at the end of the film. By belonging to an exclusive male club with its military mentality and cruel machismo, Tommy has found, in his own words, something better than thought, something even better than sex – violence'. Thus the certainties of the old institutions that once constructed the football fan have now disintegrated, and football has become but one representation of the nation in the postmodern world.

8.12 Extra time

If football is a social barometer as much as any other cultural practice, then a politicised and postmodern approach to the game could yield positive social results. If 'men and masculinity in crisis' were really British cinema's fundamental preoccupation in the 1990s, as Claire Monk (2000) maintains, then football films must reflect that preoccupation.

Perhaps the nation as a whole would benefit from a more socially inclusive game, a game less prone to self-destruction and more focused on regeneration. As John Williams (1999) concludes:

> The recent decline of overt racism in English football, the small overtures made by some professional clubs towards 'ethnic minority' support, and the apparent growth in active female support at English football matches have produced a game which now better reflects, so its supporters claim, the variability and tolerance of modern British culture.

Mike Bassett: England Manager and, to a lesser extent, *Bend It Like Beckham* and *The Football Factory* are postmodern representations of England and football. They all perfectly express male, working-class nostalgia for a vanishing past and a detached irony towards an increasingly fragmented, pluralist present. As Ziauddin Sardar (2002) states, 'We need to move away from the politics of contested identities that heighten artificial differences and towards acceptance of the plasticity and possibilities of identities that focus on our common humanity.'

At one level, national identity is now really nothing more than a commodity, a personal expression of brand loyalty. This is an uncomfortable conclusion to consider and so *Mike Bassett*, *The Football Factory* and *Bend It Like Beckham* can all be read as a postmodern puncturing of nationalist ideologies. It really does not matter what game you play, only that you do not confuse your game with reality. Indeed that is the postmodern point – reality is a game. The old categories of identity have collapsed. Football is a potent cultural artefact which, through its representations of all the social identities but for our purposes nationality, has the ability to help us identify who we are and what we want to become.

> '*They think it's all over! It is now.*'
> KENNETH WOLSTENHOLME, 1966

References

Baker, E. (1928), in 'National Character', in Jeffrey Richards, *Films and British National Identity* (Manchester: Manchester University Press, 1997).

Cozen, C., 'Sexier than Sex', *Guardian*, 27 May 2002.

Critcher, C., 'Football since the War', in B. Waites, T. Bennett & G. Martin (eds), *Popular Culture: Past and Present* (London: Croom Helm/Open University, 1982).

Eriksson, S. G., quoted in the *Sun*, 1 June 2002. With reference to England's first game of the World Cup finals against Sweden.

Hornby, N., 'Pitch Fever', *Guardian*, 29 April 1996.

Inayatullah, Sohail, & Gail Boxwell (eds), *Islam, Postmodernism and Other Futures: A Ziauddin Sardar Reader* (London: Pluto Press, 2003).

Jacques, M., 'The Age of Sport', *Observer*, 13 July 1997.

Littlejohn, R., 'We're All Americans Now: Terror in America', *Sun*, 11 March 2005.

Luckett, M., 'Image and Nation in 1990s British Cinema', in Robert Murphy (ed.), *British Cinema of the 90s* (London: BFI Publishing, 2000).

Monk, C., 'Men in the 90s', in Robert Murphy (ed.), *British Cinema of the 90s* (London: BFI Publishing, 2000).

Morrison, B., 'Painting Tokyo Red and White', *Guardian*, 4 June 2002.

Orwell, G., *Nineteen Eighty-Four* (London: Secker & Warburg, 1949).

Paxman, J., *The English* (London: Penguin, 1999).

Russell, D., *Football and the English* (UK: Carnegie Publishing, 1997).

Sardar, Z., *The A–Z of Postmodern Life: Essays on Global Culture in the Noughties* (London: Vision, 2002).

Smith, A. D., *National Identity* (London: Penguin, 1991).

Williams, J., *Is It All Over?* (Reading: Garnet Publishing, 1999).

Wolstenholme, K., World Cup Final, England v Germany, BBC1, 1966.

9. Beyond Britishness: Identity and Difference

WENDY HELSBY

In the chapter on football there is a discussion of how we might identify ourselves as Welsh, Scottish, Irish, English and ultimately British through a national sport. Here we take the discussion a stage further to look at the way that film represents groups both from within and from outside of national boundaries, beyond our 'Britishness'. This debate is currently on the agenda with Newsnight *interviewing politicians such as Gordon Brown about their view of Britishness: 'our past … British values. That's at the core of our Britishness …' (Gordon Brown in interview with Martha Kearney on BBC2, 14 March 2005)*

Susan Hayward (1993) argues that 'film functions as a cultural articulation of a nation … [reduced to]… two fundamental concepts: identity and difference.' This means that we define ourselves as a nation by what we believe we are and by what we believe we are not. Thus we achieve an understanding of our identity through a binary opposition. This section wants to show you how we construct this view of difference of nationality, but also how beneath the superficial differences of language, dress and customs there are many transnational similarities. Often we are deceived by readings of texts outside our own boundaries and we may not have the patience to read beyond difference and as a result we can be judgmental, falling back upon stereotypes. In so doing we deny ourselves the many pleasures of celebrating difference. This section reflects upon the importance of hearing and seeing other viewpoints, other representations, other nationalities.

▶ What elements could you list about a person who is British? What is Britishness? Brainstorm such a list, then divide into positive, neutral and negative groups. Keep this list to compare later with another list you will be asked to do. ●

There are two significant areas that are discussed: first, how the source of the text can deliver and influence meanings; and, secondly, how this influences the way we perceive others. But to begin with we are going to look at our concept of nation.

9.1 Britishness

The notion of identity can and does tend to difference, and at the extreme, exclusion. As a person born in Britain we are not French, American, Jamaican, Chinese or Indian … But this may not be as clear-cut as it first appears. If our parents have come from different countries, even from within the United Kingdom, how do we define ourselves then? The image of our national identity becomes muddied because we are now including race, ethnicity, inheritance and culture, in addition to the nation-state boundaries within which we were born.

So divisions are not only about us and others outside the state boundary, but also on a smaller scale how we define ourselves inside British society. There are many ways that we can be grouped. Since the Industrial Revolution a major division within Britain has been between rural and urban societies. The strength that this identity holds for some people was seen when the Countryside March, Liberty and Livelihood, was held on 22 September 2002. More than 400,000 'country' people marched in the city to proclaim themselves as different from the city dwellers. In our culture we also divide ourselves by class. The Countryside Alliance would claim that it was made up of working, middle and upper classes. But in another context, such as in the rights of workers, each class would have very different agendas. Many films have reflected the way that class divisions construct our view of society. David Lean's *Brief Encounter* (1945) focused on the mores of the upper middle classes, with the working-class characters being mere mild comic reflections of these characters. In Karel Reisz's *Saturday Night and Sunday Morning* (1960), the Albert Finney character states categorically that his credo is 'Don't let 'em [the masters] grind you down.'

Another major division within our nation is that of regional identity. The Government (June 2003) has proposed regional assemblies to underline these identities – although in November 2004 this idea was rejected by popular vote in the northeast. In addition there is the North–South divide in all the countries that make up the British Isles. If you live in Scotland, for example, you might be a highlander, a lowlander or a border person. In Wales, England and Ireland there are similar divisions. A classic comment often made is that most southerners believe civilisation stops north of the Watford Gap. Even at a parochial level one village or town estate may have a different identity to another only a few miles away. In Northern Ireland these types of divisions are built along religious lines.

In times of national crises, however, all this diversity is subsumed under that of national identity. It has been said that one of the functions of the BBC during World War II was to try to overcome regional differences and create through its radio broadcasts an ideology of one nation fighting for a single cause. Today, as is argued in Chapter 8, perhaps football serves the same function. As a result of the new world order, current government policies are trying to create a way of defining how an immigrant can be British by assessment under certain criteria. It is something that other nations, such as the United States, have done for many years.

There are also examples of identifiable groups who live inside the modern nation states created from the seventeenth century onwards, but who traverse national borders. In the United States the Native Americans belong to their own nations such as the Sioux, and these cross the official USA–Canadian border; the Inuit nation inhabits North America and beyond; the Lappish people live in countries across Northern Europe. There are also separate nations within national borders, as with Brittany in France and Wales in Britain.

But these macro groupings become more complex if we look at cultural and national identities inside the paradigm of the nation. In the case of Britain, not only do we have groups such as Welsh, Scottish, Irish and Anglo-Saxon, but also groups from Europe such as Poles and others who fled their own countries for various reasons during the later nineteenth and early twentieth centuries. There are more recent immigrant groups including Caribbean British and Asian British. The impact of this has been explored in films such as *Beautiful People* (1999), in which Jasmin Dizdar looked at many of these diverse groups living in London and explored the effects of immigration and how identities have to change.

▶ Do you agree that even in a small geographical area there can be different identities? Are there local identities where you live? ●

▶ If you were Home Secretary, what would be on your list to assess a person's right to become British? ●

▶ Conservative MP Enoch Powell gave a speech on 20 April 1968 in Birmingham where he used the metaphor of 'the river Tiber foaming with much blood' for the effects of immigration on Britain by the end of the twentieth century (Seymour-Ure, 1974).

Many groups have come to live in the United Kingdom. Do you believe we have a racially tolerant society? How do you feel about new immigrants? Do you agree or disagree with Powell's words?

If you are from an immigrant background do you feel that your perspective is different? ●

Beautiful People: beautiful people fight new battles as immigrants in London

This kaleidoscope of identities can raise concerns among older residents about protecting 'our home' national identity from 'their invasion', and often leads to a xenophobic reaction against people who come to this country as asylum seekers or immigrants, or even those who have lived here for generations but have different cultures, such as travellers (discussed in Chapter 7).

Immigrant groups have religious, racial, cultural and historical identities that are different from the Anglo-Saxon British experience. They add to the kaleidoscope of patterns in our social lives, and they illustrate graphically the difficulties of trying to define a discrete and simplistic idea of nationhood and culture. One politician suggested that one way to find out if someone was British was to ask people what cricket team they supported. He was, of course, referring to people from the Indian subcontinent, but the question could just as easily be asked of Australians resident in the United Kingdom.

Historically many of us are descended from immigrant groups such as Vikings, Angles, Saxons, Romans and their multi-ethnic armies, Normans, French Huguenots escaping persecution and Eastern Europeans following the pogroms in Russia and elsewhere, not to mention those escaping Nazi persecution. Only Celts can be said to be indigenous to these islands. Thus to try to define beyond Britishness in opposition to a nebulous idea of what it is to be British immediately puts us in a semantic spider's web. In order to begin to unravel this web a little, we need to keep in mind that nations are made up of differences, but that they also have general areas of commonality and similarities, and a generally agreed cultural 'mental set'. It is on this that the ideologies of representation of nation are built.

One good example is when we talk about 'British films'. This is in itself a problematic definition with which the Film Council and successive governments have struggled. But there is a general consensus that films made from within British culture have a different way of looking, a different style and structure, to those made about British culture from outside. Consider, for example, a film such as *Trainspotting* (Danny Boyle, 1996) which focused on youth subculture and compare it with similar films made in Hollywood. Such elements as actor-led rather than star-led, social realism, heritage, nostalgia, literary adaptations, a quirky sense of humour, and class structure all contribute to an idea of Britishness in film.

Once we understand how complex our own identity is we can then see how representation or misreading of films from others can lead to stereotyping and to misunderstanding. The purpose of this section is to begin to look at the way that groups from outside our own culture and nation are represented and how viewing texts from other cinemas can challenge, define or redefine representations of the 'other'. Other chapters in this book, such as those on football and prostitution, have referred to films outside of 'Hollywood', and we shall refer to films both from Britain and from other world cinemas, in order to reveal how such representation works.

9.2 Cultural imperialism

The concept of a nation-state may in itself have become dated with the new global economies. Many of the current debates that occur in the media are rooted in the idea of cultural imperialism. The thesis is that the West and, specifically, the United States with its large corporations are seen to be controlling and stifling the world's plurality of voices. The fact that a BBC2 current affairs programme discussed this issue shows how alive this debate is (*What the World Thinks of America*, BBC2, 17 June 2003).

It is worthwhile remembering that debates revolving around representation in contemporary media are embedded in these discourses of globalisation, ownership and technical hierarchies. McLuhan's homogenised 'global village' (*Understanding Media*, 1964) appears to be defeating the nation-state as expressed by Hobsbawm (1990) in the battle for dominance of the control of the message. There is an inevitable and inherent tension between the identity of the nation, the cultural global economy and electronic communications. It is the latter which could be the most powerful definer of future world structures and by definition of the types of representation of the world we receive. Who owns the gateway to communication may be a more important question than who is President of the United States of America.

Today the world of commercial cinema has the cultural gloss of Hollywood, at present the most powerful agency for film-making. It may be that Bollywood could challenge this supremacy in the future, and certainly Hollywood is getting rather precious about the way that the Indian film industry is taking popular American movies and remaking them in its own style. (This is rather ironic as Hollywood has frequently taken European films to remake Hollywood-style.) But in terms of the global reach Hollywood is still the main source of mass popular films for many of the world's inhabitants. This means that the world view personified by the WASP (White Anglo-Saxon Protestant) is seen to dominate the film audience. This industry relies upon its home audiences and so the messages are US-centred. Even factual stories are twisted to put an American gloss on them, as in *Saving Private Ryan*, which is discussed in Chapter 1. This gloss can also be seen in fictional films. For example, in the genre of science fiction the aliens will inevitably land by the White House or its representatives, as in the 1950s *The War of the Worlds* (Byron Haskin, 1953), *The Thing* (Christian Nyby, 1951) and *Independence Day* (Roland Emerich, 1996), and the American hero will save the day. The alien often represents a view of the 'other', someone who does not have WASP values. In the 1950s the alien represented the fear of Communism. After 9/11 this fear is more likely to be focused around Islamic religious fundamentalism.

How does this view of the world which is centred on a specific culture and identity influence the way the world is seen by audiences both American and non-American? As English speakers we find it easy to view American films and television programmes, and as consumers we are everyday users of American culture. How do Americans view the English? In American movies the English character can often be one not to be trusted. For example, English Bob, a travelling con man in Clint Eastwood's *Unforgiven* (1992), and the leader of the evil powers in *Lost in Space* (Stephen Hopkins, 1998) are both played by English actors.

But we also have other representations of Britain such as quirkiness as in *A Fish Called Wanda* (Charles Crichton, 1988) and the Monty Python films. We know that films that use this quirky or historical tourist view of Britain will be successful with American audiences, as in *Shakespeare in Love* (John Madden, 1998) and *Four Weddings and a Funeral* (Mike Newell, 1994). If you have seen these types of film do you recognise them as being a fair representation of Britain? Férid

▶ Why do you think English actors can sometimes be given the villain's role in Hollywood? If you listen to the bad characters in the *Shrek* films you will hear that they often have English accents or English ways of speaking. For example, the world 'bloody' is used by one of the lead characters. The BBFC (British Board of Film Classification) challenged the word's use in a children's film, but was told that was how the producers defined the character as English for American audiences. ●

Boughedir, a Tunisian academic and film-maker, has referred to this tendency of stereotyping other nations as the 'National Geographic' view of the world. Boughedir was referring to the way that images of Africa by outsiders focused on large landscapes, wild animals and traditional mud huts, but it can also be applied to a region such as Europe as seen by outsiders such as Americans.

Another effect of stereotyping is that we can begin to conform to the stereotype that has been created for us in the media, be it the foppish English upper classes as in the opening of *Casablanca* (Michael Curtiz, 1942), lager louts on holiday in Spain, or football hooligans (see Chapter 8). The challenge for the media is to allow viewpoints that give a varied and rounded representation and not the simple stereotype we too often see through the dominant media glasses. If each message is repeated and unchallenged audiences may have difficulties when approaching texts that have been produced from another perspective and which require reading through alternative lenses. This is particularly so if the text adopts a non-Hollywood or intransitive style (Wollen, 1972) and does not conform to the expectations of the dominant view of the world seen through those stereotype glasses. It is ironic that increasing globalisation of the media makes watching texts from other perspectives even more difficult for Western viewers who have become programmed into the Hollywood style. It is also the case that audiences from non-Western areas have also been trained into the Hollywood style of viewing. African film-makers have often seen their films rejected by local audiences in favour of cheap American films.

In order to explore these points we are going to look at two films. Both tell a story set in the past and both have a female servant as the key protagonist. One is directed by a famous American male director, while the other is by a much less famous Tunisian female director.

9.3 The pitch

As a young film producer you have two proposals to pitch to potential investors. Read them through and consider which one to choose and how you could best present them to gain funding. You will notice that there are strong similarities but subtle differences.

▶ The *National Geographic* is an American magazine. and it is worth taking the time to look at this magazine or view its website, and compare it with a publication such as *New Internationalist*. How do their views of the world differ?
- www.nationalgeographic.com
- www.newint.org ●

Boughedir commented on this in his Camera d'Arabe *documentary (1987), while Haile Gerima made a similar point at the African Cinema Conference held at the National Film Theatre, London, in 1995.*

In Chapter 6 the world of the prostitute is explored and you might like to compare the women's roles. It would also be interesting for you to keep both these films in mind when reading about representation of the family in Chapter 2.

Synopsis plot 1

This is set in a period where the country is in a politically unstable situation. A young girl is living with her mother, a single parent, who is a servant in a large house owned and occupied by a rich extended family. There is a secret about the male head of the household and her mother connected with sexual favours. It is suggested that a female servant has a relationship with one of the family. The girl is particularly friendly with the daughter of the family. As a child the main protagonist tried to learn the secret of her paternity by observing and listening to the adults. As she grows up the girl is attracted to a young male employee of the household, but she carries the stigma of illegitimacy. A party is being held by the rich family to celebrate the wedding of the daughter of the house and the girl is asked to sing. While this is happening her mother dies from a failed abortion caused by the rape by one of the heads of the household and the girl leaves the house with the young employee. The secret of her parentage is kept from her by the housekeeper even when, now as an unmarried pregnant young woman, she returns ten years later on the death of the head of the household. There is no final answer to the key question of parentage.

Synopsis plot 2

A wealthy family has a party held against a background of international political unrest. The guests arrive at the large house with their servants. One of the visiting servants is a young girl. She becomes attracted to and intrigued by a male servant. It is insinuated that another female servant, who has befriended the daughter of the house, has a sexual relationship with the head of the household. The house party is interrupted by the murder of the head of the house. A key character is the housekeeper. The girl learns that there is a secret from the past about the sexual relationship between the head of the house and the female servants, including the housekeeper. She talks to the housekeeper and the secret is revealed; we know the murderer, and the girl leaves the house with her mistress.

As members of particular cultures we share broadly similar ways of seeing, even with individual differences. This is why, if you compared your ideas about the staging and casting of

▶ Having chosen the plot you wish to pitch, prepare a proposal to gain funding. Suggest contemporary actors for the main roles and explain why you have made these choices. What type of characteristics did you give the main protagonists? What are the main elements of the location? What do these say about representation?

Have you chosen Western actors who are well known in Hollywood and located the film in a place with which you are familiar, even if only from exposure to it in the media? Just as easily as we stereotype people we can do the same with places. If you did choose unfamiliar locations, ask yourself why. Was it because of some specialist knowledge? Would it be possible to create untypical characters or would this jeopardise the verisimilitude, either cultural or generic, of the film for your audience, which in turn would jeopardise funding? Did you feel that you could use people from other ethnic or racial groups or people who had physical disabilities, or were physically unattractive? Were these types of groups absent from your proposal, and if so why? ●

the two plot synopses with someone from a similar background, the scenarios that you developed would probably have strong similarities. These mind maps are constructed through language, images and the discourses that we share and which help to create beliefs (ideologies) and which are culturally specific. This is why you will find films or other texts from a culture close to your own easier to understand than those from different backgrounds. It is not only about language and subtitles. We find it difficult to acknowledge nuanced representations of others and rely in a rather lazy way upon semiotic representations that are stereotypical.

The two synopses come from films that have already been made and, as you have seen, there are strong similarities between the two stories. They are both set in the past (servants suggest this) and against political unrest, with an upstairs–downstairs conflict. They have a young servant girl as the main protagonist, and they are based upon a patriarchal society in which an older female character, the housekeeper, holds the secrets that the young servant tries to discover. Each is set in a large establishment with many family members and in which there is a young daughter to contrast with the female servant. Each film, however, treats its narrative very differently, in both style and form. This means cinematically as well as through narrative structure. Did you notice, for example, that one had a definite, or closed, ending, while the other seems more unresolved? This might have influenced your choice of plot.

So what is the purpose of this exercise? The similarities show that human stories are not necessarily culturally specific, but their differences in style and the way they are told are. These two films are located in different cultures and the messages and how they convey them gives a very different meaning to the roles of the central characters. They reveal an objective and subjective view, a male and a female view of the world of the female servant. They reveal how different representations show us a world through different discourses. Usually we only see the one that is powerful and dominant, so this comparison allows us to see other viewpoints.

The first synopsis is of the film *Silences of the Palace* (1994), directed by Moufida Tlatli, one of Tunisia's leading women directors. It is set in one of the palaces of the beys (princes) of Tunisia in the 1950s, just as Tunisia is about to

Camera d'Afrique: Films made in Africa by Africans for African audiences represent different realities to those made by outsiders

Gosford Park: Altman reflects the oppression of working-class women in 1930s Britain through the *mise en scène*

break away from French colonial power. The second is *Gosford Park* (2002) directed by Robert Altman, a revered American director. This is set in an English country house in the 1930s. Nazism is rising in Europe and World War II is only a few years away. Both are therefore set on the brink of great social change. Both stories centre upon the way that women can be used for sexual favours in return for a livelihood.

We are going to analyse these two films to show how national cultural differences in style and form influence representation of characters and additionally how each of these films could represent a gendered difference of male and female perspective on sexual politics.

Sexual exploitation by an authoritarian male household probably seems alien to you. Did you, for example, link your 'pitch' to a location and a period where you believe that women appear oppressed? *Gosford Park* shows such exploitation happening within a twentieth-century British society, one very close to our own.

Having observed their narrative similarities, how are they so different? If you have had a chance to see these two films you will easily be able to see how each is very different stylistically, as well as in the way the narrative is told. This in turn influences the way we understand the characters and their societies. The differences that are produced by direction and context raise the issue central to representation. Who is producing the texts and for whom? In one we have an Arab woman with a relatively low budget working within a thriving but small film industry using a limited group of professional actors to explore personal issues. On the other we have a very well known American director working on a period drama with a high budget and with the cream of well-known British actors. How would a Tunisian audience understand *Gosford Park*?

Silences of the Palace focuses upon the internal conflict of the main protagonist, whereas *Gosford Park* looks more at the external observed conflict of the protagonists. Both direction and styles are significantly different. Tlatli is a director who looks at the relationship between a mother and daughter. At one point in the film their relationship changes. We see this symbolically in a scene where the mother is sitting at a mirror putting on lipstick. Her daughter Alia has been asked to sing to the beys, and she knows that now Alia and not herself will be the focus of the sexual attention of the masters. To signify this Alia comes in and sits down in her mother's place in front of the mirror and takes up the same lipstick and applies it to her face. They have both literally and metaphorically changed positions and roles. Through these personal stories Tlatli observes how the position of women in Tunisia is controlled by both cultural and economic bars.

Observing the women in enclosed spaces also conveys the theme. The women have to live within the silences of unspoken thoughts. When one of them does cry out in anguish that she hates her body the camera slowly pans over the other women, who remain silent, carrying on with their servile work, their faces expressing their thoughts. Both the incarceration and the silences are portrayed in the powerful scene when we see a symbolic shot of Alia running to the palace gates and view her from the other side holding the bars and silently screaming. This is an act that reflects her mother's as a child, going to the gates every Friday to meet her parents who never appeared, having sold her to the beys. It is also at the moment when Alia has seen her future through the rape of her mother.

Silences of the Palace is set within a country striving for a voice and for liberation from colonisation. This is a metaphor for the issue of gender, sexual power and freedom from imposed rule that the women feel in the claustrophobic world of the beys and the sexual exploitation they suffer. The scene of the rape of Alia's mother as she struggles silently in the bedroom observed by her apparently sleeping daughter is a visual metaphor for the situation of women in a patriarchal society. The camera focuses upon Alia's reaction in close-up rather than the rape scene. It is these reaction shots that give a powerful view of rape from a female perspective.

Similarly Altman bases his film upon a class system that controlled people both economically and culturally, including the use of sexual power. But his observations are as an outsider. Again there is a sexual attack on a female servant. Here the view is far more objective. The camera does not enter into the mind of the victim. The girl goes mistakenly into the room of a man who is in fact a Hollywood actor playing the role of a servant. In his arrogance the man takes this as an invitation for sex. If you compare the two scenes you will see that the Tlatli version is more telling. Why? There are obvious reasons such as context, but I would also suggest

In *Gosford Park*, the kitchen was a female domain, but controlled by men

that it is partly because you see the issue as represented through the female eyes of the daughter, rather than through the observational male and because we are seeing it through a different film language and style.

In each film groups are being represented with whom we could superficially identify. As a young or older woman or a male you might have found it easier to identify with or empathise with a particular character from each of the stories. But once these are developed through the semiotics of film language controlled by the director's view of the world they begin to develop a representation that may be unfamiliar. If you have watched the two films it is probable that the subject and the style of Altman's film were more easily accessible or readable than Tlatli's story. Altman made a pastiche of the British country house detective story, the whodunit genre made famous by writers such as Agatha Christie. The actor Julian Fellowes provided advice to give cultural verisimilitude, but ultimately the film's view is refracted through the telescopic vision of an American film-maker.

Altman has chosen a genre with a long cultural pedigree in Western culture. It contains recognisable characters and stereotypes such as the butler, the genteel but poor aristocrat, and the unlikeable victim. In its style and form it plays to the British film tradition of the literary/historical/nostalgic drama with Hollywood gloss. Before you started watching the film you would already have the mental set against which to check your understanding. Tlatli's film has none of these signifiers. From the opening it obfuscates. The narrator/

narratee positioning is complex. We move from the present to the past with only a look. For example, as the adult Alia walks through the courtyard, she turns and we cut to a point-of-view shot. But what she and we see is a scene that took place ten years previously, when she was a child. The characters and their relationships are also confusing for an audience without the knowledge of life inside a Tunisian bey's palace of the period. For example, we see the female servants washing the feet of the princes and this can alienate us because of a lack of cultural understanding. Other elements such as the music and the narrative form are also estranging. The representation of place both in *The Silences of the Palace* and *Gosford Park* are important signifiers. Both are played out in the contained and claustrophobic spaces of a large house. The entrapment of people below stairs has its parallel in the entrapped lives of the women above stairs, and is an important counterpoint in both films. In *Gosford Park* we see the ennui of the ladies; their powerlessness in terms of economic survival; the focus on superficialities such as fashion, looks, entourage rather than interests outside of the domestic. Downstairs the female servants are strictly controlled, but are open to offering sexual favours to the 'gentlemen' either for monetary rewards or because they are forced. Economic and class barriers keep them in their situations. Similarly in *Silences of the Palace*, the *raison d'être* for the wives of the beys is to provide an heir. They have luxury but no power. Their husbands are allowed sexual liaisons and favours from the younger servant women. Unlike the servants they are able to wander beyond the gates of the palace, but they are not allowed into public life. Again, their lives are bounded by the domestic. The men might sit and discuss politics or read French literature, but not the women.

So there are therefore considerable similarities of content and themes, but it is in the way that the story is told that is different. This is partly to do with the film language used, but also to do with our expectations and cultural generic knowledge. Although both talk about basic human themes – love power, birth, death – we have to go beyond the superficial differences to observe these.

Mainstream cinema favours particular narrative forms linked to genres. *Gosford Park* fits into the crime drama, so we know the type of characters to expect and how the story is to be told, with its red herrings and verbal and visual clues. But

A fruitful comparison of Silences of the Palace *with Férid Boughedir's* Halfaouine *(1990) which shows a male viewpoint of 1950s Tunisia could also be made (Ashbury; Helsby & O'Brien, 1998; Stollery, 2001).*

► *Make your own list in relation to Arabness. It is often revealing to list ideas in a form of binary oppositions: clean/dirty; aggressive/submissive; hard-working/lazy; shifty/honest; rich/poor; tolerant/fundamentalist; terrorist/freedom fighter; handsome/ugly; exotic/ordinary; comic/tragic. Look at your list. Is there a pattern building about type? If so it illustrates the way that messages whether negative or positive are repeated across the media. It indicates the power of representations of others beyond Britain, about whom what we know has been mediated. Obviously if you have an Arab background your list may well reflect this knowledge and be less stereotyped. Compare this list with the one on Britishness you were asked to do at the beginning of the chapter. What comments can you make about their similarities and differences?* ●

with *Silences of the Palace* we have to work hard, as it defies Western generic containment. It looks metaphorically at issues of independence, gender politics and transition. It does fit into the work of other Tunisian directors such as Nouri Bouzid and Férid Boughedir, but in the West we rarely see these perspectives. Films such as *Silences of the Palace* have to translate through both a linguistic and a cultural barrier when viewed through Western eyes. The difference between outsider eyes and insider eyes is important. It challenges our Western discourse of Arabness because in this film we see from an insider's point of view. In a television interview for *Moving Pictures* (BBC2, 12 March 1995), a woman Tunisian director talked about the problems of getting funding from Western sources when producers said that her view of the Arab woman was not right! What they meant, of course, was that it did not fulfil their expectations, their mental set as outsiders of the concept 'Arab woman'. It is the same issue raised in Chapter 7 on directors' views of 'gypsyness'.

9.4 The outsider – the other

Having discussed a film from an Arab country, what issues of representation do you think it raises? Is there not an ambivalence in our understanding of a culture with which we have traditionally been at odds, from the Crusades onwards? Do we not have a fascination with what appears an exotic history, with names such as Cleopatra, St Augustine and Lawrence of Arabia threaded through our knowledge of the area. How do you view people who are of Middle Eastern origins?

You would probably challenge images such as the fairy tale of Aladdin, Scheherezade and the 1001 Nights, Rudolph Valentino as the sheikh, and the dance of the seven veils as representations of the stereotyped Arab. I imagine, however, that there will still be an element of these in your image bank. All appear to me to have exotic and romantic connotations attached to them. I have visions of dark, handsome men in long, flowing robes with glamorous veiled women dressed in gossamer trousers. But there is also a sense of the unreliable and dangerous, and the image of Arab sexual exploitation of women and their control and containment by authoritarian males. Where have these images appeared? Here are some examples of films from the silent era onwards with Arab characters or set in an Arab country: *The Sheikh* (George

Melford, 1921); *Casablanca* (Michael Curtiz, 1942); *Indiana Jones and the Last Crusade* (Steven Spielberg, 1989); *Robin Hood: Prince of Thieves* (Kevin Reynolds, 1991); and *The English Patient* (Anthony Minghella, 1996).

You will be able to add other films to this list. There will also be images from television genres such as situation comedies, news programmes, dramas and documentaries such as the notorious drama-documentary *Death of a Princess* (1980) which discussed the execution of a woman in an Arab country for extramarital relations.

Today the image of the Arab in the West is often constructed through television images of violence, such as war, and cultural differences over such areas as the rights of women. Recently (November 2004) a Dutch documentary maker was murdered because he explored domestic violence inside Muslim marriages. We rarely look at texts that reveal the society from within and how it sees itself in terms of such ideas as gender politics. It is often surprising to us to hear Arab women defending practices that in Western culture we see as medieval and intolerant. What we sometimes fail to realise is that debates about gender roles, sexuality and others are also current issues inside these countries, as Tlatli's films reveal.

This underlines the fact that representation is reliant upon who creates the representation and for whom. Tlatli's film was made by an Arab woman to explore the world of a certain type of woman in her own society. Her primary audience was Arab. She wanted to explore why the generation before her had been, in general, so silent about their lives. Altman's point of view, of course, was different, and his audience was much wider. Do you think this led to a tendency to be less analytical or do you think his purpose was so different that such messages were incidental to the pleasure of the film?

9.5 Conclusion

We have looked at the way that groups from outside and inside of our culture and experience can be represented and how self-representation such as Tlatli's may be very different from the view of outsiders. The example we have used here is based upon the plot of the female servant. This has been underpinned by an understanding of the way that we develop the concept of otherness. We have seen how the media uses stereotypes in a handy shorthand to produce one-

The Sheikh: A traditional Western view of the Arab male

Recently several films have come out of the Middle East, particularly Tunisia and Iran, which provide views of this culture that counter those from Western film-makers.

dimensional images which ignore the complexity of other nations and cultures. Our understanding of the texts and how it represents people, places and nation will be very different depending upon the perspective we take as spectator, the production values, the mise en scène and the cinematography, and upon our own cultural knowledge – even upon our gender. All these meanings are part of systems of classification that help us to organise our ideas and confirm or deny the reality of the representation. If we go back to the beginning of this discussion, where Gordon Brown claimed 'the starting point is values rather than institutions' (*Newsnight*, BBC2, 14 March 2005) can we now say whether this is true, or are institutions such as cinema just as important in our ideas of nation?

References

Ashbury, R., W. Helsby & M. O'Brien, *Teaching African Cinema* (London: BFI, 1998).

Hayward, S., *French National Cinema* (London: Routledge, 1993).

Hobsbawm, E., *Nations and Nationalism since 1780: Programme, Myth, Reality* (Cambridge, UK: Cambridge University Press, 1990).

McLuhan, M., *Understanding Media: The Extensions of Man* (New York: MIT Press, 1964).

Seymour-Ure, C., *The Political Impact of Mass Media* (London: Constable, 1974).

Stollery, M., 'Masculinities, Generations, and Cultural Transformation in Contemporary Tunisian Cinema', *Screen*, vol. 42, no. 1, Spring 2001.

Wollen, P., 'Counter-Cinema: *Vent d'est*', *Afterimage*, no. 4, 1972.

Filmography

Camera d'Arabe and *Camera d'Afrique* (F. Boughedir, 1987, Tunisia)

Beautiful People (Jasmin Dizdar, 1999)

Silences of the Palace (M. Tlatli, 1994)

Gosford Park (Robert Altman, 2002)

Part Five
Conclusion

Introduction

In this book the issue of representation has been addressed in discrete areas; however, it is obvious that they interact and overlap. In reading you will have seen that cross-references have been made to other chapters and you will be aware that many of the texts cited could have been the focus for study in other areas than the one chosen.

Gender, sexuality, race, age, nationality, cultures and so on are all part of our understanding of the world. How that world is mediated is fundamental to this understanding. In the final section we show how a text can open up the issue of representation via many different points of entry. Chapter 10 reproduces an interview with one of the actors in the case study film *East Is East* (Damien O'Donnell, 1999). You will see how, through the genre of comedy, the film points to and explores many of the issues of representation around race, ethnicity, religion, family, education, gender, sexuality, culture and the nation that we have discussed in this book.

10. *East Is East:* A Case Study
(Damien O'Donnell, 1999)

PAULINE TURNER

East Is East *(1999) was produced by the now-defunct Channel Four Films. It is the largely autobiographical film of the writer Ayub Khan-Din, who fondly remembers growing up in Salford in Manchester in the 1970s and the tensions and experiences of being a member of a large family group. In the film, although the family is mixed race and references are made to racial tension between them and their neighbour Mr Moorhouse, for the children in the family 'the real problem is not how to fit in with their English neighbours, but how to fit in with their own family' (director, Damien O'Donnell).*

Watch *East Is East* and see how Ayub Khan-Din represents his life to us. Remember that Dyer (1985) has suggested to us that all representations have entertainment value.

One of the actors in the film, Raji James who played Abdul, was Actor in Residence at Portsmouth College during 2002–2003, and in a seminar held at the college had the following to say about the film and his understanding of some of the messages, meanings and representations. Pauline Turner conducted the interview.

► In what genre would you place *East Is East?* ●

10.1 On family

'*East Is East* is about a family – it's about people who like each other or dislike each other, might have an argument, might not have an argument. And it's all set near Manchester.

'It isn't just relevant to brown people – it speaks to everyone. The director, Damien O'Donnell, is a white Irishman. He had

East Is East. Westernised Muslim teenagers

very little knowledge of Muslim families before he started the movie. He also had very little knowledge of interracial conflict because he hadn't had any in his life. That said, his knowledge of cultural conflict (specifically that which has plagued Ireland) was considerable. The producer, Leslee Udwin, also had personal experiences that, while similar, were not the same as those depicted in the film. She's of Jewish heritage and had experience of interracial marriages – but is that all the film is all about?

'What would sum up *East Is East*? To me, and the way the film was eventually placed in the market, it was mainly about generational conflict, which every single one of us will go through at some point in our lives – the conflict between children and their parents. You don't have to be black, white, brown, Chinese, African – everyone goes through conflict with his or her parents, and that's where Damien had taken the film. He took something that was very personal to the writer Ayub's own life story and assisted it in becoming a great story that spoke "a truth" to a lot of people.

'There was intent on behalf of the writer (Ayub Khan-Din) to tell the story about his family, to explore the relationships and by doing so, to try to understand his father a little better, and hope to make some people laugh along the way.'

10.2 On race

'*East Is East* wasn't put forward as a general statement about the Muslim faith – it wasn't put forward as a general statement about interracial conflict. It was positioned in the marketplace as a story about generational conflict – that's it. And it was quite clearly publicised as being based on the life of the writer – so when Ayub wrote the character of George he wasn't writing a Muslim Everyman, he wasn't saying all Muslims are like this, he was saying, "This is my father."

'Om Puri, who played George brilliantly, stopped the character of George being a stereotyped Pakistani man who beats everyone up; he showed him as a man who was struggling with his inability to communicate, struggling with his own mistakes. He's telling his kids one thing when he himself has done a totally different thing – it's a complicated piece, a comedic piece, a beautifully filmed piece.

'A lot of people in the press and a lot of people in the industry were confused by this bunch of largely unknown actors (except Jimi Mistry and Chris Bisson who by now were big in the soaps) who were apparently, reasonably good – and they're quite funny and they don't just do stuff with Paki accents…. A lot of people weren't ready for this feeling that you don't have to be brown to understand that…. That you don't have to be white to play that part … so the whole idea of what is racial identity became a subsequent reaction to the film.'

10.3 How Sajid's character represents what is going on in the film

'To Sajid, what was going on in his house was what was going on in the world. Sajid spends the film inside his parka. I rip it off (as my character Abdul) and Sajid is "ready to face the world". He's scared of a lot of things – there's a big world out there that Sajid is trying to hide from, not just on a domestic level with the family conflict and arranged marriages. He's scared of being recognised as black in a predominantly white world. He describes the Shahs as "the Pakis" – Tariq also says, "I'm not getting married to a fucking Paki." A major theme in *East Is East* is the difference between Indians and Pakistanis, and Sajid is hiding in his parka. There is an actual war, commented on with venom by George, and all of this matters in the film.'

10.4 Representation in the opening scene

'It's a happy scene, watched over by their mother … yet they (the children) are clearly doing something against their

The mixed community of *East Is East*

George, the father, runs a fish and chip shop, but his roots are still in the Indian subcontinent

father's wishes…. And that thing seems to be taking part in a religious parade. You can deduce from that that the father is not a Christian, that the father is not a Catholic. His wife is. So straight away in the opening sequence of the film you have the idea that there is a conflict between the parents and the children. The idea that the mother and father have different religious beliefs, but also the idea that the children will disobey their father, that they will, as a group, and with the compliance of their mother and their mother's friend (Auntie Annie), that they will defy the father.

'[In his visual style] Damien wanted people to see that this wasn't a *Coronation Street* type story that was all going to be filmed at street level; it was a dynamic visual style. He sets the scene, the location, and introduces the idea of an entire community where there is only one Asian, one mixed-race family amongst a multitude of people.'

10.5 The final sequence

'How does it end? Pessimistically or optimistically? The thing I see in that last scene [in the chip shop] is that moment when he [George] sighs … and it gets me every time – that moment he doesn't think that she [Ella] is coming. He realises how lucky he is. I get a hint that maybe the outcome will be rosy – and I think this because the next thing you see is the kids united, having fun – with the sculpture of Peggy's fanny. It's so funny, a deliberate punchline, an almost guaranteed laugh. That line is there to lift the audience and give them a laugh to go out on. [The kids] run up the street and we have a crane shot similar to the one we opened on, but without the fear – they're running towards the chip shop. For the majority of the film they've been running away from the chip shop; now they're running towards the land of their dad – so that fear that's there at the beginning, maybe that's gone at the end. It's a wonderful way to end the film.'

10.6 Who is really in charge of representation in *East Is East*?

'Leslee Udwin as the producer made decisions about what the audience would see. She was the only person involved from day one of the project and is still involved now; the decision as to whether to make Nazir gay or not, Leslee controlled most of the publicity, even when Miramax got involved –

however, she had little influence over the marketing in the USA. She didn't like the poster – a red fez with a picture of some of the characters and the name of the film. It flopped in the States, taking only £4 million overall.

'In making any film, there are really four films: the film that's been written, the film that we actually make (including scenes which are later deleted), the film that is edited and the final film the audience see at the cinema. Even the film the director edits isn't necessarily the film the audience gets to see, marketing executives etcetera have their say. There are numerous websites out there telling you that the film represents this or means that, but at the end of it all there's the film that each viewer takes away with them, and this is often dependent on which of the characters that person "connected" with most, and, so far, it's rare for me to meet any single group who all see the film from the same point of view.'

Conclusion

As you can see from Raji's interview, *East Is East* is a film that touches on much of what has been discussed throughout this book. His comments reveal the way that representation works, such as how each spectator views the text and how each will take away from it a different reading. If you come from another region of Britain, how did the film represent Manchester to you? If you come from Manchester, did you feel the film reflected Manchester as you know it? Remember it was about a period around the 1970s, so this may have made a difference. If you come from an Asian family, did the problems that arose within the story regarding different gender roles appear to be truthfully represented?

'The two young girls who sit on the couch as prospective brides have obviously been chosen for their looks and to make a comedic moment. Do you think this is an issue when dealing with what is obviously a sensitive subject such as arranged marriages? Does it tend towards stereotyping?

'How others see Britain and our own representation as a nation can also be seen in how the film was marketed in other countries. For example, in France it was called *Fish and Chips*, partly because the chip shop is the centre of the family's occupation, but also because food so often conveys much about our cultural differences and how we view other nations. To the French the fish and chip shop is a British

▶ Visit some of the following websites for some more information about the film and for interviews and reviews.

www.popmatters.com/filmreviews/e/east-is-east.html
www.brightlightsfilm.com/30/eastiseast
www.eastiseast.com
www.kamera.co.uk/reviews/eastiseast ●

idiosyncrasy, but they also call the English 'les boeuf steak' – and we of course retaliate by referring to frogs' legs and snails.

Representation serves to make images and ideas to be seen as typical with the additional belief that they also represent the real. This is more so if deeply encoded in entertainment texts. Such meanings become embedded in our understanding of the world through convention and repetition. This can be seen as relatively harmless or harmful, but what we receive is a 'pseudo objective version of reality' (R. Williams, 1988, p. 261). This version is dependent upon historical factors and on a particular set of relationships that has been constructed but passed off as real. Understanding the processes that are involved in this construction is key to our understanding of how representation works in the media.

Reference

Dyer, R., 'Taking Popular Television Seriously', in David Lusted and Philip Drummond (eds), *TV and Schooling* (London: BFI, 1985), pp. 4–5.

Williams, R., *Keywords: A Vocabulary of Culture and Society* (London: Fontana, 1988).

Glossary

anchor Text used to confirm the meaning of a visual image.

anomic Socially disorientated/alienated.

binary opposition Theory of structuralist Claude Lévi-Strauss in which a set of values is believed to reveal the structure of a particular media text.

bricolage French term meaning the self-conscious amalgamation of different genres/styles.

capitalism An economic system based on private ownership of capital.

conglomerate A company operating within several industries simultaneously.

convergence A term for the combining of telecommunications media into an interactive experience that is accessible to everyone; can also relate to culture and lifestyle.

cultural imperialism Form of cultural hegemony enabling some states to impose world view, values and lifestyles on others. Term used by critics of American global influence to describe how the United States dominates others (e.g. by disseminating ideology of consumerism, hedonistic popular culture, or particular model of free-market society).

culture A way of life for a particular group; different groups will apply different meanings to different texts, and these meanings may change over time.

determinism A philosophical system, mainly concerned with axiological issues, for analysing cause and effect, and the individual's freedom to choose.

diaspora A dispersion or spreading, as of people originally belonging to one nation or having a common culture.

diegetic Elements of a film text that originally stem from within the narrative (e.g. a radio playing, a phone ringing, a bird singing). Non-diegetic sound is that which is added after the production (e.g. voiceover, soundtrack).

discourse A concept associated with Foucault, concerned with meanings of language and other codes according to their socio-historical context and prevailing power relationships.

dominant culture A societal group with power and authority.

elite A group or class of persons enjoying superior intellectual or social or economic status.

ethnocentrism Belief in the intrinsic superiority of the nation, culture or group to which one belongs, often accompanied by feelings of dislike for other groups.

feminist An approach associated with feminist theories; the majority of work focuses on how different media texts are accorded different meanings according to the sex of the producer or audience.

fetishism A near-idolatrous worship of certain objects. In psychoanalysis, fetishism is a pathological condition in which the fetishist, unable to acknowledge an attraction for a threatening or forbidden object of desire, finds gratification by displacing the impulse on to the object's possessions or nonsexual body parts.

functionalism The theory that all elements of a culture are functional and serve to satisfy culturally defined needs of the people in that society or requirements of the society as a whole.

globalisation Refers to a host of political, economic and cultural processes which suggest that any separation between national groupings is increasingly less distinct.

hegemony A concept devised by Antonio Gramsci to outline the way in which the dominant classes in a nation maintain power over subordinate classes either by coercion or consent.

heritage Body of practices that are handed down from the past by tradition.

hyper-real Apparently more real than the real world.

icon A highly valued person or product in popular culture.

ideological state apparatus (ISA) According to Marxist Althusser, this relates to institutions that generate ideologies that we as individuals (or groups) then internalise and act in accordance with (e.g. schools, religions, the family, legal systems, politics, arts, sports); these organisations generate systems of ideas and values.

ideology Derived from Marx, this term describes the implicit message and value systems in operation in media texts that is characteristic of a particular class or group, usually related to how power is distributed within society.

institution A company who are involved in some aspect of media production; there is usually a system of values, apparent by the way in which the texts are produced.

intertextuality A relationship between two or more texts, be it implicit or explicit, which influences the reading of the existing text.

language A system which uses signs (or signifying systems); these signs can be iconic, indexical or arbitrary.

mediation Altering the meaning of a 'real' event by applying media technology, rendering the representation partial or selective.

metaphor A figure of speech in which an expression is used to refer to something that it does not literally denote in order to suggest a similarity.

mimetic Apt to using imitation.

mockumentary Text that subverts the generic conventions of a documentary in a fun, ironic manner.

negotiated reading A reading of a text where the dominant values are broadly accepted, but readers will be prepared to argue with certain elements of that reading.

oppositional reading A reading of a text where the 'preferred reading' is wholly rejected by the reader.

the other Freud and later Lacan discussed how our psychology creates our identity through opposition to another.

paradigm The common sense range of alternatives which fit into a particular slot within a structure.

patriarchy A form of social organisation in which a male is the family head and title is traced through the male line.

popular culture Prevalent, current trends in arts, customs, beliefs etc. favoured by the majority in a society.

postmodern A contemporary movement in the arts which celebrates surface and style as opposed to content; an ideology about the contemporary world.

preferred (or dominant) reading The intended reading of a 'closed' text where a particular reading is preferred to others, it is the intended reading.

propaganda A systematic effort to persuade, involving the deliberate presentation of a one-sided argument to a mass audience.

Propp, Vladimir Developed an analysis that reduced fairy tales to a series of actions performed by the *dramatis personae* in each story; he argued that all fairy tales were constructed of 31 plot elements, which he called functions, and that these elements consistently occurred in a uniform sequence. This theory can be employed when undertaking a textual analysis of a film text.

realism That which may be considered the most 'real' in the recording of the world; a representation which purports to be truthful.

representation The process by which members of a culture use signifying systems to represent ideas and produce meaning.

repressive state apparatus (RSA) According to Althusser this is the mechanisms for insuring that people within a state behave according to the rules of that state, even when it is not in their best interests (in regards to their class positions) to do so (e.g. the police, the criminal justice and prison system); through these 'apparatuses' the state has the power to force you physically to behave.

scopophilia Literally means the desire to see/pleasure in viewing; in psychoanalytical theory it refers to the unconscious processes at work when the spectator views the screen; feminist theory asserts that pleasure is derived from the gaze (usually male) of the character whose point of view is within the film together with the pleasure derived by the spectator gazing upon the female body – the woman becomes fetishised.

semiotics The study of sign systems.

sign A word or an image used to represent an object or an idea.

signifier A sign referring to an object or concept.

socialisation The process whereby individuals are made aware of the behaviour that others expect of them particularly with regard to the norms, values and culture of their society.

stereotype A highly opinionated, biased and simplistic characterisation which helps audiences to understand a narrative; stereotypes may change according to shifting political cultural context.

stigma Symbol of disgrace or infamy.

subculture A set of cultural characteristics shared among a group within a society that are distinct in some ways from the larger culture within which the group exists, but also have features in common with the larger culture.

sub-genre A genre within a genre that has a particular specific common theme (e.g. 'slasher' horror movies; 'fallen woman' melodramas).

synergy When two different media texts work simultaneously to promote one another.

trope A single unit or idea.

verisimilitude The appearance of truth or reality; the quality of seeming to be true.

voyeurism The act of viewing the activities of others unbeknown to them, giving the spectator a degree of power over the spectacle.

Index

UNDERSTANDING THE MOVING IMAGE

UNDERSTANDING FILM TEXTS

Patrick Phillips

Part of the Understanding the Moving Image series, *Understanding Film Texts* aims to make the ideas and procedures of film studies both accessible and ordinary. Using a variety of critical approaches to film texts, the book is grounded in the experience of the student as a cinema-goer. It is organised around three non-specialist experiences of film: story, character and spectacle. This lively first book by an experienced teacher of film studies provides a stimulating first step in approaching film as an area of serious study.

ISBN 0-85170-799-8 pbk

UNDERSTANDING THE MOVING IMAGE

UNDERSTANDING REALISM

Richard Armstrong

The second book in the Understanding the Moving Image series,
Understanding Realism examines the complex relationship between the
moving image and appearance and reality. Richard Armstrong's in-depth
treatment considers in turn the roles that narrative, genre, audience and
ideology play in relation to realism in mainstream and independent film.
Written by an experienced film studies tutor, it provides an accessible
overview of a concept key to the understanding of contemporary media.

ISBN 1-84457-062-2 pbk